THE CHINESE JUGGERNAUT

THE CHINESE JUGGERNAUT

HOW THE CHINESE CONQUERED SOUTHEAST ASIA

Uli Schmetzer

TIZULI

TIZULI

PUBLISHER: Tizuli Publishing
EMAIL: ulischmetzer@gmail.com
WEBSITE: www.uli-schmetzer.com

Copyright © Uli Schmetzer 2010
First published January 2011

The moral right of the author has been asserted.
All rights reserved. No part of this publication may be reproduced, stored in a retrieval system, or transmitted in any form or by any means (electronic, mechanical, photocopying, recorded or otherwise), without prior written permission of the copyright owner.

CATALOGUING-IN-PUBLICATION DATA

AUTHOR	Schmetzer, Uli, 1940–
TITLE	The Chinese Juggernaut: How the Chinese conquered Southeast Asia
EDITION	1st ed.
ISBN	978-0-9806375-2-6 (pbk.)
SUBJECTS	Schmetzer, Uli, 1940–
	Foreign correspondents—Australia.
	Journalists—Australia.
	Journalism—Political aspects. Foreign news.
	International—Australia, China, Europe, Indonesia, Malaysia, Philippines, Thailand, USA.
	International—Finance, Trade, Immigration, Social aspects.

EDITOR: Jayaram Nughalli
DESIGN AND PRINT MANAGEMENT: Reno Design R30007
DESIGNER: Graham Rendoth | www.renodesign.com.au
COVER ILLUSTRATION: Dragon © RealRockin | dreamstime.com
Opposite page: Chinese character symbol 'Lu' (prosperity)
PRINTING: CreateSpace

CONTENTS

Acknowledgements   9

Introduction: Diaspora and Destiny   11

CHAPTER **1**   **INDONESIA: THE POGROM**   17

CHAPTER **2**   **AUSTRALIA: NEW MOUNTAIN OF GOLD**   73

CHAPTER **3**   **THE PHILIPPINES: THE CHINESE TAKE-AWAY**   131

CHAPTER **4**   **MALAYSIA: COLD WAR**   181

CHAPTER **5**   **THAILAND: INTEGRATION OR DOMINATION?**   235

Epilogue: Are the Chinese coming?   245

ACKNOWLEDGEMENTS

This book is based on personal interviews and my own experiences in reporting the anti-Chinese riots, kidnappings and persecution of ethnic Chinese as well as their amazing conquest of Asia's wealth during my fifteen years as foreign correspondent in Southeast Asia. Many of the interviews took place in the late 1990s. Some were updated later, others remain valid today. The people interviewed were often candid, not afraid to be quoted by name, not afraid to be politically incorrect or un-diplomatic. Such people are a rare breed today in our PR-conscious societies where lies, half-lies and convenient replies are not only fashionable but acceptable.

When I reread these pages I am stunned by the frankness and honesty of those who offered their insights and opinions 'on record'. I thank all. This book is dedicated to every one of them.

And a special thanks to Jayaram Nughalli for his gentle editing of the book.

However, I owe a special debt to those who led me to subjects that graphically portrayed the hardships, the persecutions, the idiosyncrasies, past and present, of the Chinese Diaspora in Southeast Asia. I want to thank particularly my good friend Michael Sheridan in Bangkok, Alf Strano in Innisfail, Australia, Myra Sidharta in Indonesia, the courageous Teresita Ang See and that wise owl Washington SyCip in the Philippines. Included among those special people is Francisco (Frankie) Sionil Jose, the celebrated Filipino author now officially declared a "National Treasure."

He pestered me year after year during our annual reunions: "Have you written that book about the Chinese yet?" Frankie is now in his 80s so I figured I'd better write the book before he haunts me from the grave.

— ULI SCHMETZER

INTRODUCTION

DIASPORA AND DESTINY

Over a relatively short period, much of the wealth in Southeast Asia became concentrated in the hands of a minority of ethnic Chinese. Chinese minorities came to own the majority of private assets and to dominate the retail industry in the region. The fortunes of the Chinese peaked during the golden years of the Asian boom in the 1980s and '90s. Frugal, skilled and industrious, the Chinese in the Nanyang (Southern Ocean) took advantage of an unprecedented era in Asia's history, a boom that was mainly of their making.

Perhaps the most significant achievement of the Nanyang Diaspora, one that will haunt history for a long time, has been the financing of China's economic miracle.

This phenomenon superseded all predictions and remains unrivalled in human history. It was only possible thanks to the huge influx of funds and know-how from the Overseas Chinese, mostly from Southeast Asia.

From the late 1980s until the late 1990s the Chinese in Asia supplied an estimated 80 per cent of all foreign funds invested in communist China.

The wealth of the Diaspora and not the comparatively paltry funds from the United States, Japan or Western Europe became the real locomotive for Deng Xiaoping's vision of hauling China onto the world stage as a key player. Like most Chinese, he saw such a role as being consistent with the size of China's population and the past achievements of the Chinese people. Deng's great leap into capitalism or what he subtly called "Socialism with Chinese Characteristics" unleashed the commercial energy of his people, an energy that had only been anaesthetized by Maoist dogma.

But the great leap has also created a sense of nationalism reinforced by the clout of a military modernized by the same method. Today China feeds its people on a dangerous dish of destiny, a fare that more than once inflamed global conflicts in the past.

In this emergence of the oriental giant, the overseas Chinese from Southeast Asia have played a key role as financiers, technocrats and a bridge to the outside world.

The Chinese Diaspora is by no means a homogeneous society. Its members come from different parts of China, though their forefathers originated from mainly three provinces—Guangdong, Fujian and the island of Hainan. Their loyalties remain first to their families, then to their clans and villages and only finally to their Chineseness. Over the last decades, however, they "globalized" their commercial networks (before the term became popular) to link Southeast Asian nations with a largely invisible ring of economic interests forged by merchants and entrepreneurs who live in different parts of the Diaspora but collaborate like secret societies or commercial mafias. This ring has come to be known as the Bamboo Network.

The lock and key on this ring is China.

Despite occasional saber rattling, Beijing does not have to conquer its Asian neighbors by military force. The overseas Chinese have already commercially colonized virtually all of these neighbors. In fact the Bamboo Network, perhaps the world's most formidable commercial mafia, easily exceeds the assets and commercial activities of the Jewish Diaspora.

An Australian Government study in the 1990s at the height of the Asian boom found the Chinese in Southeast Asia generated a Gross National Product two thirds that of mainland China while Hong Kong, Taiwan and Singapore have combined foreign reserves larger than that of the United States or Japan and almost equal to that of the 1.3 billion Chinese.

By the turn of the century, the 56 million Chinese in Southeast Asia— nine per cent of the region's population—had conservatively estimated cash assets of US$2,000 billion to US$3,000 billion. The Asian economic meltdown in the 1990s hardly affected the wealthiest of these taipans.

Before the boom went bust they had moved the bulk of their cash assets out of the region, mainly to the United States.

The statistics are even more baffling if one remembers the Chinese are a small and sometimes persecuted minority among the Asian nations whose economies they dominate today.

The following figures are often disputed or diluted by Southeast Asian governments, which do not wish to frighten their citizens with Sinophobia when their main trading partner and creditor is the People's Republic of China. The figures are based on surveys in the late 1990s when the Diaspora's participation in national economies in Southeast Asia was at its height. The Chinese share in national economies may have been reduced by the subsequent economic crisis but there are those who argue the share is much larger today.

In Indonesia about seven million ethnic Chinese, making up three per cent of the total population, controlled 78 per cent of the private capital and over 50 per cent of the country's trade by the end of the 1990s.

Eleven to 14 per cent of Thailand's population is ethnic Chinese but they own 62 per cent of the private economy and nine-tenths of all investments in commerce and manufacturing. Half the financial resources of Thai banks and the majority of corporate assets are in Chinese hands.

In the Philippines 1.5 to 2 per cent of the population are ethnic Chinese but they control an estimated 55 per cent of the private economy and own 120 of the largest 300 enterprises.

In Malaysia the Bumiputra laws have tried to limit Chinese ownership and have given preference and business concessions to Malays. Around 33 per cent of Malaysians are ethnic Chinese but control 65 per cent of the private economy and 44.9 per cent of all companies despite the limitations of the New Economic Policy.

Vietnam sent out to sea 500,000 ethnic Chinese during the Boat People exodus in the late 1970s but the 4 per cent of the population which remains Chinese—and stayed behind—has already cornered an estimated two thirds of the fledgling private economy, mainly in Saigon (Ho Chi Minh City).

Three out of four Singaporeans are Chinese and own 95 per cent of the island-state's economy. Ninety-nine per cent of Taiwanese are of Chinese descent and they own 100 per cent of the economy. Until it was handed over to China in 1997 the British colony of Hong Kong had a population 97 per cent Chinese who had a 90 per cent share of the colony's wealth.

As a minority, hated and envied for its disproportionate wealth, the Nanyang Diaspora increasingly looks to China for protection—and guidance—as did the former Communist Party of Malaya which carried out an armed struggle in Malaysia during four bloody decades, a struggle that ended only in 1989. Sooner or later anti-Chinese riots like those in Indonesia could afford China the excuse to intervene by force in the affairs of its neighbors and so extend territory in that part of the South China Sea already shown on many Chinese school maps as part of a Greater China.

Before the accumulated wealth of the overseas Chinese modernized the motherland, China had for a while been a backward, isolated and ignorant society. Then, in 1979, Deng advocated his Open Door policy. It took another decade—and muscle flexing on Tiananmen Square—before Deng's policy bore fruit and attracted the flood of investments from the Nanyang Chinese.

The influence of the overseas Chinese on China's recent history is no anomaly. Funds from the Diaspora have steered the destiny of China for the last century. Diaspora money accelerated the fall of the empire, financed the Republic, padded the anti-Japanese war chest and helped build the Other China, the one in Taiwan. Today Diaspora money has metamorphosed mainland China.

The dedicated struggle of the Chinese to possess and control the riches and resources of the countries in which they have settled is as fascinating as the futile efforts of these countries to keep the Chinese settlers out or dispossess those who gained a disproportionate share of the total wealth.

In the war over resources and control of economic assets the Chinese at home and abroad have shown no mercy for competitors or concern for the environment.

They are truly a human juggernaut.

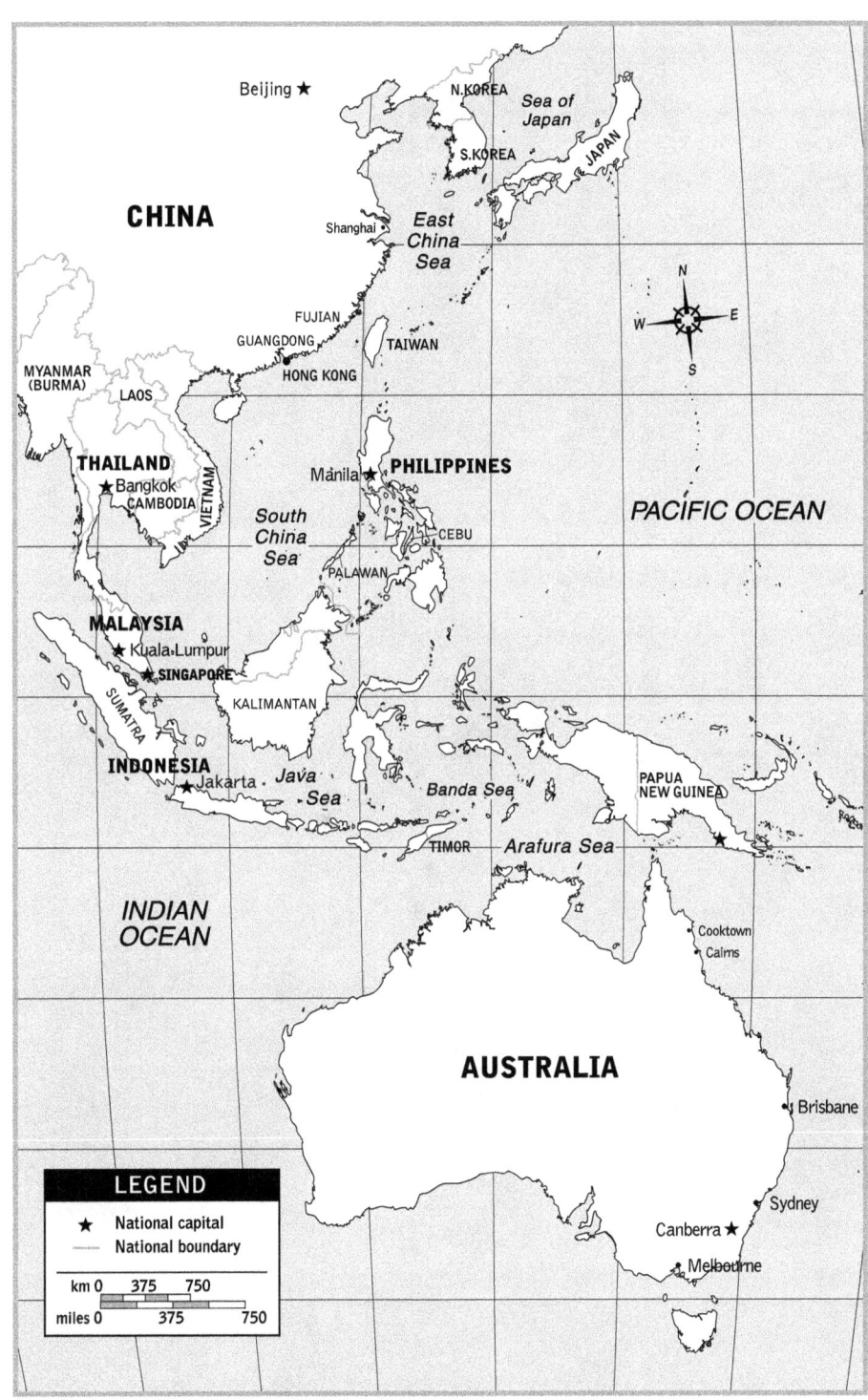

CHAPTER 1

INDONESIA: THE POGROM

In the weeks that followed, a time span during which she tried to erase from her memory all that had happened, Anne Chung had frequent mental flashbacks to the morning of May 13, 1998. It was the most agreeable part of her memory, the only recollection that had remained clear. All that happened later merged into a nightmare and would remain so, perhaps forever. With some luck, in time she would no longer feel their spittle trickle down her cheeks as they showed their final loathing, not for her body, which they had brutally abused, but for her ethnicity. Perhaps scabs would grow over the scars of their violence, their brutal intrusion into her most intimate privacy, their coarse jokes and throaty calls upon their God, the searing hurt of their frenzied bucking, their sweaty palms and drooling lips. Right now the scabs were fragile. The slightest jolt burst them, exposing a mental wound that oozed and would do so if she lived to be a hundred.

It had been a morning like most other mornings around the Pantai Indah Housing Complex in West Jakarta. It began with the creaking noise of shutters being raised. Anne never understood why the shutters were never greased but allowed to squawk, loud enough to jar the marrow in a dead man's bones. The first shutter was always the signal for the rest to be raised since no one in Chinatown wanted the competition to gain an unfair advantage on the day's trading.

The housing complex had mushroomed out of the rukos, also known as shop-houses, the traditional Chinese wall to wall shops located on the ground floor with family living quarters upstairs. Many shopkeepers, prodded by sons and daughters demanding more comfort and less hardship, abandoned the upstairs living space and moved their families into the modern rabbit warren of the housing complex. Soon the move became a matter of status. The new generation found it more fashionable to work in the ruko but live in the complex.

Each ruko is a private empire run by a patriarchal or matriarchal figure, assisted by sons or daughters. Native serfs carry out the strenuous chores. These workers are people the Chinese privately call Kaffirs, a derogatory term for colored natives borrowed from the Dutch. The Dutch colonizers of Indonesia had always looked down on the Kaffirs and defined them as bone lazy, sloppy and mentally sluggish, people who received money with one hand and spent it with the other, or, if they could manage, spent money in advance. On the other hand, the Dutch considered the Chinese a different kettle of fish, a thrifty and industrious people. One could not always trust the Chinese to treat you fairly, but they got the job done.

The 17th century Dutch governor Jan Pieterszoon Coen wrote: "There is no people better than the Chinese, too many of them cannot be brought to Batavia (Jakarta)."

As a man of action, Coen outfitted fleets to "capture" as many Chinese as possible from their trading posts and bring them to Batavia to populate and run the Indies for their Dutch masters. Soon the Chinese managed Dutch plantations, worked as tax collectors and supervisors for the Dutch and in the process began to consider themselves if not as good as their masters, at least far superior to the locals.

Now and then the Dutch had to massacre a few thousand Chinese to keep the rest in line and reduce their excessive arrogance.

Anne could not remember her family without cheap native labor, people like Muhamad who had been around since the days of her childhood. They were quiet, unobtrusive men and women, ready to carry out any task. She could not recall Muhamad or the others ever being mistreated: they were simply there, like the walls, the sacks of rice and the cash register in which her mother kept just enough notes to make change.

Her mother was determined to make a daily profit. Sometimes

she would raise the price in the afternoon if the morning had been slow.

From the very beginning of their existence in the Diaspora, profits had always motivated the Chinese. They collected more tax than the colonial masters had ordered and pocketed the surplus. They loaned money to natives at a salty interest rate to compensate for defaulters. If the natives fell behind in their tax payments or in their loans, the Chinese bought their land or took it over in lieu of payment.

By the time the Dutch were eased out of Indonesia, only about three per cent of the country's population was of ethnic Chinese origin and yet many of them had become powerful landowners. This irritated the natives and contradicted the ideals of independence with its nationalist slogan, "Indonesia for the Indonesians". Sukarno, the father of the young nation, found receptive ears with his argument that he had not wrested the country from the Dutch to have it fall into the hands of the Chinese. Hailed by his compatriots, Sukarno dispossessed the Yellow Colonials of their rural estates and banned them from owning land. Some 200,000 ethnic Chinese, many born in Indonesia, went back to China, distraught, dispossessed, bitter and often as poor as they or their forefathers had arrived in the Nanyang, the Southern Ocean.

Once in China the unfortunate refugees were soon stuck with the label "Capitalist Roaders" and treated as recalcitrant reactionaries by Mao Zedong's fanatical Red Guards.

Those Chinese who remained in Indonesia were forced off the land and had to move into urban areas, taking with them whatever money or gold they had managed to salvage. Like all people uncertain about their permanence in one place, the Chinese converted their assets into gold whenever possible and sewed it into the clothing of their children to hide it from marauding natives.

Those who did manage to keep a stake and had been brave enough to stay in Indonesia soon flourished again, this time as urban shopkeepers, pawnbrokers and moneylenders, services in great demand but despised by those who made use of them. During this time, Indonesia's Chinese earned the label a Thai prince once gave them: "The Jews of the East." Muslim fundamentalists who upheld the Koran's ban on usury preached against "the yellow infidels violating the Koran and misleading the faithful". But these zealots soon discovered religion had blind spots when fellow Muslims fell into debt, required funds to start a new venture or were desperate to patch up an ailing one.

The label Jews of the East would stick. With the advent of the Internet and the globalization of news it even became a banner under which the Diaspora aired its many grievances and made its demands for reparations. The Chinese have always had an uncanny knack of turning adversity into advantage. By 1998 the Chinese all over Southeast Asia talked of their "holocaust". The appropriation of the term infuriated the Jews who have always jealously guarded that term for themselves.

The torment of the Chinese was not over once Sukarno took away their land.

In the mid-1960s Colonel Suharto wrested power from the nation's founder Sukarno with a bloody witch-hunt for communists, a ruse that gained him the tacit approval of the Western powers. They saw the shrewd Indonesian as a staunch ally in the Cold War against Soviet expansion in Asia, unlike his predecessor Sukarno who had openly flirted with Moscow and professed socialist ideals and admiration for a Soviet style economy.

Suharto would rule Indonesia for 32 years with an iron fist while the United States and the West virtually ignored his brutal regime. The West stood by and watched when Suharto invaded and annexed East Timor in 1976 after the Portuguese withdrew from the sandalwood island they had run for 460 years, mostly with silk gloves and patient tolerance. Unfortunately for the East Timorese their island had become a vital Cold War asset. Not only was it on the doorstep of Australia, it lay along the route of U.S. nuclear-armed Polaris submarines, a route the Pentagon felt must remain "friendly" if the Cold War ever exploded into a Hot War.

During the 23 years long guerrilla war against the Indonesian armed forces, a third of the native Timorese population perished. The persecution was particularly cruel for the strong contingent of Chinese who had settled in East Timor, trading in sandalwood, which is highly coveted in Asia. Most of Indonesia's military commanders won their epaulets, stars and medals in the bloody campaigns in East Timor. The unfortunate island became a stepping-stone to promotion and recognition. The guerrilla war was barbaric on both sides and the Chinese were often caught in the middle.

In the rest of the world no one blinked.

Long before his invasion of East Timor, Suharto launched his own pogrom against the Chinese. Human rights organizations estimate Suharto's so-called anti-communist purge in the mid 1960s was responsible for the deaths of 220,000 people, a good portion of them ethnic Chinese accused of working as a fifth column for their Maoist masters in Beijing.

But the Chinese are irrepressible and perhaps humanity's best survivors, honed to survive famine, disease, deprivation and persecution. It did not take long before Indonesians found themselves in debt once again to the "yellow whites".

The debts grew rapidly and coincided with the golden age of the Chinese in the Diaspora, the years of the Asian tigers and the bamboo network. During this period the commercial acumen and clanship of the Chinese reached their full capability. In just over a decade, trade by local Chinese, their know-how and their funds dominated the entire Southeast Asian region. Hardly a deal was made, hardly a shipment moved in the region without Chinese say-so. No project had any hope of being launched without Chinese participation or intermediary activity. No bank or financial institution facilitated loans without the nod from one of the Lords of the Rim as the Chinese in Southeast Asia have been called.

As a child, Anne saw her father's modest grocery store quadruple its income in just a few years. She recalled her father built an annex behind the store. Then he bought a stake in one of the new shopping malls owned by a consortium of Chinese. He left the running of the store to his wife and to Anne and concentrated on procuring items for the supermarket in the shopping mall.

These supermarkets soon became targets for popular wrath. Street peddlers suddenly saw their source of supply eliminated when Chinese networks paid peasants a portion of their crops in advance with the proviso that all production must be sold exclusively to their supermarkets. The Chinese even collected the produce from the farm, saving the farmers the tedious trip, often on bicycles or buses, to sell their goods in the city. As more and more supermarkets mushroomed in the major cities of Indonesia, tens of thousands of street peddlers lost their livelihood or found their income depleted. The rancor of these disgruntled peddlers was easily inflamed.

The Chinese monopolized the food retail industries in similar ways all across Southeast Asia, in Thailand, Malaysia, the Philippines and wherever they gained a foothold. But nowhere did the Diaspora flourish more than under Suharto's autocratic regime, an anomaly in a nation that had persecuted the Chinese and weaned Indonesian children since colonial days on anti-Chinese prejudices.

Caught by the momentum of their unexpected prominence, the Chinese ignored the envy their wealth elicited and the danger signals gathering like monsoon clouds. Worse, they separated themselves from the natives even more.

As soon as the supermarket began to pay off, Anne's father had taken his two daughters out of the State school and entered them into the new Chinese schools that had been banned but were now quietly tolerated by the Suharto regime. These new schools had become status symbols among the Chinese, just as the new residential villages had become evidence of a family's superior financial rank and the modern residential blocks had turned into symbols of growing wealth for the Chinese bourgeoisie, the shopkeeper class, which was now graduating to the supermarket class.

Anne and her little sister Nan loved these shiny new schools where they were treated with respect, where no one taunted, teased or pushed them, a school without native classmates who never let you forget you were Chinese, a no-good and greedy outsider and above all a guest in "our country."

The teacher she remembered most was a Mister Tan who came from Taiwan to teach both Mandarin and English. A dapper little man with a pencil-thin moustache, Mister Tan wore elegant dark suits and carried an ivory-handled umbrella he opened during monsoon rains and also in the tropical sun. His classes were crowded with teenage girls in the front rows. Like the rest of the girls, Anne had a crush on Mister Tan, although the little fop showed no romantic interest or preference for any of his adoring female students. He was her first and only secret love. Anne knew her choice of husband would be regulated by her parents. The two, aided by relatives, guarded her virginity and passion closely to ensure any pent up teenage romanticism would have only one outlet—for the man they would select as a "good match" both in financial and ethnical terms. By the time she was mature, a girl might almost accept any man presented by her parents as the outlet for her suppressed sex drive and romanticism.

Within a year, the mooned-over Mister Tan from Taiwan was replaced by a Mister Lim from Sichuan province in China. The commercial climate had changed. As Indonesia's powerful new trading partner, Beijing insisted that in order to promote more lucrative trade and investment ties, it was necessary to educate the new generation of Indonesia's overseas Chinese with teachers from the mainland and not from Taiwan. Mister Lim was rigid and dogmatic. He had a face like an old monkey and wore dark Mao suits. He was not popular and Anne moped for months for the little fop who had been sent back to Taiwan.

The change in teachers was significant and coincided with the growing clout of China on the international stage and particularly in Southeast Asia. The Diaspora's economic and political rise was closely related to China's economic and political rise. Beijing's power and muscle straightened the backbone of the Diaspora and added to the confidence, and often cockiness, of the overseas Chinese. Napoleon had once compared China to "a sleeping giant", better left slumbering. Now the giant was awake and the speed of its development, unprecedented in the history of humankind, amazed the world and stimulated the entrepreneurial spirit of the overseas Chinese.

The motherland and the Diaspora had long coexisted in symbiosis. The phenomenon had its irony: In imperial days the overseas Chinese were considered traitors for defying an imperial ban on emigration. Anyone who returned from the Nanyang could be executed for treason. The Dragon Throne was not popular in the Nanyang, one reason why overseas Chinese rescued and financed Sun Yat Sen's fledgling republican movement in the early 20th century. Once successful, the Republic relegated the emperor and his costly court to the confines of the Forbidden City. When China was invaded in the 1930s, it was the Diaspora that filled the war chest, financing resistance to the Japanese invaders. After World War II, the financial investments of the Diaspora allowed tiny Taiwan and Chiang Kai-shek's nationalists to stand up to Mao's communist China.

Until modern times, China's attitude towards its emigrants was scorn, indifference and hostility, consistent with that of the Ming and Manchu emperors who were afraid anyone who left the realm would conspire against the empire from abroad. An imperial decree in 1712 proclaimed:

"THOSE OF THE OVERSEAS CHINESE WHO STAYED ABROAD PERMANENTLY ARE LIABLE FOR CAPITAL PUNISHMENT AND WILL BE EXTRADITED BY THE PROVINCIAL GOVERNORS FOR PROMPT EXECUTION."

As late as in 1894, near the dusk of the empire, the court considered the overseas Chinese "outlaws beyond the pale of the Chinese emperor's authority". China refused to accept The Hague Convention of 40 nations held in 1930, which prohibited any state from extending its jurisdiction over its citizen living in another country of which the citizen is also a subject.

As the power of the imperial dynasties waned, the fear that emigrants would help the rebel cause grew. As it happened this fear was well founded because the emigrants considered the court their mortal enemy. Only a new regime could change their outlaw status and allow them to return home or at least be accepted as equals.

In time Communist China became more astute. Proclaiming "common interests" but in reality coveting their money, Beijing encouraged the Diaspora to visit the motherland or even retire there.

(The State of Israel follows a similar strategy, promoting itself as a must holiday or retirement home for Jews in the Diaspora. Like China, Israel has immensely benefited, financially and politically, from the Jewish Diaspora, especially the one in the United States. Neither China nor Israel would be at their current development level without the financial support of their ethnic brethren abroad. Not surprisingly, both countries treat these nest eggs around the globe as if they are part of their own population. China considers the Asian Diaspora as a species of frontier Chinese in the Nanyang, the vast Southern Ocean region.)

Since 1980, the overseas Chinese invested 80 per cent of the $167 billion in foreign funds that came as investment into China by the end of the century. They carried back to the motherland a large part of their wealth from abroad as soon as Deng Xiaoping lifted the bamboo curtain to the Middle Kingdom with his historic open door policy which made it clear that making profits was no longer banned or considered evil exploitation of the working class. In those early days of the switch in China's economic policy, the Diaspora provided the managerial skills and investments that boosted

China's muscles. The Nanyang's devotion to the motherland, coupled with instincts for a good, quick deal, would help propel Mao's children from a backward, underdeveloped communist nation into a capitalist powerhouse.

Today, should China ever wish to annex any of the territories in the Nanyang, it would find available an efficient ethnic administration of loyal local Chinese ready to run these new territories just as Hitler found them in Poland and in Czechoslovakia where generations of German immigrants, always loyal to the Fatherland, had settled, prospered and often economically dominated these countries. But unlike the Germans of the early 20th century, the Chinese want trade with as many nations as possible, especially those in their vicinity. While Chinese emperors demanded an oath of allegiance from these nations recognizing the Dragon Throne as the supreme sovereign, the new rulers of China no longer demand such recognition. Instead they demand access to buy into and exploit the natural resources of these countries. In other words, so China argues, exactly the same right of access the United States has enjoyed for almost a century. When this access is not granted, the Chinese can be ruthless in their retaliation. This was illustrated in the case of Rio Tinto executive Stern Hu. A Chinese court in Shanghai sentenced him to ten years in jail on charges of bribery and spying in China on behalf of the Australian mining conglomerate. China badly seeks a stake in Rio Tinto's iron ore mining but has been rebuffed—so far.

The pragmatic official policy in China vis-à-vis the overseas Chinese has been unable to eradicate the private feelings of mainland Chinese. The mainlanders look down on emigrants as people who have failed to attend to their filial duties, failed to care for aged parents and failed to worship at the ancestral tombs. Such people can never claim to be true sons of the Yellow Emperor. At the same time there is considerable envy. These foreign cousins prospered while the mainlanders had to struggle through idiotic political campaigns, the disastrous agrarian policies and the famines caused by Mao's harebrained policies.

Whatever ordinary citizens privately felt, successive Chinese governments had no intention to surrender jurisdiction over citizens who migrated. Chiang Kai-shek's Kuomintang government realized and recognized the importance of keeping the overseas Chinese on board. In 1932 the Kuomintang created a ministry for overseas Chinese. This ministry strongly encouraged and sometimes even financed or subsidized Chinese abroad to maintain the Chinese language, schools, hospitals and cultural activities. The Kuomintang also appointed overseas Chinese to its Legislative Yuan and the Control Yuan, the upper and lower houses of parliament.

Mao too realized early the enormous financial potential of the overseas contingent. He might have remembered their vital contribution to the nationalist cause of Sun Yat Sen between 1907 and 1917. Mao's first People's Consultative Conference, founded as a pro-communist talking shop in September 1949, included 18 overseas Chinese delegates. It proclaimed: "The Central People's Government of the PRC shall do its utmost to protect the legitimate rights and interests of Chinese residing abroad." The communists insisted that all Chinese abroad retained their Chinese citizenship.

In 1951 Zhou Enlai said: "The lawful rights and interests of these people, as a result of unreasonable discrimination and even persecution on the part of certain countries, cannot but arouse the serious attention and deep concern of the Chinese people."

The following year, at the first National People's Congress, Chou Enlai expressed the hope that all Southeast Asian countries would respect the legitimate rights of their Chinese citizen. He also promised to settle the question of dual nationality.

By this time both Taipei and Beijing fought not so much for the souls but the purse strings of the overseas Chinese. The Taiwanese were winning the contest easily among the rich overseas Chinese. Given the choice, the overseas Chinese, a group motivated by economic gains, had no intention of investing in the Spartan Maoist society which frowned on private wealth, was persecuting landlords, rich peasants and affluent merchants. On the other hand, the pro-Maoist members of the Diaspora usually came from the poorer classes, mostly young people inflamed by the doctrine of equality and solidarity the communists preached.

It took three decades and a radical switch in economic policy before Deng wrenched the overseas investors away from Taiwan.

Beijing was quicker, however, to settle the passport question. Under the Sino-Indonesian Dual Nationality Treaty of April 22, 1955, free choice of nationality was offered to all overseas Chinese. The Treaty included the unusual step of offering the same choice to women, perhaps a concession to Mao's proclamation that half the earth is held up by women. Under this treaty a husband could opt to remain Chinese, a wife to become a citizen of the host nation. Diasporas everywhere have always loved to have it both ways.

Zhou Enlai urged the overseas Chinese to be good citizens wherever they chose to be. He also virtually pledged that Chinese citizen who opted to retain Chinese nationality abroad, would not indulge in political activities in Indonesia or Malaysia. He renounced China's right to interfere in the internal affairs of Indonesia while Indonesia promised to protect the rights and interests of its Chinese citizens.

That neither side would respect any part of the accord was a foregone conclusion. But China, bleeding in North Korea and on the verge of its first major purge at home, the Hundred Flowers Campaign (when Mao called on academics to freely air their criticism and then had all punished when they did) was anxious to maintain peace with its neighbors and dedicate itself to internal stability. At the same time the Great Helmsman preferred to have his overseas Chinese naturalized rather than see them repatriated to a struggling China.

In 1978, once China had opened its doors, ethnic Chinese from all over Southeast Asia made pilgrimages to the homes of their ancestors. These visitors paid indirect homage to a system few of them respected or had faith in. But nearly all of them saw the enormous potential of a billion strong market they understood better than anyone else in the world. The stability guaranteed by the harsh, rigid and intolerant rule of the Communist Party was the best collateral for investors.

But the real boom of Diaspora investments came only after Chinese troops killed hundreds of demonstrators around Tiananmen Square on the night of June 3-4, 1989. The victims, youths and workers, knew little about democracy but saw a momentary weakness in the system they felt could be exploited to advance their own personal fortunes. Only a few idealists saw the student movement as an opportunity to redress the many injustices of a cruel and often bloody police state.

The world was shocked by the televised killings. For years afterwards Chinese officials, in moments of rare candor, would ask me why the West was so obsessed with the so-called "Tiananmen Incident". Had the West not realized the shootings of a few prevented a period of horrendous chaos in China and had saved the lives of millions of Chinese who would have surely perished, butchered in the struggle for the spoils of the communist system in a country notorious for bloody upheavals? Had the West not realized that if law and order had broken down an estimated 100 million people would have spilled across China's borders to seek their fortunes abroad, mainly in the West? Didn't Washington remember Deng's visit to the White House when President Carter asked him to be more generous about allowing exit visas for his compatriots and the wily Chinese leader is said to have replied: "Mister President how many million do you want?"

The Chinese are a pragmatic race, more interested in opportunities than ideals. Few Chinese people truly mourned the victims of the Tiananmen massacre but many privately lamented the fact the troops had stifled any chance of change and the opportunity for non-party members to piggyback on such a change closer to the center of power and its privileges. The situation was different in Hong Kong: There, to march for democracy was safe and beneficial to one's credentials in those days. Besides, many Hong Kongers secretly cherished the hope that massive demonstrations could persuade Britain and the West to renege on handing over the colony to Beijing.

Only a few hundred of the tens of thousands of mainland Chinese "students" who obtained refugee status abroad had anything to do with the Tiananmen movement. The rest saw a golden opportunity to go abroad thanks to the international compassion created by the "massacre".

At home, by reasserting its authority, the Communist Party won the confidence of the overseas Chinese. While Western banks and enterprises pulled out or retrenched their commitments in China following Tiananmen, the Chinese in the Diaspora poured in more money in the following two years (1990-91) than they had done over the previous decade. Chinese accountancy wizard Washington Sy-Cip explained it bluntly to me in Manila one day: "We were convinced the communists were there to stay and China would not go the way of the Soviet Union, as the Americans might have wished."

With the confidence in China's future came the subsequent pilgrimages of overseas Chinese to their hometowns. Local authorities laid out the red carpets for them, desperate for investment funds after

Tiananmen so they could maintain, at least partially, an economic growth rate which they saw, rightly, as the main safeguard to ensure their hold on power.

But these pilgrimages had a second scope: The overseas Chinese were anxious to perpetuate their names and achievements in the villages and towns of their ancestors. The visitors built schools named after themselves, restored ancient temples destroyed by Mao's Red Guards during the Cultural Revolution and financed joint ventures to manufacture their products with cheap local labor. Some came at the last moment, on stretchers and under oxygen tents, to be buried in the native soil with the spirits of their ancestors. Their mausoleums, with air conditioning and toilets, encouraged a lucrative funeral industry. For hard cash the undertakers catered for the desires of the moribund, anxious to exchange a life of hardship on earth for an existence of comfort in the realm beyond.

The return of the overseas Chinese, as investors or moribund, brought back old traditions in a China where Maoism had outlawed burials as a waste of good land, discouraged religion, banned ancestor worship and instituted the common practice of cremation for the dead.

Now the investments and the nostalgia of the Diaspora constituted the economic backbone for entire provinces as China turned from state ownership to private enterprise, from the iron rice bowl of cradle-to-grave state care to blatant capitalism. The party camouflaged this Dengist ideology with the mollifying phrase: "Socialism with Chinese Characteristics". Privately it was known as "capitalism with communist characteristics".

The prodigals' return to the motherland, feted, favored and featured, was the ultimate gratification for years of hard toil, cruel deprivations and sometimes bloody persecutions abroad. Few overseas Chinese— or emigrants of any nationalities for that matter—have resisted the age-old dream of going back home, as a Chinese saying goes, "dressed in silken robes".

In the motherland, half a century of communism had not erased the commercial acumen and natural tendency of the Chinese to pry on each other. Astute mainlanders welcomed the cousins from the Nanyang with open arms and then set about plucking these golden geese of as many feathers as could be extracted. After all, had not these rich cousins enjoyed the good life abroad while those left behind fought tooth and nail to survive the traps of political campaigns and Mao's economic blunders?

In the beginning, federal and provincial governments granted ready concessions for cheap land, cheap labor and tax exemptions. The rich cousins were celebrated at public banquets, coddled at private parties and asked to contribute to all kinds of worthy causes. In time the welcomes wore thin and the concessions became loaded with levies, all disguised as federal evils though they were mostly local scams.

Ever since Deng's Open Door policy turned millionaires into national heroes by the late 1980s, the great majority of China's people became obsessed with affluence. To achieve wealth, all methods are considered fair and worthy tools in today's China: Crime proliferates, cheating, lying, exploiting, taking bribes and kickbacks are acceptable ruses and practiced despite the occasional public execution of a swindler or official on the take. The Maoist slogan about honesty and social equality have become, like every other Maoist dictum, a mere tool for convenient lip service to a dogma whose credibility died during the first purge of its critics in the 1950s, long before Deng's ascent.

Twisting the truth, turning black into white and white into black has been a Maoist forte since 1948 and most Chinese will argue the Communist Party remained in power thanks to these methods. What was good for the gander yesterday was good for the geese today.

In Deng's Brave New China, provincial leaders imposed levies on wells dug by peasants, demanded buffalo, cow and corn taxes, all in order to raise funds for industrial projects that filled mainly their own pockets. If the peasants were slow or unable to pay, thugs were sent to reinforce the demand; furniture and livestock were confiscated and sold in lieu of taxes. Sometimes the thugs dragged away a son or a daughter to serve out the tax debt in servitude. Over a short period of time the entire social fabric of Mao's socialist system collapsed, replaced by unprecedented greed and cruelty. The code of common welfare was ridiculed and replaced by the unofficial slogan: Everyone for themselves. Mao's China, where everyone was supposed to be equally poor, was buried by Deng's new slogan: "To get rich is glorious."

The new heroes of China were no longer hardy tractor drivers or barefoot girl doctors, their hair braided, their cheeks rouged. Hero soldiers like Lei Feng no longer split wood for the aged and rescued children from forests and fires. The new heroes feted in the *China Daily* and the *People's Daily* were China's first millionaires, the rags to riches tales of humble peasants now living in luxury villas and driving imported cars. These paragons of capitalism were the models for the new socialist species.

For the Chinese on the mainland, all Chinese in the Diaspora were millionaires. It was everyone's personal duty to discover how the rich cousins had done it.

Fleeced in the motherland, the Chinese investors were also in trouble in their adopted countries where the local media criticized them for taking the wealth earned in countries such as Indonesia, Malaysia, Thailand and the Philippines to invest in China.

Before the great Asian boom, the Vietnamese had already attempted to purge their nation of Chinese co-nationals. The Boat People "encouraged" to flee Vietnam in the late 1970s and early 1980s were almost exclusively ethnic Chinese. Thousands perished in the exodus when their rickety boats sank. Others were cruelly butchered, raped and dumped into the sea by pirates and natives. Before they were allowed to leave Vietnam, the Boat People had to pay corrupt authorities and boat owners in gold for the right to run away. Once paid off, the Vietnamese Navy and police turned a blind eye.

But only a decade after the exodus, those Chinese who remained in Vietnam—no more than 1.5 per cent of the population—already owned nearly 50 per cent of the private wealth of a country in which capitalism and communism coexist. The achievements of the Chinese in Vietnam are truly astonishing and a tribute to their diligence and their ability to survive and flourish in adverse conditions.

The issue of capital flight to China remained on the back burner until the Southeast Asian boom went bust. Suddenly governments provided statistics: In the 1990s alone, some $80 billion from the region found their way into projects on the mainland. The same capital, kept at home, could have sustained the ambitious infrastructure and development projects that became the Achilles heel of Southeast Asia when currencies plunged against the U.S. dollar and overnight the repayment of loans, pegged to the U.S. dollar rate, became too expensive to honor.

The worst affected nation was Indonesia where Suharto, in need of finance, had turned to the wealthy Chinese and made them partners in concessions that helped both sides to dizzy heights of affluence over just three decades.

The unholy alliance between Suharto, his clan and the rich Chinese was never based on love or respect but undisguised avarice. The alliance is known as Cukongism. Its modus operandi was simple: The Chinese created enterprises in which Suharto, his six children and senior generals became partners. In return the regime doled out monopolies and concessions to their Chinese allies. No major Indonesian concern could expect to survive without the name of a Suharto family member or one of his senior generals on its board of directors.

Anne remembered her father had difficulty persuading his bank to extend a loan he required to pay his share of the new supermarket. "Dad didn't want to go to the Cukong-Chinese because he knew they would want a share of the market in return for the permit and the loan. So he went to his friends. But no one seemed to have that kind of money or wanted to risk it with a man who had been only a small time grocer and now had big ideas. I guess there was also a pinch of envy involved. Why should Dad get out of the rukos when all of them were still in the rukos?"

In the end Anne's father went the route of most of the ambitious Chinese. He threw in his lot with one of those connected to the Suharto clan and for a 25 per cent share in the market the permit and the loan came through, ironically from his own bank which had denied him the loan in the first place. Someone high up had obviously given the approval.

Anne recalled that whenever her father was tired, he would complain about Cukongism, lamenting that he was doing all the work while the fat cats were taking a quarter of all the profits. Worse, he said, he had to pay back the loan, which meant the fat cats had not even invested a single rupiah for their 25 per cent perpetual share in the supermarket venture.

Cukongism was highly profitable for those involved.

And there were many. The Chinese quickly spread their commercial dominance to the entire Southeast Asian region, creating the so-called Bamboo Network, a loose alliance of movers and shakers imperative to any major deal. The Network had no need to stage expensive and long-winded feasibility studies or hold project presentations, conferences and legal contracts that involved a battery of expensive lawyers all flown to a common destination and housed in expensive hotels. For the Bamboo

Network, a single phone call between taipans sufficed to raise tens and sometimes hundreds of millions of dollars for a project one of them had in mind. These deals were made on one taipan's pledge to another. According to a Chinese friend who had been involved in such deals the conversation went something like this:

"Hey! This is Long in Singapore. I have a concession to build a 15-storey hotel not far from Orchard Road. It's a 150-million-dollar project. I can offer you a third, Lim, if you're interested. Sugarman Chu in Malaysia is already in for a third. Interested? Good. I'll send you the details. How is the family? Good. Say hello to your son and tell him next time I'll give him a stroke-a-hole and still beat him. Bye for now."

This was the way deals were made and no one would renege on his word if he or she ever wanted to do business again with the Bamboo Network. The few who put together loss-making projects are either dead or are minor players in the Asian Rim today. Some, like Lucio Tan in the Philippines, have redeemed themselves by making good the losses suffered by their associates.

It was the Chinese who taught the Indonesians the art of creative bankruptcy in which the government closes both eyes as directors and major shareholders salvage their own funds while ordinary depositors and shareholders go home empty-handed. In these bankruptcies it was usually the Indonesian partners who bore the brunt of any publicity. The Chinese remained behind the scenes. Sometimes their names were not even on company records.

Losses were covered up or swept under the table by a censored media.

"Indonesian generals have developed a world-wide reputation for catastrophic financial losses but are rarely scolded," wrote author Sterling Seagrave, long before Suharto bowed out.

Cukongism has two faces: In Indonesia, the Chinese control the economy and the army protects them in return for kickbacks. In Thailand, the army controls commerce but the Chinese run it for them in return for kickbacks.

The most successful Cukong is Liem Sioe Liong. He was born in 1916 in Fujian province in China, left his village at the age of 20 and arrived in Java where he started off as a humble peddler of peanut oil working in a rich uncle's venture. Eventually he made Kretek cigarettes which—so many

Indonesians still allege—were not only spiced with cloves but laced with opium to make smokers dependent. From there he graduated to wartime smuggling for the Indonesian army.

During his transactions, he befriended a young colonel named Suharto who badly needed funds to promote his ambitions in the armed forces and create the kind of loyalty that comes with largesse. The colonel had a great thirst for power and money. Liem and the Bamboo Network had a great thirst for opportunities. The Network supplied the funds and once in power Suharto rewarded Liem and his cronies with monopolies. But Suharto made sure he or his family had a stake in every enterprise.

These initial monopolies formed the basis of Liem's financial empire, the Salim Group whose enterprises and banks now circle the globe: a typical product of the heady days in Southeast Asia in the 1980s and 1990s when paupers and peasants in China were turned into millionaires virtually overnight.

In those days astute peasants roped into joint ventures graduated from bicycles to Mercedes limousines, a rural worker with a line in toy exports tooled around the austere Chinese capital in a red Ferrari and a communist cadre built his own horse race track with a stand for 10,000 spectators. Then he added a golf course next door, all just outside Beijing. A humble logger from Guangzhou migrated to Borneo in the 1980s and became the billionaire timber king of Asia a decade later. Peasants in blue Mao suits were buying Armani in the new boutiques of China, proudly displaying the labels on the sleeves like medals of distinction. Girls in quilted trousers and jackets bought their new western wardrobes by pointing to the pages of the Italian and French fashion magazines every new boutique had on display.

The China boom spread across Southeast Asia.

Suharto made sure his own nest and that of his rapacious children was suitably feathered. By the time he resigned under pressure from student demonstrations and street riots in May 1998, his family assets were estimated between $30 billion and $40 billion—ironically the exact amount Indonesia required as a loan from the International Monetary Fund (IMF) to rescue and kick-start its stalled economy.

Before the crash, Cukongism had become so successful banks all over the world loaned money to Chinese entrepreneurs on the simple pledge—

sometimes no more than a rumor—that one of the Suharto children or the Dictator himself was backing the project for which the loan was intended. A letter by Suharto's business-minded daughter Rukmana to the owner of a two-bit Jakarta taxi company was good for a $250 million loan from the Hong Kong branch of Peregrine Investments. The loan eventually bankrupted the Hong Kong branch and badly hurt Peregrine's partner, Chicago's First National Bank.

During the so-called Asian miracle, the Chinese front for the Suharto clan blatantly milked a gullible global banking system, often operated by inexperienced protégés with grand expectations. The greed of these young brokers, their lack of morals and the blatant flouting of accepted banking norms became the main culprits of the Asian financial disaster.

These European and American whiz-kids who recommended and often authorized the huge loans on which Southeast Asia's economic bubble inflated were often the sons and daughters of ordinary western workers. Thrown into the hot pot of a bubble their older peers no longer understood, the youngsters were misled by the initial windfalls and the prospect of rapid promotion. In contrast, their clients and advisers were the sons and daughters of ethnic Chinese whose genes had been laundered through generations of mercenary affairs, often murky and often muddy, but nearly always profitable and nearly always at someone's expense.

The whiz-kids became welcome fodder for the Chinese. The carrot of tasty dividends and interest rates the borrowers tangled under their nose proved irresistible. The "kids" took the bait with the most common shortcut: Grossly inflating the collateral assets of their clients. This way a two-bit taxi company was suddenly on the books as a multi-million dollar transport industry.

By 1998, the Chinese made up barely three per cent of Indonesia's 202 million people but owned more than three quarters of the country's private wealth. It was not an isolated phenomenon. A year earlier Henry Tsang, the China-born deputy lord mayor of Sydney told me 70 per cent of all private wealth in the Pacific Rim area was owned by the Chinese Diaspora, which constituted only seven per cent of the total population in that region.

Privately, Indonesians bickered about the disproportionate distribution of wealth. Publicly however, resentment remained muted as long as the economy forged ahead, jobs were available and basic commodities were subsidized for ordinary mortals, all waiting on the sidelines for their share of the spoils from the boom.

Not everyone kept quiet. For Islamic fundamentalists in a Muslim country, the Chinese were poison. Every now and then during Friday prayer, an imam would thunder invectives against pig-eating infidels living amidst the faithful. He would say their usury and greed kept the Prophet's followers poor while the unholy ones flourished. The ranting resulted in periodic mob violence at villages and towns. Chinese shops and homes were looted, smashed, burned, their owners often beaten up. These riots were obviously considered a safety valve by the regime. It allowed the mobs to vent their frustrations whenever the economy went sour.

Usually, after a few hours, the riots were smothered by the armed forces. Now and then a particularly militant clergy would be arrested to dampen the ardor of other zealots. He would be tried for violating the law against racial discrimination or the law against inflaming ethnic ill feeling. Punishment was soft. Often the case was simply shelved. Suharto had no wish to tangle with the fundamentalists, although he was determined to keep them in line.

For decades these sporadic outbursts of violence against the Chinese had become accepted in Indonesia, just as the wave of kidnappings of ethnic Chinese in the Philippines was seen by Filipinos as an unfortunate but understandable way to readjust the wealth gap. The Vietnamese for their part argued that the ethnic Chinese Boat People had been the country's "bloodsuckers".

The Chinese came to the Wihara (temple) in Rengasdengklok only at night to light joss sticks and leave food at the plinth of the Buddha's statue. They named the place an "assembly hall" to appease Muslim sensitivity. Their prudence did not save the Wihara from being ransacked and torched early in 1998 during a riot sparked by the imprudence of Liu Chi, the wife of a butcher and known for her irreverent tongue. Liu tongue-lashed a Muslim youth named Hendra Kurnia when he beat his drum outside her home at 3 a.m. to celebrate the end of Ramadan, the period of the fast.

"You stupid dog!" she shouted. "You crazy pig!"

Mrs Liu's outburst, not unusual in the circumstances, was passed from mouth to mouth, embellished, exaggerated and dished up as an example of how these infidels blasphemed against the Koran. The lady's intemperance was welcome fodder for riot provocateurs who always ply their trade when times are harsh and when they know the authorities are ready to activate the anti-Chinese safety valve: Allowing the rabble to let off steam by looting goods from stores owned by the Chinese.

To disguise the real purpose of the riots, the mobs usually claim to act in the name of Islam and to safeguard their faith against encroachment by alien religions.

Within hours, Mrs Liu's story mobilized the town. Peasants armed with pitchforks, cutlasses and axes streamed into Rengasdengklok from the countryside, alerted by youths on motorcycles who had raised the alarm.

The mob came into a town in which nearly every shop was owned by a Chinese family, a town that until just 20 years earlier had been totally Indonesian. Then the first Chinese family bought property and within a few years all up and down the main thoroughfare, the shops came to be owned by the Chinese. The native Muslims had moved a mile out of town into ramshackle huts bought with the money left over from the spending binges they had indulged in after selling their town properties to the Chinese. The Muslims bred cattle and grew rice, which they sold to the Chinese shops. The Chinese also lent money, paid in advance for the harvests of the Muslims, those now living on the fringe of the town. The usual religious rabble-rousers had no difficulty stirring up these Muslims, religious issues serving as an excuse to cover the rancor of their lost shops and their growing debts to the Chinese.

The Buddhist Wihara became a symbolic target.

In no time the crowd had smashed the statues of minor deities, tossed the joss stick holders into a fire and reduced the woodworks to tinder. In the rampage that followed, a Protestant church and 48 Chinese homes or shops were stoned, burned or looted along the main thoroughfare of the rice growing town just 40 miles east of Jakarta.

Finally, a cheering mob decapitated the Buddha figure, dunked the head in the sewage canal, tied a rope around the neck and strung the head from the archway to the temple compound. There the Buddha head dangled, still dripping as the mob ran up and down the main street accompanied by locals pointing out the houses and shops of the Chinese.

A month later, the court in the district capital of Karawang sentenced Mrs Liu's husband, Liu Kim, 55, to three years in jail for inciting a riot. He took the blame for his wife's intemperance to save her from going to jail, not a place from which a Chinese husband can expect his wife to return unblemished.

The excuse for the riots had been no more than a peccadillo.

Anti-Chinese riots are no novelty in Indonesia. They date back centuries. The Dutch now and then launched purges of their own against their Chinese subjects. The Indonesian nationalists denounced the Yellow Whites as colonial lackeys of the Dutch. After independence thousands of Chinese were massacred as "communists" in the 1960s. Today the Chinese are victims of their own thrift and wealth.

In the 1990s Nely Tan, a prominent professor of sociology, believed the riots are a safety valve for social frustration. "The Chinese shops are all along the main streets," she points out. "They are visible and vulnerable. What the rioters really want is to strike at the government. But like the man who wants to hit his boss and ends up beating his wife, the mobs are picking on the Chinese."

Professor Tan's explanation is typical of a Chinese upper class member who refutes any suggestion that native Indonesians actually do loathe the Chinese. Tan and others want to believe the riots are a social accident, the Chinese only unfortunate victims of circumstances. There is a terrible parallel to the elite class of Jews in Nazi Germany who also explained the anti-Semitic excesses as a temporary phenomenon of thuggery.

Their excuses are always wishful thinking, contradicted by reality.

In fact it is difficult to find a native Indonesian who has something good to say about ethnic Chinese. Those who do show tolerance are like the Jakarta taxi driver who blurted: "I don't like the Chinese but without them I wouldn't have this job."

Ong Hokham, a history professor at the University of Indonesia, attributed this racist prejudice to the fact that the Chinese dominated the country's distribution apparatus and all aspects of the retail trade since colonial times. When their rural holdings were closed in 1959, they became urban street vendors. During the Asian boom the Chinese on the street graduated to supermarket owners. Overnight agrarian produce was presold to the Chinese and their supermarkets. These transactions cut into the livelihood of middlemen and street vendors who find it easy today to rally a mob against the Chinese and their despised supermarkets.

Charges against the Chinese proliferate: They have never participated in any nationalist movements; under the Dutch they exploited the natives as tax farmers, pawnshop brokers and opium distributors. In the old days the Chinese laced the food of their workers with opium to get them addicted and control them through vice. Today the Chinese are accused by popular belief of lacing with opium a Chinese brand of clove cigarette so smokers will be addicted to the brand. After all, so the argument goes, the Chinese lace their food all over the world with a chemical additive to make it more palatable—and addictive.

The accusations go on and on: The Chinese cooperated with the Dutch. The Chinese sent their children abroad for education. The Chinese ruined the economy and native business. They turned on their friends: They helped bring down the government after it had made them billionaires with preferential treatment.

Back in 1965, during the anti communist massacres—when many of the Chinese were murdered as Maoist agents and Indonesians were caught up in a tidal wave of xenophobia—the use of Chinese characters, language and culture was banned even though the constitution outlaws racial or religious intolerance.

Despite this tolerance law, most Indonesians are candidly anti-Chinese in private. One of Indonesia's most distinguished academics once told me: "The Chinese are like locusts. Once they have a foothold they eat up everything and won't be content until the field is barren."

Some Chinese people seem to agree.

"We can never get enough. We want it all. If ten projects are up for grabs the Indonesian is happy with one or two. The Chinese wants 11," said Sofyan Wanandi, one of Indonesia's new taipans and chairman of the Gemala Group.

His assessment of the voracious nature of his race was borne out at Rengasdengklok. Twenty years ago, so Ety Wisuda remembered, the shops on the main thoroughfare were all owned by native Muslims. Now every shop and store is owned by Chinese immigrants who arrived in droves from Western Kalimantan (Borneo) and Sumatra, where they or their forefathers had settled, mainly illegally. Even the lucrative prawn farms and the timber yards, the town's main industries, are in Chinese hands. Ety's husband runs the local bus service.

"The Muslims now live out back," she said, pointing to the vast expanse of rice paddies and thatched huts behind the town. "They have small farms or rent them out to the poor."

Ety lives opposite the Wihara. On the night the town ran amok, she fled through the back door and hid in the home of an Indonesian neighbor. She listened with chattering teeth as the mob stoned her home and then ransacked it, dragging furniture out onto a bonfire.

"The men who led the mob shouted into megaphones: "Chinese!" and pointed fingers at our houses," she recalled. "Some Chinese had converted to Islam and painted "MUSLIM" on their walls. Their homes were stoned all the same."

Two days after the riots, Rengasdengklok looked as if nothing extraordinary had occurred, except for the scorch scars on the torched shops. The smashed windows and shop fronts had already been boarded up. The word "MUSLIM" in huge black letters was daubed prominently on homes and fences, not just in Rengasdengklok, but also on buildings in villages and towns nearby.

Like Ety, the rest of the Chinese returned after taking refuge with relatives in Jakarta or with compassionate neighbors. All of them remained uneasy, particularly after a mullah toured the town on the back of a truck. Looking like a prophet with his white beard and wind-swept black gown, he exhorted citizens over a megaphone to donate funds for a new mosque. The Chinese knew the appeal was meant for them only, a subtle way of raising protection money with a tacit assurance there would be no further riots, at least for the time being.

The situation is similar in many towns all over Indonesia where the Chinese own most shops, supermarkets and factories. Across Java the batik industry, the trademark of old Java, is now in Chinese hands. Of Indonesia's 100 major conglomerates, 80 are owned by ethnic Chinese, according to the estimate of Gemala chairman Wanandi.

"Sure, the Chinese own more than two thirds of the private wealth of Indonesia but half of that belongs to the president (Suharto)" argued Christianto Wibisono, director of the prestigious Business Data Center in Jakarta. He spoke before the riots broke out.

The symbiosis created by Cukongism has certain benefits for any regime: In times of social unrest it is convenient to blame the Chinese for ravaging and usurping the nation's resources. The Chinese know this. But the advantages outweigh the risks. After all, relations with Suharto and his cronies were a sure short cut to fortune. Few Chinese people pass up a short cut, no matter how dangerous, as long as the stakes are high.

Most of Indonesia's taipans became rich by taking risks—and shortcuts:

Prayogo Pangestu emigrated from China on a slow boat to Borneo. He worked in the forests as a logger and plantation hand and invested all his wages on a chain saw eight years later. Soon he could afford to buy his first plantation. He became known as "The Lord of the Forest," the timber king and second richest man in the country.

Rattan tycoon Mohamad "Bob" Hasan was born The Kian Seng, son of a Chinese wholesale merchant. He became Suharto's golf partner and Mr Fix It.

Apart from being the rattan king, he owned four shipping lines, was part owner with one of Suharto's sons of the now defunct airline Sempati Air as well as two banks. He was also a partner with a Suharto son in the government concession to build Indonesia's national car. The car, the Timor, was really built by South Korea's Kia Motors and was virtually wholly imported. As the designated National Car, it was however exempted from steep import taxes imposed on all foreign made vehicles. When the car failed to sell, despite its cheap price tag, a letter from the Ministry of Transport went to every major company in the country, setting a "quota" for the number of Timor cars it was expected to purchase.

"I wouldn't be where I am today without my friendship with the President," Hasan has candidly admitted in the past.

In 1998 Mr Fix It was called in to broker the dispute between two of the President's children over partnership in the Busang gold mine in East Kalimantan (Borneo). The children desperately coveted a share in a gold mine that had been promoted as the find of the century. Not much later the mine myth exploded after allegations that its test samples of gold had been doctored with alien gold dust to dupe investors. That was after the mine's Filipino geologist took a swallow dive from a helicopter flying him to an inquiry. Before he plummeted to his death, he took off his expensive

Rolex watch and left it on the seat. The incident was officially recorded as a suicide.

Before the mine and its geologist became a casualty, Hasan had elaborated a formidable formula to divide its profits: Nusamba, Suharto's $5 billion private foundation (in which Hasan had a 10 per cent stake) would own 30 per cent of the gold mine. The government would take 10 per cent. The Canadian exploration company, Bre-X, would have to share its 45 per cent stake with Suharto's eldest daughter, Siti Hardijanti Rukmana. The remaining 15 per cent would go to Louisiana based Freeport-McMoRan Copper and Gold, the operator.

The formula was not unusual in an Indonesia in which all productive enterprises were carved up in similar ways, where the Chinese were considered the best insurance for economic development and the best partners. The Chinese did the work while their silent native associates simply signed.

Using the Chinese to become rich is not a novelty in Indonesia.

Back in the 18th century, the Dutch outfitted fleets to "capture" the precious Chinese from their coastal trading posts. Some of these posts dated back to the 9th century and the Chinese had no intention of exchanging their lucrative trade—porcelain vases swapped for spices—for labor under the Dutch. Swords and guns were required to bring the Chinese to Batavia.

A few decades later, in 1740, the Dutch, like the Spanish in Manila, would massacre 10,000 Chinese in Batavia when "the Chinamen" became too numerous and too demanding. In China, Manchu emperor Chien Lung was informed of the massacre but he replied: "These people are deserters of the Celestial Empire. They deserted their ancestral homes and sought benefits overseas. The court is not interested in them."

The Dutch settled their Chinese captives in the old Chinatown at Glodok near the port in Jakarta. Glodok still thrives, inhabited by poor Chinese, newcomers from the islands and China. They come with hopes of opportunity and good guanxi (contact) to make their own fortunes. But it is Pluit, the new Chinatown of the well-to-do middle class, which is one of the symbols of achievement for the 56 million Chinese in Southeast Asia.

Even Pluit is symptomatic of the Chinese quest for wealth in which no one, no matter what their ethnicity, is spared.

The swamp at Pluit was bought and developed by Endang Wijaya, an ethnic Chinese with three years of schooling but a knack to persuade bankers to give him loans without collateral and officials to grant him concessions. His associates argue he bought off the wrong officials, an error that cost him a three-year prison term. From inside his prison he not only continued to develop the swamp into a kind of Beverly Hills but there are those who swear they saw him guzzle drinks at cocktail parties in Singapore and Hong Kong while he was supposed to be behind bars.

Wijaya's new Chinatown has terrible flaws: The tamed swamp keeps flooding during the rainy season. A murky lagoon separates Pluit from the smelly fish market at the next door shanty town, an ocean of corrugated iron roofs and misery inside the front doors. On Pluit's edge, a puffing power station spreads a spider web of high-tension cables right across the roofs of the new rich. Kneeling lepers on the pavement hold out arm stumps at passing luxury limousines with smoked glass windows in which rotund Chinese kids drive to skate at an ice rink in Pluit's shopping mall.

Rags to riches tales were common among ethnic Chinese in Suharto's Indonesia, a country that could boast a seven per cent annual growth rate, deemed a positive legacy of Suharto's long tenure.

In just two decades, Sofyan Wanandi had turned a single retail store selling batteries into a commercial empire, which posted a $1.5 billion turnover in the 1990s. His Gemala Group had factories in Britain and the United States and offices around the world. Wanandi is a debonair, articulate man who plays golf and tennis every week. His office is a restored colonial mansion where he was once kept under guard as the notorious Jakarta student leader whose movement spearheaded the fall of the socialist leaning Sukarno in 1965. He bought the mansion for nostalgic reasons.

"There is a lot of jealousy because we ethnic Chinese corner all the market, tie up every venue, buy it up, turn it into a monopoly," he said. "For our own good, we have to farm out to sub contractors, to give others a chance so that the gap between us and the Indonesians will narrow."

Before the big bust, Wanandi, like everyone else, saw no end to the bonanza. Just months before the economy collapsed he told me: "The sky is the limit here. I am already into pharmaceuticals, oil, chemicals and automotive parts. You can't help making money in this country if you work closely with government policy."

He said this without blinking or blushing.

The severity of the riots escalated after July 1997 when Indonesia's economy began its rapid slide into a crisis that ended in a full-blown recession. Within months, the rupiah had nose-dived from 2,500 to the U.S. dollar to over 17,000. Money became scarce and companies could not pay their workers. Firms laid off workers. Livelihoods evaporated.

The truly wealthy Chinese were not caught napping. The problem was partly of their own making as they and their native business partners had moved liquid assets abroad months earlier, mainly to Wall Street, which suddenly saw an astonishing influx of Asian money. Bimantara Group executive Peter Gontha told me he estimated that the capital flight from Indonesia and Southeast Asia injected $600 billion into the U.S. stock market. The result was not unexpected: America's economy flourished, not by its own momentum or any improved productivity, but thanks to the influx of the runaway Asian funds. In those heady days the U.S. greenback reigned supreme across the globe.

By April 1998 only eight of Indonesia's 230 banks were still considered "healthy". With the exception of a handful of export-oriented companies the rest of the enterprises were now technically bankrupt. A nation once considered Southeast Asia's powerhouse and the richest in natural resources went begging to the International Monetary Fund and the World Bank for a bail out.

As usual the economic crisis affected the poor far more than the rich. Basic commodity prices went through the roof, one in three workers lost their jobs, savings were quickly exhausted and the fear of imminent starvation loomed large.

The dismal economic situation stoked anti-Chinese sentiments as it had always done in the past. Subtly inserted news items warned shopkeepers against price increases outside the approved government limits. The Chinese were not mentioned but everyone recognized the reference to "shopkeepers". Attention was drawn, again without naming names, to people who benefited from the country in good times but as soon as the tide changed, took their money abroad. And there were learned arguments that the flight of capital had precipitated a crisis of confidence, the root problem of the economic debacle. Indonesians knew who the culprits were. No one pointed the finger at the Suharto clan and their cronies whose money had long since joined the exodus of Chinese funds.

The dictator's moribund regime was not the first to throw the Chinese to the wolves in a last ditch effort to save their own skins. The majority of Indonesians have been nurtured on anti-Chinese sentiments from the day they were born and long before the Republic was created. The Chinese were perfect targets.

Ironically the Chinese did nothing to cure this prejudice: By nature aloof and arrogant, they made no effort to treat the natives better than inferior wretches. Worse, previous wiser Chinese generations had carefully hidden their wealth, pretending to be poor or barely surviving, rarely moving out of the rukos in the boxed streets of the various Chinatowns. The older generation wore the same rags the natives wore, pedaled the same bicycles and carted loads on the same tricycles as native neighbors. Even those who had made fortunes made sure no one suspected their wealth.

The new generation was different. Emboldened by Cukongism, educated at prestigious Western campuses and accustomed to the best that money could buy in the West, the sons and daughters of the old Chinese merchants cast off the ways of their forefathers. They ignored the age-old warning of Chinese sages that man's worst enemy is envy.

This new breed became ostentatious: The sons and daughters of the taipans and wealthy shop mall owners zipped about town in imported luxury cars, drank at the most expensive bars, ate at the best restaurants and spent their holidays overseas "because there is nothing to see or buy in this country". These Chinese playboys and playgirls lived in palatial homes in new Chinatowns such as Pluit on the way to the airport or posh residential villages fenced off and barricaded to the outside world by armed security guards.

Chinese homes in these exclusive residential areas were clustered with imported Italian marble, Venetian chandeliers, Brussels lace and French decor, all tossed together in a mélange of bad taste, between cheap rattan chairs from grandfather's days and tables from aunt's kitchen. Despite their wealth, the new rich Chinese never acquired a sense of modesty and aesthetics, an attribute only found among the Mandarin class. The homes of the newly rich had heart shaped pools copied from early Hollywood films. The pools were rarely used for swimming but for breeding carps and other marketable fish. The parsimonious owners saw no reason to waste good water and space without deriving some material benefit. Most

Chinese villas have no gardens or parkland but are packed against each other, wall to wall, like the Siamese twin houses in Chinatown.

"In most Chinese thinking, gardens and parks are a waste of space," Myra Sidharta, a Chinese academic and writer once told me. "We Chinese think you could build another room over that space and rent it out." At the time we were visiting a wealthy Chinese lady in Jakarta in her palatial new home. She proudly showed off her chicken coops in the backyard and the carps in the pool. On marble floors imported from Italy stood tacky old rattan chairs, family heirlooms.

Chinese prejudice for the natives survived best in the ruko, a labyrinth inhabited by the petite bourgeoisie and the Chinese proletariat who consciously separated themselves from the "Kaffirs." In contrast the new rich Chinese generation mingled with their native partners, sampled native charms, no longer self-conscious but convinced their wealth made them part of the elite.

This novel extroversion by the new generation of affluent Chinese did promote integration. On the other hand the ruko dwellers however were determined to keep the race pure and the language Chinese. In the ruko, intermarriage was tantamount to betrayal and disgrace. Copulating with "one of them" would be, as Anne's father often told his two daughters, "like sleeping with the pigs".

∎

Anne remembered she had opened the shutters, still wearing the white shift in which she slept. She had no time to change because her mother was furious. She had seen the next door neighbor ease up his shutters with as little noise as possible.

"Move, move, move, girl!" her mother shouted: "Or that bellyaching Ikman Wong with his false smile will convince those stupid Kaffir housewives his cooking oil is of better quality than mine and his rice is imported from Thailand and not stolen from the pigsties of Bandung."

Anne hurried down the narrow staircase before her mother hurled her felt slippers. Mother was determined any early bird customer must have the choice between her and Fat Wong's shop. When it came to business it was everyone for himself in Chinatown and her mother was not beyond telling customers weevils had been found in Fat Wong's rice and his cooking oil was stretched with turpentine.

It was one of the great satisfactions of life for one Chinaman to damage another Chinaman's business.

■

Farida Gunawan was driving at a crawl through Chinatown when she ran into the mob at the intersection. She clicked the automatic door locks on the BMW and tacitly thanked her husband for having ordered the model with the smoked windows. It hadn't taken her more than a few seconds to realize the mob was in pursuit of Chinese. She sat quietly. She did not toot her horn as did other drivers caught in the blockade. She had no intention of drawing attention. The natives had an uncanny ability to recognize a Chinese even from behind, by their waddling walk.

A small energetic woman in her late forties, Farida is the archetype of the Overseas Chinese. They operate best when conditions are worse, when laws are nebulous and rules not implemented, when the status quo resembles a Wild West-Last Frontier scenario, when opportunities beckon from every corner because conditions are virgin, lawmakers are inexperienced and commercial life is novel. Such ideal conditions existed in China and Southeast Asia during the 1980s and most of the 1990s.

It was not the first time Farida had been at the receiving end of anti-Chinese riots. As a teenager in 1966 she remembered hiding at her grandmother's plush residence. She saw Chinese stores ransacked in the 1970s and again in 1984.

But this time it was different. This time Farida, tucked in behind the cushioned steering wheel of her BMW, realized the rioters were well prepared.

"There was nothing spontaneous about the whole thing," she recalled.

Before the economic crisis crippled Indonesia's building industry, Farida owned and operated three factories on the northern outskirts of Jakarta. One of them manufactured bricks, the other tiles and the third timber door frames. During the boom years these materials were in such demand she hired extra day labor to cope with the orders.

Yet, by early 1998, judging from the fate of her competitors, Farida should have been bankrupt, battered by what the World Bank called the worst collapse of a nation's economy since World War II. The recession followed by a depression left one third of Indonesia's labor force of 90 million unemployed and turned a 7 per cent average annual growth rate into minus 15 per cent.

On the outskirts of the capital the jobless set up food stalls to eke out a living. Millions were scraping through on savings or with the help of rural relatives. Millions more escaped from mega-cities like Jakarta, Jogjakarta and Medan and returned to their rural villages and towns. Survival in the countryside was easier, the cost of living lower and the fertile soil provided enough to feed the extra mouths for the time being.

Farida, an architect by profession, quickly deduced the immediate future for architects and builders was gloomy. She saw a future plagued by chronic unemployment and food shortages, a future with more anti-Chinese riots. She prepared herself. Like her ancestors had done for generations, she adjusted.

First she moved her two teenage children out of harm's way to a campus in Perth, Australia. Then she recycled her assets to serve a different market while keeping the construction machinery for better days.

"Despite the anti-Chinese riots, I didn't want to leave the country. What would I do abroad? And I didn't want to leave my workers who depended on me," she said.

Within weeks she converted the 1.5 hectares around her timber frame factory into a vegetable garden. Soon she was selling its produce at the local market. At the same time she converted the tile factory into a poultry farm using bamboo scaffolding from construction sites to build chicken coops. Then she converted the tubs of her brick factory into fishponds. She turned factory furnaces into egg hatcheries. With imported fertilizers now far too costly, she used the chicken manure to fertilize the vegetable plots and imported a breed of Australian worms she set free on a municipal garbage dump. The worms' metabolism metamorphosed the dump into manure for the vegetable farm. Then she "imported" in her handbag Silky Hen eggs from Australia and hatched them. The much heavier Australian chicken sold at three times the price of the native variety.

Farida admits she learned all the techniques from books. This way she succeeded in keeping her 38 workers employed. Not one of them lost their job or had their wages cut. She even lent money to her day laborers to lease land and cultivate rice with the proviso all surplus and chaff had to be sold to her as chicken feed and fish fodder.

Finally she converted her tile factory into a Fitness Centre using the bricks she could no longer sell for partitioning, the door frames and timber, now rotting in storage, for structures, floors and décor. She knew Jakarta still had enough rich people ready to be pampered.

On that May morning she might have congratulated herself for making the successful transition from construction to agriculture and body molding. Instead she was trembling inside her luxury car, cursing herself for not taking out the old jeep, a far less conspicuous vehicle, that morning. From now on, she promised herself, the BMW and the Mercedes would have to stay in the garage.

■

It was around nine o'clock when Anne first noticed a crowd had gathered outside the rukos down the street. She always took a handful of biscuits and a pot of tea to the storeroom for Muhamad, the thin, quiet Javanese factotum who had his early morning break around that time.

Muhamad was not there. That alone was strange. So she went outside to see if he was busy with the cart. That was when she saw the crowd.

Anne took a few steps towards the mob gathered outside Lao Tzi's tailor shop. At the head of the mob were three or four young men waving heavy sticks like sabers. One had an iron rod with a flat spike head, the kind used to pry hub caps from car wheels. He was using it now to bang at the tailor's shutters, yelling words Anne could not make out. She took another few steps forward, then froze.

"Death to the Chinese!" the young man was shouting.

Another youth, this one with a military crew cut and a loud harsh voice berated the mob: "What's the matter with you folks? These Chinks have sucked your blood for generations. Their time has come. Let's get rid of them!"

When no one moved he went on: "Don't stand around looking stupid! These bloodsuckers robbed you for years. What about their high prices? What about the high interest on your loans? What about the money they sent out of the country? Hey, these Chinks break our laws and what are we going to do about those pig-eaters? What shall we do? What must we do? Yes, yes, yes: Kill them, Allah Akhbar! Allah Akbhar!"

This time the crowd shouted back: "Allah Akhbar!"

Anne rushed into the shop. She vaguely recalls the sound of shutters going down on rukos next door; her mother pushing her aside as she hauled down their own shutters, her father running into the house from the supermarket and ordering her to stay upstairs and to look after her younger sister. Then the mob was outside, banging at the shutters. She heard voices: "Kill the Chinese pigs! Let's have us some pretty Chinese chicks for fun! Come out, Chinaman! Come outside. Now!"

And then someone yelled: "And bring your pretty white daughters!"

Upstairs, from the barred window, Anne and her sister Nan could see the mob entering the Pantai Indah housing complex, a 15-storey high edifice almost entirely occupied by ethnic Chinese. Her parents had also bought an apartment some months earlier but had rented it out, much to Anne's disappointment.

She could see people running up from floor to floor, banging at doors. Some of the occupants had left their apartments and were climbing to higher floors, gesticulating, crying, yelling for help as they climbed, ever higher, pursued by men taking two steps at a time.

Down in the street young men armed with crowbars had jimmied open shutters and smashed down doors. The crowd surged forward. Soon the first of them re-emerged, doubled over with rice sacks on both shoulders. Others carted lamps, television sets, radios, hi-fis, cartons filled with tins of cooking oil and tins of tuna and sardines. A man was trailing the electric cords of two steam irons, impervious as the cords bounced across the pavement. Another lugged a small washing machine on his back. An old woman, limping but anxious to have her fill, slipped into Lao Chong's shop and hauled out a tin of salted biscuits just before a young man in a green shirt hurled a Molotov cocktail through the shop window.

Seconds later the plastic bottle filled with kerosene exploded. Flames licked at Lao Chong's shop. Looters were still running through the flames into the shop, anxious to salvage the last goods. Some emerged, their sarongs smoldering, their hair singed, hugging their booty. A grinning tricycle driver who used to wait outside Anne's school for hires, now triumphantly held up Lao Chong's beloved water pipe, an heirloom from his grandfather.

There was no sign of the old man or his grand-daughter, Ezi who helped run the shop, cooked and kept the place clean. Lao Chong preferred his granddaughter to a native servant. Besides he didn't have to pay Ezi.

Much later, when the nightmare came her way, the youth with the crowbar would boast to Anne: "We tossed that squawking Chink girl into the flames until her sickly white skin was crispy brown. Then we put honey on her and ate her. Now you wouldn't want that to happen to you, would you? So just lie back and enjoy it. And don't scream. I hate girls screaming. Understood?" And he had roared with laughter.

But that was later, after the stores burned, after the supermarkets went up in flames, after billowing smoke blanketed the city from 5,000 burning shops and supermarkets, after 1,200 people had been killed, many of them fried to a frazzle as they looted the supermarkets and shopping malls.

On that day, as Anne watched the horror approach, the Indonesian capital seen from the air as I flew in resembled a smoldering garbage dump and it seemed unlikely anyone could walk alive out of the billowing smoke.

At street level, however, tens of thousands of looters and freebooters, moving ant-like with their cargo, hurried to safety before the squads of pyromaniacs set more buildings aflame. Neither police nor soldiers were to be seen in a country where police and soldiers had always been ubiquitous. The arsonists, backed by mobs or small groups, had moved freely from place to place as if following a pre-ordained blueprint. There seemed to be no limit to the amount of plastic bottles filled with gasoline on which rags stuck into bottlenecks served as wicks.

The noise, the shouting and the crackling of the flames were so loud hardly anyone heard the pitiful cries for help. These came mainly from inside the blazing supermarkets where looters were trapped by their own greed and the speed of the fire as it spread once the first Molotov cocktails had been tossed through broken doors and windows. Those who set the fires moved quickly and quietly, motivated less by revulsion for the Chinese than hatred of the supermarkets which had taken away their livelihood as street vendors.

Two days later, when some semblance of order was restored, firemen and volunteer rescuers plucked more than 800 charred corpses from the supermarkets. Many were young women the authorities identified as "shop girls caught in the conflagration". Most of these "shop girls" were ethnic Chinese, nearly all of them naked, a circumstance the authorities attributed to the flames which seemed to strip Chinese shop girls while leaving the corpses of native looters dressed in their scorched attire. But few people in those days argued with official logic.

Anne had long given up watching the staircase in the building complex. What she could see was too horrid. Yet her mother had no such qualms:

"They've got the newlyweds," she reported at one stage.

"He is being kicked around like a football.

"Now they're holding her down, tearing off her blouse, rolling down her jeans. Ahhh! Two are holding her arms, two her legs. Now they're pushing one another... Oh, damn it... I can't see anymore."

These were neighbors.

Anne had turned away from the window after the incident with the girl. She knew her. Her cries would haunt her forever. She was about 12 or 13, a thin, pretty little thing who talked little but had a reputation as an egghead. A burly man with a swarthy face had carried her onto the landing like a trophy. He clasped her from behind carting her like a rag doll. He roared with laughter. He laid her down along the stairs and while he was unbuckling his belt another man was covering her mouth with kisses, holding her head in a tight grip. A third man was ripping her dress and fondling one small, barely developed breast. Then the big man pushed them aside and lowered himself.

Anne had turned away but she could hear the young girl's anguished cries drifting from the landing across the street: "Mummy! Mummmy! No! Nooooo! Mummy... Mum... Mum... it hurts, Mum it hurts. Make him stop... ."

Then Anne had clasped both hands over her ears.

"I wanted to scream, many times myself," she recounted later, "but Mother slapped me: 'Quiet,' she said. 'You want to bring those kaffirs over here when they're so busy at Old Tzi's shop and on the landing?' "

■

Farida realized the demonstrators were accompanied by two pickup vans. The loading tray of the blue van was stacked with plastic bottles. The other van, a faded green, was loaded with quarry stones smashed into small pebbles. One young man picked up a stone, the size of a tennis ball, and hurled it at a ruko. The stone smacked against the iron shutter and fell back on the pavement.

"Help yourself," the youth cried, gesturing towards the van. A few men came through the crowd and picked up stones.

"Let's break it. Let's see what goodies these Chinks hide!"

"Yeah, yeah, break it open," someone else yelled. "Burn the Chink shop!"

"Break it! Break it!"

Stones, like hailstones, pelted against the shutter. Someone brought a crowbar and began to lever at the locks. Soon the shutters gave way and the crowd surged forward tearing away the last obstacles, kicking down the wooden door, pushing and shoving to be first into the haberdasher's shop. A husky Chinese came running down the street. "We'll give you money, we'll give you money. Please don't loot it. Please... ."

He had no time to say any more. A skinny runt of a teenager had sneaked up behind the man and with a belt began to flagellate him. He struck hard and fierce with violent anger and when he tired, passed the belt to another youth. First the man had yelled, protecting his head. Then he had begun to whimper. Soon he collapsed.

One of the youths took a bottle from the back of the van and held a lighter to a rag dangling from its neck. The bottle arched into the shop. Seconds later there was an explosion, followed by screams. People stumbled outside.

During the pandemonium a youth wearing a very short crew cut, of the kind obligatory among the military, moved along the line of cars trapped in the commotion. He banged at windows and shouted: "Any Chinese in there?"

He was an ugly youth with a coarse face. He used his fist to beat at car windows and Farida prayed he would tire before he reached her car. Behind him, appendix-like, trailed six young men, slouched and straddle-legged, banging iron wrenches against car chassis. Farida recognized the type: The young thugs from the local Mafia who collected illegal tolls at intersections and for parked cars. In time these types graduated to debt and loan interest collection and then to the protection racket. If they did well they got promoted to "rub-out men" and finally, if they survived their stint as killers, they could become a minor boss in one of the district gangs of the Organization.

"Any Chinky-Chinks in there?" The Crewcut's eyes squinted at the smoked glass as if he might discern the truth beyond. Farida went stone cold. She knew she would have to open the window to avoid suspicion. If she could only change her Chinese looks for a moment. Or pretend. Or bluff. But these natives had an unerring sense, something they were born with and grew up with. They could spot Chinese even in the dark.

Just then someone shouted an obscenity from across the street where a regular rusty passenger bus was caught in the traffic jam. Some of its passengers had spilled out and were standing around, mingling with other people caught in the blockade. One of the passengers, a gangly teenager with long black hair, was pointing at the back of the bus: "She's Chinese, the bitch, a real haughty-toughty Chinese bitch, if you're looking for one."

The gang suddenly lost interest in the line of cars. Dodging between stalled cars the youths rushed towards the bus followed by a crowd of the curious. The Crewcut boarded and a few moments later re-emerged dragging a girl of about 14 still dressed in her school uniform, a short green skirt and a white blouse. The girl whimpered. Crewcut dragged her along by the scruff of her blouse:

"Lookey, lookey here, what we've found" he yelled. "Now what do we have here? A real white Lily! A real Chinese pussy! Dressed up in a mini, white socks to boot."

There was laughter from the crowd and a few shouts of encouragement.

"Now, boys," Crewcut yelled, pushing the girl in front of him. "Wouldn't you like to feel that nice white skin of the little Chinky? Touch those soft white teats?" He poked at the budding breasts with a stubby finger.

The girl retreated and began to whimper.

"Now who wants a little of that milky skin?"

The crowd had fallen silent. The girl, both arms crossed over her breasts squatted on the pavement. A little puddle formed between her legs. She was sniffling into her lap and trembling the way leaves do in the breeze before the monsoon rains splash down.

"How about a little bit of Chinky pussy?" the Crewcut yelled, turning around to look for takers.

He lifted one boot carefully and advanced it into the gap below the green skirt. Tongue out, concentrated, he nudged her private parts with the tip of his boot—once, twice, harder, harder and then with a final kick he sent her sprawling across the pavement.

"No takers for that virgin pussy and all that white skin?"

"Kill the Chinks. Kill the bastards!"

The shout came from his companions, right on queue.

The crowd muttered, indecisive, perhaps embarrassed; the girl was so defenseless, so young.

Suddenly a man stepped forward.

He was a tall, middle-aged man in a blue overall, the kind mechanics and welders wear on the job. He had elbowed his way through the crowd and confronted Crewcut: "You should be ashamed," he said in a loud voice. "She's only a little girl."

Before Crewcut had time to answer he had walked up to the girl and lifted her up by one elbow. "Come," he said: I'll take you home."

"Chink-lover!" the Crewcut yelled. "Let's get that Chink lover!"

But no one moved.

■

Frans Winarta's house stands in a residential village guarded by boom gates and men in uniform who demand to know, "who are you?" and "where 'you going?" Drivers leave an ID before the guards allow them to proceed to the inner sanctuary, a cluster of ostentatious villas, trimmed road aprons, high walls and spiked iron gates that slide open and shut by remote control. The guards first telephone the host to verify the visitor is welcome. Sometimes, on request, a guard trails visitors by motorcycle to their destination.

In their luxury "villages," with close circuit television eyes and electronic sensors, the Chinese are swaddled in a security blanket that costs a small fortune every month in payments to police and army officers, the men who guarantee added protection. When the urge is upon them and when the situation merits it, these types have no compunction in knocking at doors with the demand: "Sir, we need another 100,000 for food this week."

No one has the courage to turn them down.

On May 13 the security simply evaporated. Most guards did not show up for work. Others were seen riding off towards the Plaza Arion market stalls as fast as their 50 cc motorbikes could carry them. They left behind a residential village at the mercy of the gathering mobs.

As a third generation ethnic Chinese, a man born and educated in Indonesia, Winarta has accumulated a reservoir of bitterness and self-irony that comes with experience to victims of discrimination and small daily indignities. As a teenager he became an addict of the legal profession after he had read Harper Lee's *To Kill a Mocking Bird*. Once he had graduated, he soon discovered the law was no springboard into politics for the Chinese. His native colleagues subtly undermined his ambition to form a political party and his campaign to be elected to a more prominent post within the Human Rights Committee of the Lawyers' Association. The natives closed ranks to elect one of their own. He always lost in the secret vote despite his undoubted energy and qualifications. Behind his back, he knew, they argued it was bad enough the Chinese dominated the country's retail and distribution networks without them also dominating politics.

Efforts to keep the Chinese from power and away from politics started early.

A short amiable man, Winarta complains that even in primary school "I was always asked for a citizenship certificate. It was part of the screening out of the Chinese and it was so annoying because on my mother's side we are fifth generation Indonesian and on my father's side third generation Chinese. I was born in this country. I don't even speak Chinese. My family comes from the Tan and Chen clans of Fujian but we integrated and adopted Indonesian names."

A man who has traveled extensively and studied in Holland, like most of Jakarta's elite, Winarta is no bigot. He candidly admits the Chinese have racist prejudices themselves.

"Dating back to colonial days the Chinese considered the natives as inferior with the exception of kings and sultans. Chinese captains and mayors considered themselves equal to whites. For generations we Chinese lived like a superior race. Then there is the fact that most of us live better than the native Indonesians, that most Chinese are Buddhists or Christians while the natives are Muslims. So there you have issues of friction. And if that's not enough, we stand out from the rest because we separate ourselves.

"We are even divided among ourselves. The Totok Chinese speak Chinese and often hold dual citizenship. We Parnakan Chinese were born here and consider ourselves Indonesians and good citizen. The Totoks are mainly an uneducated lot and they do tend to monopolize business for their own benefit and their own race. The Parnakan Chinese are more integrated."

On that Black May 13, a Wednesday, only one news item gave Frans Winarta satisfaction: It was the graphic report of how a mob stoned, looted then burned the private villa of Liem Sioe Liong without the authorities lifting a finger to save it.

The former peanut oil peddler turned billionaire thanks to his friendship with Suharto, was the champion among crony capitalists. Like the medieval German Fugger family of financiers who bankrolled kings and princes in return for royal concessions, Liem built a financial and commercial empire in alliance with Suharto and the dictator's six children. His Salim Group consisted of 400 companies, employed 150,000 workers and had annual sales of US$11 billion. The Group owns the United Savings Bank in California and has vast interests in China. Liem, perhaps afraid the bonanza could end with Suharto's death or resignation, moved a large part of his holdings overseas, much of it to California.

The rags to riches fairytale began when Suharto gave Liem a monopoly on flour milling for his PT Bogasari Flour Mill in the late 1960s. A subsequent survey claimed Bogasari was charging three times the world price for milling. From that concession Liem cornered the Instant Noodle market which now dominates Southeast Asia as the most popular fast food product with a potential consumer market of 600 million. His Salim Group became the world's largest buyer of wheat. Thanks to similar concessions, the Group dominates other basic products, among them Indonesia's cement industry, vital to the construction fever that accompanied Suharto's economic vision of a New Order focused on economic development. The Group's Bank Central Asia, the largest private bank among Indonesia's 240 banks, gave Suharto's eldest daughter and eldest son a 17 per cent stake. Another son is an equity partner in the Group's 5,000-acre Batam island industrial development scheme in Singapore.

But when the hermit billionaire celebrated his golden wedding anniversary in 1997, he prudently moved a million-dollar banquet to

Singapore. He was respecting an old dictum among a generation of early Chinese immigrants who felt wealth creates envy and is best served by maintaining a low profile. The new generation, the sons and daughters of the empire builders, has no such scruples or false modesty.

Their homes are not in rundown Chinatowns with narrow alleys and smelly sewage canals but in Manila's plush Greenhills and Jakarta's new Pluit residential zone. They occupy new offices on Bangkok's Silom Road, Jakarta's Jalan Sudirman and Manila's Ayala Avenue. These Chinese "princes" and "princesses" are no longer illiterate like their immigrant fathers or grandfathers but educated at Harvard, Princeton, Oxford, Kellogg, Sydney or Melbourne universities. They no longer spend frugal holidays in battered Chinatown homes but own condominiums or villas in the United States, Canada, Australia, Singapore and Hong Kong.

Pluit was once a swamp. Today it is the site of palatial multi-million dollar homes with satellite dishes the size of radars on the roofs. It has a smart shopping mart with an ice rink so the sons and daughters of the well-to-do can skate in the tropics just like the sons and daughters of the oil-rich sheikhs in the Arab world can skate on rinks built in cities amidst deserts.

At Pluit, fat Chinese kids, stuffed by doting parents and grandparents, are chased by native nannies. The spoiled, precocious and ill-mannered kids spit, kick and curse their nannies while their parents do not see, hear or seem to care. The Indonesian nannies hate the Chinese but need the jobs.

The Hollywood style pools and split level mansions are a long way from Glodok, the old Chinatown with its drab maze of dark back-to-back houses, bustling markets in winding alleys, places where the Chinese plied their trades in colonial days.

The wealthy Chinese have learned to move fast out of harm's way. Liem was safe in the United States when the mob turned on his small central villa, a home that itself was a tribute to his frugal Totok ways. From his villa in California, the taipan of taipans watched the Indonesian capital go up in smoke and saw his former mentor and business pal Suharto lose a nation he had made subservient to his will and his greed for 32 years. He heard and saw on television student mobs chant, "Hang Suharto" and attach misspelled slogans on the facade of parliament saying, "Suharto and Crownies Go to Hell." The shouts and slogans were nothing short of a miracle after three decades during which calling "the Old Man" a pompous ass or a glorified peasant was punishable with jail or a spell in the police torture chamber.

It is unlikely however that Liem, the shrewd, egocentric billionaire, wasted any tears over the demise of his mentor. Most of his own funds had moved long ago and his Salim Group had invested more abroad than at home. He had seen the writing on the wall. Like other taipans, Liem appeared to have scant loyalty for his adopted country. Besides, Suharto had become grumpy and suspicious with age. He often blamed his Chinese connections for the country's economic pains. The old friendship had long gone. What kept it glued for so long was mutual greed.

"It was good to hear his house burned down," Winarta said. "The man deserved it. He has never cared about any other Chinese. He has never felt guilty about anything that happened to the Chinese. He was only interested in himself and his commercial empire. The mob did well to torch his home."

That reaction was typical of the Parnakans. Elegant and articulate, they see themselves as the cultured Mandarin faction of Indonesia and consider the Totoks peasants who work 22 hours a day to become rich. There is a perverse irony in the Parnakan-Totok relationship: If Germanized Jews were nonplussed when the Nazis included them in their anti-Semitic pogroms, Indonesia's Parnakans never accepted their national credentials were open to challenge. Like the Germanized Jews 60 years earlier, the Parnakans could never understand why the authorities and the populace relegated them to the level of "those Totok ethnics in the ghettos". In their jokes, Totoks are uncouth throwbacks, steeped in anachronistic traditions, people who refuse integration, worship old gods and won't allow their children to marry the locals.

Liem is a Totok

The taipan had no problem passing through Singapore, ushered in by a government known for its kowtows to money rather than compassion. The same small City State imposed a three-day visa limit on ordinary Chinese, the not-so-rich, when they sought a safe haven from the turmoil in Indonesia. Singapore had enriched itself on trade and deposits from the region's Overseas Chinese, particularly those in Indonesia, yet the moment trouble broke out, it had no intention of sacrificing any part of its regulated comfort and financial welfare. It had no wish to become a refugee camp for an exodus of ethnic Chinese from Indonesia.

Run like a corporate state, Singapore does not waste money on compassion but is paranoid about cleanliness. Singaporeans were ordered to smile because it attracted tourists. Singaporeans have also been ordered to flush toilets or face heavy fines. Clearing one's throat and spitting out the mucus in public, an old Chinese habit, incurs a hefty fine, so does smoking at bus shelters or busy streets as well as tossing away cigarette stubs. Hours after Philippine Airlines closed down in September 1998, Singapore Airlines tripled its cheap fares to Manila. The price hike devastated the lives of thousands of poor Filipino domestic helpers in Singapore who were no longer able to fly home to see their families on cheap tickets. "It was purely a business decision," a Singapore Airlines spokesman explained, before international pressure forced the airline to lower its Manila fares again.

Winarta sent a strong letter of protest to the autocratic and patriarchal government in Singapore. He called the three-day visa a travesty of justice, a social barbarity and reminded Singaporeans they were fellow Chinese and had done well for decades as bankers and suppliers to their ethnic cousins in Indonesia. Now the chips were down, so how about some solidarity?

He knew he was talking into the wind.

On May 13, however, Winarta was more concerned with survival.

He assumed correctly that the shrewdly guided mob hysteria, manipulated by factions inside the army intelligence, would become one of the worst nightmares for the ethnic Chinese. Only this time, many Parnakans decided they were not going to be slaughtered without opposition. The determination to resist came from a new generation, educated, self confident and aware that in a modern interdependent world, with Internet communications and mobile phones, pogroms have adverse effects on a country's business ratings and can no longer be cloaked in secrecy.

The Chinese men who armed themselves with whatever was handy—pick axes, kitchen hatchets, wrenches, crowbars and ornamental daggers—made a vow that the mobs would only pillage their houses and ravish their women over their corpses. No one wanted to die but no one wanted to kneel in front of ragged Muslim toughs turned into zealots by fanatical mullahs calling on the faithful to redress grave insults to Islam. No one had the stomach to beg for mercy while thugs raped their daughters and wives invoking the name of Allah to justify their crimes.

Winarta recalls: "I armed myself with a dagger. There were others who said they had shotguns ready, which they had buried for just such an occasion. We never understood why we should not be allowed to own shotguns to defend ourselves. We gathered what weapons we had and took up guard at the main gate. Then we waited and waited... ."

While the men waited at the gate for a mob that never came, neither that night nor the next, 1,000 kms north on the tip of Sumatra, a youth named 'Sixth Wong' had organized his own vigilante committee. He too had decided it was preferable to fight for home and family against the rampaging mobs in Medan, a city notorious for its anti-Chinese riots.

Accoring to human rights organizations some 8,000 Chinese people in Medan in 1953 had been killed and their homes and shops wrecked or burned. Chinese blood courses through the veins of one in four residents in Medan. The large presence of the Chinese is one reason perhaps why Muslim Indonesians blame the infidels, whose numbers are growing by the year, for anything that goes wrong in the city.

When the riots started in Jakarta the Chinese in Medan formed vigilante committees to confront the mobs. In a letter to a friend, Sixth Wong wrote: "The media portrays these bastards as the poor and hungry but I don't see any shortage of food. Many sold the food (they looted) for half the price later on the street. Have you ever seen the hungry in any part of this world loot and rob shops and sell the loot afterwards?"

The vigilante committees fought the mobs off so well that human rights groups later said only three Chinese women had been reported raped in Medan. The battle between natives and Chinese prompted the quick intervention of special army units from Java who entered the city to restore order. The army immediately issued a decree proscribing the bearing of swords, spears and hatchets, the favorite weapons of the vigilantes.

"So yours truly had to switch weapons, from a samurai katana (sword) to a hockey stick," the Sixth Wong lamented in his letter.

After years of standing by while the mobs violated their homes, ransacked their shops and decimated their families, the determination of some Chinese in Jakarta and Medan had saved their lives. The resistance was indicative of a new pride and bravado among an ethnic group that felt, as the Jews must have after the creation of Israel, they were no longer alone and now could count on support from a bigger brother.

The Asian boom and the emergence of a new consumer conscious bourgeoisie enriched the Chinese who have always functioned best in frontier atmospheres where the playing field is not yet level, monopolies are not illegal and laws are porous. Yet the fabulous wealth of the taipans stoked racism among Asian natives who complain the Chinese are boorish, cruel bosses and usurers. One placard carried by demonstrators in May 1998 read: "Destroy the Chinese. They are murderers and robbers who plunder the country's money that belongs to us." In a 1991 paper on "Masalah Cina" (the Chinese problem), Siswono Judo Husodo, the former minister for Transmigration and Resettlement listed the six cardinal sins of the Chinese in Indonesia. He wrote: "There are those (Chinese) who treat Indonesia solely as a place to live and earn a living; those who still speak only Chinese; who view Indonesian citizenship as only a legality; those who feel superior towards other population groups; those who pay more wages to fellow Chinese than to the natives and those who congregate in communal exclusive areas."

Yet Chinese influence in commerce has become so predominant Indonesians have learned to count in the Hakka or Hokkien languages and use words from the kinship talk of the Chinese.

Not surprisingly, the Chinese in the Diaspora are not only victims of native prejudices but are divided by their own class consciousness.

"When I came to Jakarta as a student the Parnakans (mixed blood Chinese) complained I had no manners, I was uncouth, not refined like them. They felt superior because we Totoks (pure Chinese) arrived later. Yet most of the tycoons are Totoks. Like all immigrants, they felt it was important for them to become rich," said Myra Sidharta.

She came from the small island of Belitung off Sumatra where her grandfather, Au Yang, landed in 1881 to work in the tin mines. These were turbulent times with famine in China. Only the lucky and courageous managed to board overloaded boats to the Nanyang.

It was a rough time also in Indonesia: Chinese batik factories kept their native workers in hole-in-the-wall dormitories and supplied them with opium to enslave them. (In China in the 1990s, expatriate Chinese textile and shoe factory owners locked their workers into dormitories sleeping

200, with bunk beds stacked to the ceiling. Thousands of these workers have died when fires broke out in their dormitory.)

The new rich Chinese did not wish to remember their poor, cruel and often tragic past. The last Chinese "captain" on Belitung burned the historic archives containing the stories of the immigrants.

"He said it's better this way," Sidharta recalled.

Indonesia's fortunes have in fact see-sawed with the fortunes of the Chinese.

In 1953 Jakarta imposed a trade ban on Chinese in rural areas. In Medan on Sumatra the military confiscated 8,000 Chinese homes yet the then foreign minister Subandrio rejected a protest from Maoist China with the now famous quip: "China should not offer protection to a group of capitalists and monopolists in Indonesia."

The trade ban took away the livelihood of half a million Chinese. One in five of them returned and resettled in China where in 1966, Mao's Red Guards would cruelly persecute many as outcasts contaminated by foreign devils.

Their exodus had a disastrous effect on the Indonesian economy. Shortages in basic commodities, black marketeering and rampant inflation dogged the country. It eventually led to the fall of Sukarno in a military coup in 1965. In the coup's wake, Chinese schools were burned, Chinese writing and signs were banned and thousands of Chinese lynched or beaten to death as alleged "communists". A decree ordered them out of the country by August 8, 1966.

The decree was later suspended.

Ironically it was Suharto's New Order government which heralded the golden age for the Chinese in Indonesia. Their commercial know-how and their networking were badly needed to achieve his ambitious economic plans. Chinese influence blossomed under Cukongism.

"It's a wonderful formula," said Wibisono the business consultant: "The natives take no commercial risks but become signature entrepreneurs earning millions each time they sign. The Chinese become rich enough to buy a minister or a general."

Suharto himself began to "squeeze" his Chinese allies. In 1996 he imposed a decree ordering all companies whose turnover exceeded $4.5 million a year to pay two per cent of their profits into the president's

Namusa Fund which was intended to supply cheap loans and relief to the poorest sector in the country. In reality it was the president's private pork barrel.

No official funds ever found their way to Rengasdengklok. Like in most Indonesian towns, the Chinese community was expected to supplement the miserable police wages with "contributions" that amounted to levies. The Chinese, who are Buddhist, Taoist or Christian, were also expected to make generous donations to build new mosques.

"We never argued. We just gave," Ety Wisuda explained.

Her six children have all gone to Indonesian colleges on the income from her husband's private bus company. Yet when her children marry, she hopes they will find "the right partners," preferably other ethnic Chinese.

"Marriage is also a matter of financial well being," she argued.

Like all middle class Chinese, she is adamant the family will remain in Rengasdengklok, riots or not. "This is where our home and property is. My family has lived here for over a 100 years. One of my grandmothers was a native. We like it here."

In a part of the world where Chinese still keep a Kitchen God, she was cradling the head of a Chinese deity salvaged from the rubble across the road. She was keeping it for a future when the Wihara would be rebuilt. She looked startled when someone suggested it might be wiser not to rebuild.

The Chinese in the Diaspora always rebuild.

■

Inside the Pantai Indah complex, pandemonium reigned.

The graphic account of the atrocities was never fully exposed to the public. Nearly all the victims of rape kept their identity a secret and the victims of looting and burning were too scared, at least for some years, to make an official complaint at a time when it was obvious that army intelligence and some army units masterminded the pogrom while common thugs had served as foot soldiers and executioners. The most barbaric excesses occurred when mobs ran amok, as they always do when the law is suspended and base human instincts are given free rein.

Chinese minorities anywhere rarely come forward to file complaints with the authorities who, so the Chinese insist, will not only ignore them but may pass these complaints on to the offenders who in turn may take revenge. Some Chinese who privately thanked journalists for exposing the atrocities did so with unsigned letters or no address. Over generations, the Chinese in the Diaspora have found it more convenient to stay away from the authorities, to keep a low profile and take abuses and material losses in silence. This was the accepted price for operating in an alien environment that remained alien as the result of the Chinese refusal to assimilate.

The government could not deny the visible evidence of the rampages that left its scars throughout Jakarta. However the authorities angrily rejected the charges of rape and classified them as inventions by people bent on damaging the nation's good image. Both the police and the military continued to deny rapes had occurred despite documentation by human rights groups of 152 cases in which all the victims refused to give their names. A senior police chief argued Indonesians simply did not commit such atrocities. He forgot that in one supermarket alone hundreds of people burned to death after thugs set the place on fire. And he forgot that 1,200 had died in the violence, many of them beaten or kicked to death by the same thugs who would not think twice about raping a woman during the turmoil.

Over the weeks the charges and denials gathered force. At the same time navy and army intelligence sources admitted special units had been involved in the riots, inciting the mob and commandeering the local gangs. Someone had been anxious to promote chaos so the armed forces could come to the rescue of the nation. Suspicion fell heavily on Suharto's son-in-law, the ambitious special forces lieutenant-general Prabowo Subianto. He had hoped, so insiders claimed, that salvaging the nation from the marauding rabble with his troops would give him the prominence and stature to replace the aged dictator, his father-in-law, as Indonesia's new president.

Since no Chinese rape victim had come forward, the authorities were on safe ground with their denials. Unfortunately, Chinese society considers "saving face" the sacrosanct duty of any family member. In the introvert Chinese culture, rape is a shame that not only spoils the victim but disgraces the entire family. It is in the interests of everyone to deny the act. In the narrow, anachronistic minds of the Diaspora, a mentality that survived from the old days, a woman raped has become worthless. If she were single she would have no chance of a reasonable match. If engaged to be married, her fiancé's family would dissolve the engagement. If she is married, the disgrace would be unbearable for a husband, if made public.

The intrusiveness of the Chinese has no limits: If her fate were known, people would point her out in the street as the woman who was raped. Most Chinese would not blame her for what happened but despise her for making it public.

Torn between their outrage and the confines of their culture, some of the victims resorted to the anonymous cyber space or told close friends to publicize their ordeal.

Myra Sidharta, who interviewed some of the families of the victims, was shocked by their stubborn reticence. "We saw mothers whose daughters had obviously been raped and shockingly mistreated but still insisted nothing had happened to the girls. One kept telling us her daughter would still go to her wedding a virgin. It was sad, even for a Chinese like me."

Most of the victims were shipped out of Indonesia as quickly as possible if their parents and relatives could afford the fare. The majority went to Australia and Canada as students. The less affluent headed for Singapore. The bulk however had to live out their ordeal at home and pretend nothing had happened.

On the night of the rampage, Anne recalled the horror of sitting behind shutters in the dark and listening to sporadic screams, not for help but for mercy because by then everyone knew help was not coming and the only hope was to escape with one's life. She trembled as she squatted on the floor and listened to the piercing screams of women or girls in terrible fear, in abject horror and finally in what must have been insufferable pain. She said the screams were always quickly smothered as if someone had placed a hand over the person's mouth, or a pillow or a cloth. Then someone else would scream and then their scream would be muffled—until someone else, somewhere else was squealing and begging.

In mortal pain or in mortal fear people's vocabulary becomes very limited. "Most of the shouting was no, no, noooo and pleasssse... ." Anne said: "I can't remember any other words. I thought why are they not shouting 'you bastards, you pigs or you animals?' but I guess you can't call these people animals because animals don't behave like that, only human beings are capable of doing these things. Animals don't gang-rape.

Only humans do that."

The rapes and the beatings in the residential zones inhabited by the Chinese were not made public. The media concentrated on the fires which had enveloped Jakarta behind a smoke screen and threatened to wipe out entire suburbs as they spread to non-Chinese property. For days the rapes and killings were kept quiet while the focus was on those looters who had died in the supermarket fires and the poor shop girls who had burned alive, their naked corpses fried to a frizzle. The entire media network concentrated on diffusing shock-horror scenes from the conflagration, obviously to scare off pyromaniacs and alert public opinion to the danger of torching shops and homes. Those behind the plan to massacre the Chinese had suddenly realized their plot had spiraled out of hand and was now in danger of turning the entire city into rubble.

"We were behind the shutters for a long time," Anne recalled. "Gradually the noise died down and my father and Uncle Cheah carefully opened the shutters and peered out. 'They've gone' my Uncle said and then opened all the shutters. We walked outside. What we saw I won't ever forget. There were five or six bodies sprawled in the courtyard of the residential block next door, smashed bodies because they had been tossed from the floors upstairs. I remember two bodies had no heads. Fanatical Muslims use swords, the swords of the prophet they call them, to behead infidels. They believe their swords become blessed by the prophet and so are the prophet's swords. It's mad, but they really believe in these fairytales.

"My little sister Nan was sobbing and my mother put her hands over Nan's eyes. I wanted to look away but I couldn't. The horror was like a magnet. I remember everything was very still. No one was shouting or making a noise. It was as if the air had been suspended. Then we heard people moving on the fire escape on the apartment block closest to the rukos. We saw two women and a man. The women were almost naked, their clothing in tatters and one had blood all over her face. The man was trying to help them down the escape ladders but the women couldn't move. Uncle Cheah and my father ran to help them. We also walked towards them to help, that's why we didn't see some of the men sneaking up on us. It was only then that we heard their shouts. We had been discovered. One of those pigs had stayed behind and he had obviously alerted the others... 'Run, run,' my father shouted. 'Run back into the ruko, run.'

"We ran with all our might. Not only us but some of our neighbors who had also come out to see what had happened. But the mob was coming at us fast and first they caught Nan and then they caught Mum and me because we tried to free Nan. They grabbed us by our long hair and pulled us along. Two men dragged Nan into the nearest ruko. The others were chasing the rest of our neighbors who were all running in different directions. I think they must have caught all of us and if someone reached the ruko they smashed the doors down. That's the last sound I heard from outside, the smashing of doors.

"Two men had dragged me into one of the ground floor apartments where I saw one of our neighbors, Tundaleen, being raped. They held her standing against the table with her face pushed onto the table top and her bottom sticking out. One of the men raped her from behind and the others urged him on, all anxious to have their turn. More men were coming through the door. I knew her well. She was 20 years old and engaged to Tomtom, the son of the greengrocer. She survived the rapes but he did not marry her. I remember she yelled and one of the men hit her in the face with his fist. The muscular young man who was raping her had not even lowered his trousers.

"I saw all this before three men lifted me up and carried me off to a room where I was dumped on the carpet. The men began to unbuckle their belts. I was stripped naked. They just tore my smock and my panties off, then a man with hardly any teeth in his mouth stood over me. He had a knife in his hand and he waved it in front of my eyes. I did as I was ordered and closed my eyes. Then another man was on top of me.... There was a terrible pain and I can't remember anything else because I must have fainted...

"When I regained my senses I saw another body on top of me. He was covering my face with kisses and then he bit me and the pain was terrible and I must have fainted again.

"When I came to I was naked on the carpet. Not far from me on the floor I saw my aunt Emmy. She was also naked and moaning. I didn't see Nan and I didn't know what happened to Nan because I was taken to a hospital where they gave me a lot of drugs and I was sleeping for days. Poor Nan. She was only 12 years old."

Only Uncle Cheah had witnessed Nan's ordeal. She struggled

furiously and cursed the men who had pinned her down on the sofa. The more she ranted the rougher the men became, tearing off her jeans and her T-shirt and snapping off the bra. Uncle Cheah was being held down and forced to watch. He pleaded with the men to let Nan go. He promised to give them money. He said he had lots of money if they let Nan go. But the men laughed at him and said they would get his money anyway—and also have Nan. The men drew straws as to who would deflower her. Uncle Cheah said a fellow wearing military boots won the draw and roared with glee. He didn't even bother letting down his trousers and he raped Nan while the others held her arms and legs and told him to hurry up so they could have their turn. At one point Nan managed to lift her head and she spat into the rapist's face. The other men laughed and the rapist, infuriated, took a switch blade knife from his pocket, clicked out the blade and stabbed Nan again and again, in a frenzy. As he stabbed her he was shouting. As blood spurted from Nan's chest the men around her turned quiet and then hurried out of the room, just dropping Uncle Cheah on the floor. He was left beside Nan's corpse.

Anne knew nothing of her sister's death when she regained consciousness in Pluit Hospital. "I woke up with my head feeling like it was three times the normal size and my body seemed not a part of me anymore. I guess it was the drugs they had given me. My father came to visit me every day and cried with me over what had happened to my mother and to Aunt Emmy. They said Nan was alright but they didn't want to talk about her when I asked what had happened to her. My father was already talking to Uncle Cheah about how to rebuild the supermarket and where they could get the loan. He said it was a good time to reopen the supermarket because people had to eat, even in a depression.

"After four days of treatment my condition started to improve. Then, with a sad look my father told me what had happened to Nan and I nearly fainted again. My father still couldn't see very well because he had been hit with a wooden club. He told me we were not going to tell anyone what had happened to me or to Mum or to Aunt Emmy. We could say the mob had beaten us but we must never say we were raped.

"And that's what we did. We kept quiet. I still work at the ruko, my mother still looks after the cash register and shouts at Muhamad who has come back to work for us. Aunt Emmy stays at her parents and never leaves their house. She only has her sister for company. My father and Uncle Cheah have rebuilt the supermarket. And Nan now lives in a small mausoleum we built for her at the cemetery. I guess I will be working in the ruko for the rest of my life. I don't want to work in Dad's supermarket because there are too many people there. Oh no, no man has asked me or will ask me to marry him because everyone knows but no one talks about it because we have never said it happened and Mum keeps telling everyone we were beaten up and fainted and then the mob left us alone. Even if a man asked me I would say no. I couldn't honestly face a husband after what they did to me, now could I?"

In December 1998, seven months after the riots, the Indonesian government finally admitted the rapes had occurred and military personnel had been involved. It appeared most of the military personnel implicated in the riots had been Special Forces, many of them former fighters against rebels in East Timor where rape of rebel women and civilians had virtually become institutionalized. As always, the authorities promised an investigation. In Indonesia such investigations usually turn into a whitewash. Sometimes the authorities find a few scapegoats from the lower ranks.

GLOSSARY

Cukongism: Business relationship between ethnic Chinese and native Indonesians

Fugger: Medieval family of bankers famous for financing imperial wars and crusades

Kaffir: Derogatory term used by Dutch South Africans for black people

Nanyang: The island regions of the South China Sea

Parnakans: Mixed blood Chinese

Ruko: Chinese residential quarters with shops downstairs and living space upstairs

Taipan: Super-rich Chinese entrepreneur and a key player of the Bamboo Network

Totok: Pure blood Chinese

CHAPTER **2**

AUSTRALIA: NEW MOUNTAIN OF GOLD

Taam Sze-Pui arrived in Cooktown, Queensland, Australia on a steamer from Ny Chuen Village, in Guangdong province. He was 20 years old, thin, gullible and desperate for a better life.

Like every other Chinese on the boat he had trusted in the men with placards on their backs, men who had paraded around his hometown and in loud voices offered Travel-Now-Pay-Later fares to Xin Jin Shan, the fabulous New Mountain of Gold. Where this Xin Jin Shan was located the men with the placards indicated only by pointing towards the horizon and rolling their eyes. It was enough to keep everyone mystified and tingling with anticipation.

One of these men with placards on their backs had whispered in Taam Sze-Pui's ear, as if he were offering exclusive and privileged information: "In Xin Jin Shan the streets are paved with gold and all you have to do is scrape it off the sidewalk."

The news made Taam burp with excitement.

In the same confidential tone the man continued: "After you've paid back your fare it's all yours. What? The gold you fool. Young man, you'll come home in silken robes and they'll carry you through the streets in a litter of blue brocaded cloth and your servant will shout: "Make way for Taam Sze-Pui the great mandarin from the New Mountain of Gold. Yes, my boy: People will kowtow. And you, in your magnificence, will toss gold coins at their feet.

"So what do you say?"

Taam had signed up on the spot, ignoring, like tens of thousands of other impoverished and overcrowded Chinese, the imperial ban that no subject of the emperor could leave the empire and that successful "fugitives" must be executed if they returned. However, imperial officials in the far flung empire had a way of turning a blind eye towards those who left and those who came back—as long as their palms were suitably greased.

Taam left no heavy heart behind in Ny Chuen Village. His family was not unhappy to see him go. He was one less mouth to worry about. Even better, he was a family asset wandering somewhere out there in the Nanyang, an asset that could make the family rich, one day. Besides, who could blame a young man like Taam for leaving the village? As the youngest son he had no legitimate claim to the six mu of land his father owned. The land and the house would go to the eldest son. Taam's destiny as the youngest was either to join the Imperial Army, as cannon fodder, enter a Taoist temple as an acolyte or in servitude, or be bonded out to a wealthy landlord or mandarin.

One way or the other his future in China was not bright.

Ny Chuen was a cluster of mud brick huts, some with a central courtyard, some without. Its residents cohabited under one roof and in one large room with pigs, hens, dogs and ducks. Space was so restricted that in some homes eight to ten people camped on mats in a single room. In the winter the families crowded onto and around the kang, heated by a charcoal fire below. The big sow was reluctant to make space for those who had to camp next to the kang. The father always had the central part on the kang, next to him his wife or favorite concubine. The rest bunked in concentric circles according to their social status in the family hierarchy. Being the youngest, Taam was always among those furthest away from the kang. His oldest brother and heir to the land was so close to their father he would tell the other brothers next day how the old man had wheezed and puffed as he plowed inside the young concubine, trying to sow his seed. At night Taam himself would stay awake and listen to the furtive love making of the couples who had to be quiet and quick in the cramped conditions.

The hurried mating in crowded rooms even today is often blamed for the unsatisfactory love life of Chinese women who rarely reach a climax and often find sex a detestable chore with only one acceptable outcome: To procreate a son. Women in China are often in an unseemly hurry to proceed with the act and have this bothersome task done with. A sociological study as recent as in the 1990s found only one in three Chinese women ever experienced an orgasm, a word that does not exist in Chinese vocabulary and had to be substituted by the question: "Did you ever experience any pleasure?" In Taam's days in the 19th century only men were supposed to feel pleasure and women were barely one rank above domestic animals. Until recently a man hardly had time to catch his breath before the woman next to him had her drawers back on and was stretched out, prim and proper.

Over the past decade, greater contact with the outside world and the availability of pornography and sex education has made women in China more aware of what they have been missing. The one in three statistics might no longer be realistic but in Taam's days it was probably far higher.

Many of the people of Ny Chuen were so poor fathers sold their daughters as concubines to wealthy peasants or leased their sons out as bonded laborers.

A few months before Taam signed up, a young man named Chu had left for the Nanyang. Before he was able to set sail, Chu as the oldest son in his family was obliged to satisfy the code of filial duty. Chu was aware failure to carry out his obligations would damn him among the spirits of the ancestors and earn him the scorn of his contemporaries, who would shun him. There was no place in the Nanyang where the Chinese lived to which news from villages back home was not carried by word-of-mouth with every new arrival. This information network was facilitated by the fact that the Chinese tended to congregate abroad in groups from the same village or region.

Before he left, Chu hoisted his little brother Tzi on his shoulders and hiked from village to village. He was hawking the boy to a farmer or a landlord for a lifelong contract. If the boy was lucky the farmer might adopt the purchased stranger and make him his legitimate heir. But usually the purchased boy was treated like a slave.

Chu finally found a couple who examined his little brother closely, opening his mouth to see if his teeth were straight and not yet blackened by cavities. The wife squeezed the boy's arms and legs to test their sturdiness and the farmer finally gave the child a good kick in the bottom. He seemed satisfied with the yelp of pain. The boy's lungs were healthy.

Chu took the money from the sale to his widowed mother. In a world where sons have to look after their parents or be forever damned, Chu could now set sail. His mother had been provided with a reasonable livelihood.

Ironically his little brother had been visibly excited by the prospect of living in the larger home of the peasant couple who bought him. He had no idea how bonded laborers were abused at times, physically, sexually and mentally. People did not talk about this dark side of the bondage system. And those who had been victims rarely complained in a society that tolerated abuse quietly in order not to lose one's own face and that of one's family. Worse, perhaps, it seemed that once handed over as bonded labor, the individuals lost all rights to humane treatment and their fate was at the mercy or the vicissitudes of the buyer.

A week after he had signed up, Taam Sze-Pui boarded the steamer together with several hundred other compatriots. Their only luggage permitted was a haversack containing their sparse belongings and some victuals. Most of the other men were equally convinced a gilded future awaited them in the Nanyang. But their initial enthusiasm was quickly dampened by the sea journey: The passengers were crammed into the cargo hold among sacks filled with spices and bales of cloth. They were allowed above deck only once a day for fresh air. A watery meal was ladled out every evening.

Taam did not make friends on board.

Once, an older man asked him: "Who is your patron?" Taam had shrugged his shoulders. "I'll be met at the dock," he replied. The older man had shaken his head. "A slave driver for sure," he had said.

Taam had walked away in disgust. He did not want to hear his benefactor insulted.

Half way through the journey one of the men became sick. He vomited and trembled and the ship's crew moved him to a single berth. Next day he was missing. When his friends plucked up the courage to inquire what had happened to their countryman, one of the ship's European officers explained in a matter of fact way that the man had died during the night. To avoid contamination, he was tossed overboard.

"A sea burial," the officer had said.

The passengers obviously considered this a reasonable explanation. No one complained. But from that day on Taam sneaked into a quiet corner and vomited each time the sea was rough. He always added an extra spring to his step on deck in case one of the crew thought he might be weakening.

When the steamer docked in Cooktown, Queensland, Australia, a bunch of surly colonial immigration and customs officials came aboard. Their manners and language were coarse and they treated the coolies as inferior creatures descended from an inferior world and offered the privilege of admission to Her British Majesty's colony. The customs men shoveled through the men's haversacks, tossing out their meager belongings with the disdain of people who do not care and are not held responsible for what they break or spoil.

"Got any opium, Chum?" one of them asked Taam.

An immigration officer with a nose tip the size of a potato was in charge of the register. He listened to Taam's name and scratched his head. "Blimey!" he shouted to his companions: "Them coots 'ave names 'ike farts." He roared with laughter at his own joke and wrote down in the register: TOM SEE POY.

It was a far more convenient monocle for Anglo-Celtic ears than Taam Sze Pui. The new name would stick to Taam for the rest of his life. From that day until he died he was Tom See Poy in Australia.

He was lucky. Other newcomers were inevitably named Ah Song, Ah Lim, Ah Wang because when they were asked: "What's your name then, mate?" The peasants stammered "Ahhh" before stuttering out the family appellation.

Like everyone else, Tom See Poy had come alone to Australia, the land known as Xin Jin Shan, the New Mountain of Gold to distinguish it from California which was known to the Chinese as Jiu Jin Shan, the Old Gold Mountain where the gold rush had already petered out by the 1850s.

In its wisdom the British Crown had decided to restrict Chinese immigration to males to avoid "proliferation among the yellow race". The Crown wished to ensure that Her Majesty's Terra Australis remained a white settlement, unadulterated by oriental heathens or colored races. Right now however the new colony was in dire need of cheap labor and additional diggers to scrape gold from the wilderness. Gold and sheep were laying the foundations of a penal colony that had the makings of an affluent nation.

Few people had voiced any faith in the future of this god-forsaken colony at the end of the world, a place to which the Crown sent rebels, rabble and petty thieves, fettered by ball and chain. Many of these transportees were poor wretches accused of theft before English courts. They had no money to contest the harsh verdicts, passed down for petty offenses such as stealing a loaf of bread, picking a gentleman's pocket or poaching a squire's hare. Transportation for Life was common in those days and served a dual purpose: To populate a virgin colony and rid England of troublemakers, rowdy rabble and the growing hoards of the poor. Those sent as overseers, officials and troopers to administer the penal settlement did not come from the cream of English society and were renowned for a taste for brutality, which they were able to indulge in fully in a far away colony. Early White Australia rarely questioned the excesses of the authorities or the abominable stupidity of its leaders and squatters.

The East Coast of this forsaken southern land had been discovered barely a century earlier by Captain James Cook who immediately took possession of the entire continent in the name of the British Crown. Those who followed him showed scant love for the land or its inhabitants but an insatiable appetite to amass as much and as quickly as possible, no matter at whose cost.

A century after it fell into British hands the colony thrived but needed more labor. The Chinese were excellent workers and meticulous gold diggers although they had one drawback: Judging from the experience of the Dutch in Batavia and the Spanish in Manila the Chinese, nicknamed in Australia "Chows", had a nasty tendency to riot for their rights, once their numbers were sufficient to muster a mob.

How then could one exploit the talent of these Chows for hard work but keep their numbers down?

The authorities found a fiendish solution: Chinese men were allowed to enter the colony but Chinese wives and single women were banned. Six decades later an independent Australian nation would use similar restrictions to "whiten" the Aboriginal race. The racial and religious zealots took mixed-race children away from their Aboriginal parents, stuffed them into orphanages or foster homes and specified that as adults, these children could only mate with whites or other mixed-race partners. The idea, officially, was "to breed the blackness out of them".

The no-women regulation was highly effective: Between 1887 and 1920, only 18 of the 1,575 Chinese in the northern town of Cairns managed to get married.

In the 1880s, official statistics show the presence of 38,000 Chinese in Australia. Only 11 of them were officially female.

Still, reports from the gold fields claimed the Chinese had a good number of Chinese whores in their joy-houses. These ladies of the night had apparently arrived disguised as men, not a difficult task considering the hairless nature of Chinese faces of both sexes and the boyish physique of many Chinese women. Immigration officials did not subject the new arrivals to a sex test. They would have surely done so had it ever dawned on them.

Some Chinese men solved the problem of no women by sharing one "wife". Frequently she was a former white prostitute well beyond retirement age and with no prospect of a pension. These women were the white man's leftovers. The Chinese Chums "jumped" them just as they had "jumped" the claims on the gold fields once these had been abandoned by the white diggers. Other Chinese men took up with Aboriginal women known as gins. Yet by law the Chinese were not allowed to marry a white or a black woman and white diggers and natives became furious when the Celestials strayed across the racial divide.

An old digger named Tommy Doughtery recalled the punishment when a Chinese man was discovered fornicating in a whore-house: "The Chow would get a good thrashing and so would the brazen hussy that'd allowed him her favors."

Australia, in its colonial bigotry, was determined to be known as a white continent, even though there were more than a million Aboriginal people on the land when the white man arrived in 1788. The colony stubbornly refused to import Indian labor, which was available in surplus on the British-run subcontinent. The colony's white bigots were afraid the Indians would leave a dark genetic smudge on Australia's official whiteness.

Not long before Tom's steamer moored in the Endeavor River at Cooktown, a group of Aborigines had kidnapped two Chinese gold diggers. The Celestials had enraged the tribe by persuading two young gins to live with them. The story, carried by word of mouth, was that the natives cooked the two Celestials alive and then ate them, leaving only their queues and skulls as testimonials of the feast. The news spread through the gold fields like a bush fire. As a result many Chinese abandoned their black paramours.

By the turn of the century prejudice, discrimination and the law had virtually disqualified the Chinese from partaking in carnal pleasures. The white man did not even want them hanging around white brothels and the Chinese joy-houses near the gold fields had vanished when the digs became exhausted. Deprived of these basic joys of life as well as a family, a basic need for any Chinese, many of them sought pleasure in other ways.

Around 1900 the Australian customs and excise police estimated at least one in four Chinese workers in Australia was seeking solace in opium. Opium smoking became a daily routine, a way to escape from sexual frustration, the lack of family life, homesickness and an alien society. Puffing the pipe was as common as breakfast or dinner. Most lodging houses kept extra beds for smokers. Common belief soon had it that all Chinese were opium addicts, carriers of leprosy and other unmentionable diseases.

This kind of prejudice was inherent in contemporary Anglo-Saxon society. English literature portrayed the Chinese as diabolic villains, people not to be trusted and, of course, inferior to the Caucasians, particularly the British, a race whose empire was now girdling the globe, making alien species subservient to London. Sax Rohmer's *Fu Manchu*, Dickens' *Mystery of Edwin Drood* and the opium den in Oscar Wilde's *The Picture of Dorian Gray*, created a prejudice that has survived to this day.

By the time Tom See Poy landed in Cooktown, the Anglo-Celtic mining fraternity in that new boomtown on the York Peninsula had closed ranks against "the Chows". The miners gave the likes of Tom as hostile a reception as possible in the hope the news of their welcome would deter more Celestials from trying their fortunes on the gold fields. Once in a while the mobs managed to stop Chinese miners from setting foot in Cooktown, a town that mushroomed out of the bush like a stray orchid after gold was discovered in 1873 along the Palmer River.

The miners' blockades forced the steamers from Hong Kong and Guangdong to raise anchor and plod along the coast as far south as Port Douglas or Cairns to unload their human cargoes. The hapless Chinese diggers, tired and weak after the long sea journey, would then have to fight their way overland to the gold fields, slashing through virgin bush and dragging their packs over rugged ox-cart tracks. Many perished, waylaid by cannibal natives who had apparently developed a taste and a predilection for smooth, hairless Chinese flesh, far more appetizing to their palate than the bristly, blotched and freckled bodies of Irish miners and carriers.

The Chinese presence on the goldfields had fanned racism long before Tom arrived.

In 1876, a report by the Palmer River Warden P.F. Sellheim alleged, perhaps with much exaggeration, that 17,000 Chinese were scattered over a 2,000 square mile river area with only 1,400 Europeans present. Steamers were bringing in as many as 1,000 Chinese per journey. There were Chinese riots when the authorities insisted the newcomers had to be quarantined for months at Fitzroy Island, a hostile place, already crowded with 2,000 Chinese who had to camp in the open without tents. Many Chinese died on Fitzroy Island.

The media reported that the situation was turning from bad to worse on the gold fields. Starving Chinese working in mobs robbed, murdered and beat up shopkeepers, carriers and miners, just to grab their tucker. Chinese gangs ambushed white diggers to steal their gold. Chinese mobs kicked whites out of their claims and, conscious of being a majority, refused to pay mining fees. Thousands of Celestials took over large tracts of land for their own prospecting and allowed no other race to stake a claim.

"It is no longer a question of repelling an invasion," said the *Cooktown Herald* in May 1876, "but to defend, not alone our hearths and homes, but our very lives against the invaders who swarm around us."

These reports were obviously exaggerated and their aim was to curb the influx of the Chinese or what the media called the Celestials into Australia, especially the gold fields. Acting on the paranoia thus created, the authorities in Brisbane imposed a heavy poll tax on new Chinese arrivals. Together with the dwindling gold, the tax slowed down the invasion. For the next century, however, the hair on the neck of Australians would bristle at the mention of Chinese migration. Many Australians considered it a miracle the north of their country was never taken over by the "Oriental Chums" (another term the miners used for the Chinese).

On the day Tom's steamer slipped into the Endeavor River at

Cooktown, the white miners were well into their cups.

All day the carriers had been offering the men free drinks. The carriers had their own motives to stop the Chinese invasion: Their ox and horse teams carted supplies to the gold fields at huge profit. The new arrivals would be under contract to Chinese merchants for years before their fares were paid off. These merchants already owned two thirds of Cooktown and rented out their coolies as porters to the miners. The cheap labor undercut the white carriers and took away a fair chunk of their transport business. Both the carriers and the Chinese merchants had worked out long ago that supplying the gold rush was far more lucrative than digging for the precious metal in the wilderness.

So once the steamer was sighted by the lookout, the carriers offered fresh rounds of free drinks and whipped up gruesome tales of the evils and illnesses of the Chinese. The story was basically the same: The Celestials spread disease among the white race and practiced heathen habits. The diggers readily accepted these stories. Gold was running scarce along the Palmer and no one wanted more Oriental Chums to compete for the little that was left.

According to one report a carrier named Robertson had been strutting up and down Main Street all day brandishing his new breech-loading Snider rifle which fired a bullet that made a hole four times the size of those from the old .303.

"I shot lots of 'em blackfellows down in Victoria and there ain't noth'n to stop me shooting 'em yellow-belly Chinks," Robertson shouted.

A batch of sailors on shore leave had joined him. Their cutlasses gave his words a sinister appendix. The mood was ugly. There wasn't a white man in Cooktown, either in the catering business or out on the claims, who was not feeling the pinch of a rush gone sour. Many a good mate had sold his pick and shovel, his pan and billy for just a few more days of grub to live on. Times were tough without more Chinese making them tougher.

"Toss the buggers into the water!" someone yelled.

"Yeah, mate" added another voice: "Let's drown them blooming Chows."

"Ain't no place for the blighters."

"Bloody drongos who'd let 'em in ought to be tarred and feathered. Strewth, mate."

When the steamer docked, the miners strung ropes across the gangplanks. Then someone had the bright idea to make some cash from the affair.

"Let's put a levy on all Celestial Paddies," the shout went up.

The idea found instant approval.

Extorting the Chinese was no novelty. Disgruntled miners and their leaders had bandied the scheme for months, arguing that news of a levy would reach Hong Kong and discourage other Celestials from heading to Gold Mountain.

Aboard Tom's steamer the captain saw the mob of rowdy miners milling on the quay, fists raised and making unmistakable gestures for his vessel to move on.

"Trouble brewing, lad," the captain said to his first mate.

He was an old sea dog familiar with the situation.

"Gentlemen," he called over the bullhorn, addressing his human cargo politely for the first time: "In my esteemed opinion I think it would be better to head for a more friendly port. We are going to have trouble here, gentlemen. You are not wanted."

An interpreter translated the words into shrill Cantonese. "There's good land to be had near Port Douglas, gentlemen," the captain went on. "Good jobs to be had on the new plantations. Good pay for good workers. A man can make a fortune in these places."

The captain, who had done his fair share of oriental Runs, was mentally counting the fee he could pocket from farmers in Port Douglas and Cairns for the delivery of each member of his cargo. Labor was at a premium there. The new farms couldn't grow enough food to supply the gold fields and Chinese workers were coveted help on the farm. They could be depended upon, unlike the Aborigines, a nomadic people who would go on walk-about without warning and usually when needed the most. The natives were not deterred by the threat of being put in chains if they walked off a station or a farm.

Still, the captain's suggestion found no favor among the coolies who saw the promised mountain of gold vanish and with it their dream of going home in silken robes. Shouldering their haversacks, the coolies made a dash down the gangplank. The crowd of miners, a formidable phalanx, pushed them back. In the melee a Chinaman named Ah Long received a broken nose after he had hurled himself against the picket line and right into the roundhouse swing of a burly Irish carrier.

Once again the captain beseeched his passengers to consider more hospitable shores. The coolies chatted excitedly among themselves. Some appeared to change their minds. This was not the kind of reception they had expected. Weakened by the sea voyage, they had no stomach for a brawl.

Before a decision could be made, there was a commotion on the wharf as the representatives of the Chinese merchants arrived, flanked by the law, a tall constable with a handlebar moustache and a revolver in one hand followed by three Aboriginal trackers armed with rifles. The new arrivals took no notice of the jeers from the miners but elbowed their way rudely to the gangplank. Obviously the Chinese merchants had no intention to see their investments sail off to Cairns or Port Douglas where they would never see them again. These men were labor, bonded to their masters by their fare. Each arrival knew there would be retribution against families back home if he broke the bond. Besides, the law, its palms generously crossed, tended to be on the side of capitalism as it always is, in this case the Chinese merchants.

In the free for all that followed, shots were fired into the air. The miners lurched back and the Chinese saw their chance and charged down the gangplank. Their landing soon turned into hand-to-hand combat the police could not prevent.

Tom's haversack was ripped from his back and vanished in the crowd. It contained all his worldly goods, a change of clothing, a wok, two pairs of chopsticks, a kettle and a small statue of the village deity. When he finally broke through the ring of white miners, his only possession was the shirt on his back, a pair of pants, the sandals he wore and three Chinese coins in his pocket.

Bruised and bewildered, he walked into Cooktown.

He came into a frontier town built on the Palmer River gold rush and as mixed in architecture as it was in the origin of its inhabitants. He saw scores of his countrymen hurrying along streets and alleyways with carrier poles slung across their shoulders, moving in that minced half-run, half-walk gait of the Chinese porters. No one gave him a second glance in a town that was home to 18,000 Chinese who made up two thirds of the local population.

In his colorful book *River of Gold*, Hector Holthouse wrote:

"Overnight a tent town sprouted on the steamy, mangrove shores of the Endeavor River, and within months it had grown to the second busiest port of Queensland. Its sole business was Palmer gold. Men and women of every race and nation jostled in its streets. Banks and stores stood cheek to jowl with shanties, brothels, and gambling dens. Its Chinese citizen outnumbered all the others put together and in their bazaars they were predicting that Cooktown was about to become the Canton of the South."

In Tom's days, Cooktown was still wealthy. Horse drawn carriages careered down stone-paved streets. Gentlemen in toppers bowed to ladies veiled in lace. Silk-gloved hands held pink parasols to fend off a scorching tropical sun. Tom would find out later the dainty creatures he so admired were not ladies and the dandies who escorted them were not gentlemen. The town had 94 licensed pubs and just as many brothels, a Chinese town council of elders and a temple fully imported, piece by piece, brick by brick, from Guangdong.

Tom approached an elderly Chinese scrubbing down a hefty hobbled horse. He named the merchant who was supposed to meet him. Without pausing in his chore, the old man pointed over his shoulder and muttered something in a language Tom did not understand. The fellow was definitely not from Guangdong. He was obviously one of those country bumpkins from around Hong Kong, illiterates with bad manners and uncouth faces.

He headed off in the direction indicated in search of the man who could do with him whatever he pleased for the next few years until his fare was paid off. The thought never occurred to Tom that he could have walked away, found a paying job and escaped years of unpaid toil and pain. The thought never occurred to him because the retribution for his family back home would have been terrible. Just as bad would have been the family's shame that a member had reneged on his contract.

Today Cooktown is a sleepy hollow, a mere shadow of its Chinese days when the coolies arrived as bonded labor to the local representatives of the Chinese merchants in Guangdong and Hong Kong. These men could hire them out not only as porters, cooks or laborers but also as "Aboriginal bait" for the white convoys heading through hostile bush to new fields. In the annals of the time it is reported the Chinese were asked to walk behind the convoy, at a good distance. The Aborigines would always attack the Chinese who were easier prey and apparently tastier.

Today a rusty coastal tramp is moored where Tom and the Chinese disembarked. Outside the Cooktown Hotel a cluster of rowdy Aborigines gulp down the contents of stubby beer cans. Sturdy men and women, they are the descendants of the fierce Merkin, cannibals from the Torres Strait who, so reports claimed, had a predilection for Chinese flesh during the gold rush days. Alcohol offered by profit-minded white men and social welfare offered by the bad consciences of successive Australian governments have devitalized them.

The last Chinese store on Main street, Hip On & Co, closed in 1951. The last Chinese, a bent frail old man with a wispy chin growth whom no one remembers by name, died in 1957 after a hermit's life. There is no visible sign of the old Chinatown. It stood in a part of the town the Aborigines named "The mangrove where the sand flies live". The spot is now a public park.

Today Cooktown has only three pubs and 912 residents who know nothing about an era when white supremacists thundered against the "disease-riddled, opium-smoking Chows." The Chinese temple was pulled down long ago and its deities, scattered in the bush, ended up as dolls for the local toddlers. An occasional tourist carted off the elaborate temple carvings until Hans Looser salvaged a few of the relics for the local museum. Looser was a soldier in Hitler's Wehrmacht who decided to migrate to Australia after the war. He bought himself a German map to determine where he should go. The map still showed Cooktown as a major Australian city. When Looser finally arrived at the city of his dreams, he found only a hamlet at the end of a dirt track.

Undaunted, the German remained. For 31 years he sounded the bugle for the *Last Post* in Cooktown's Anzac Parade, the Australian anniversary to commemorate the fallen soldiers of two world wars. In 1994, however, two elderly housewives protested against what they considered a gross offense to the war heroes—having an enemy sound the *Last Post*. Looser resigned.

Cooktown has been dying slowly, decade by decade, ever since alluvial gold petered out along the Palmer and northern rivers. The Chinese drifted south to the farms. Those who had money for the fare went back home. Before the Chinese left they built a memorial to commemorate the thousands of coolies who had starved to death on the remote gold fields, were robbed, shot, clubbed to death or eaten by cannibals.

The memorial is overgrown by shrubs and hard to spot at the rear of the Pioneer Cemetery. It hides behind bushes, gum trees and the stately tombs of the white men and women hailed as the trail-blazing pioneers of Cooktown. At the front of the cemetery, engraved on weather-beaten rock and granite tombstones, are the names of doctors, matrons, bankers, parsons, priests, seamen and the odd European aristocrat driven across the Ocean by his family's penury or an unusual sense of adventure.

The Chinese have no names, only a monolith as a memorial. The hazards and discrimination in Gold Mountain did not deter more Chinese from seeking their fortune. So many arrived, their presence triggered the Cooktown Scare—fear of a Chinese takeover.

The Scare inspired a plethora of petitions, which in turn led to the White Australia policy, one of the first decisions of the newly created Commonwealth of Australia in 1901. The advocates of the policy told the new nation the Chinese had sent back to China two thirds or 10,000 tons of all the gold found on the North Queensland strikes. This was deemed intolerable. Worse, it was proof the Celestials had neither love for the new nation nor any intention to remain—in retrospect not surprising given the welcome they received.

The White Australia supporters complained that the coolies, who were organized in disciplined work gangs, had raked the gullies and ravines for gold, locust-like, leaving not an ounce of the precious metal behind. No one admitted, of course, that the methodical Chinese system to scourge the gold fields was a far more thorough and successful way than the hit-and-run prospecting of the white diggers who usually dug shafts, exploited them laterally and abandoned them as soon as the pickings ran thin.

The White Australia policy doomed further Chinese immigration. Its harsh terms limited immigration of so-called "Celestials," "Asiatics" and "Kanakas" (Pacific Islanders) until Canberra shelved it in 1973.

To save face before the international community, the authorities devised a fiendish ploy: Any colored person was able to apply for immigration and was granted residence if he or she could pass a language test. The test could be in any language. Thus a Chinese person may be tested in Swedish, an African in Chinese. Hardly anyone ever passed the test and Australia remained smugly white. In 1957, Labor Party Migration Minister Arthur Caldwell was asked in parliament why he refused permission for two Chinese to join their families who had lived in Australia for decades. Caldwell made the famous reply: "Two Wongs don't make a White."

His retort became the toast of the nation. In their heart of hearts Australians have not changed their attitude towards non-white migrants or black natives. Isolated on their vast island in the Southern Hemisphere, most Australians suffer from latent xenophobia, a condition of fear that others will snatch what they took from the natives and stole from a land that never stopped giving. In recent years economic realities and a more tolerant world have forced Australia to pay lip service to racial equality and colored immigration. Nowadays Australians bristle with indignation if someone suggests the country remains raked by racist sentiments and intolerance towards non Anglo-Celtic ways of life. No one publicly admits envy persists against anyone willing to work harder than the laid-back Aussies. Prejudice remains towards the Aboriginal race, the native victims of one of the world's sleaziest genocide campaigns ever invented by white colonizers and covered up for almost two centuries.

Australia is still run by people with Anglo-Celtic names although more than half its population comes from non-English speaking nations. The Anglo-Celtic still mocks "the others" and when confronted, calls this "good-natured teasing." Any criticism of life Down Under is still rebuffed with Neanderthal logic: "If you don't like the country go back to where you came from."

A new wave of Chinese has rolled into Australia. The newcomers are far more confident than their predecessors, aware of their own values and the geopolitical reality that the fifth continent is now shackled, by hook or by crook, to Asian markets after Mother England set its white colony adrift in return for European Market membership. At London's Heathrow Airport colonials from Down Under are grilled as thoroughly these days as any third world arrivals. Mother England has no stomach for the descendants of its own outcasts.

This contemporary wave of Chinese to disembark in Gold Mountain continent is not made up of indentured coolies but members of the taipans of Southeast Asia and the Pacific Ring. They come from a region in the world where the Chinese make up only 7 per cent of the native populations but own 70 per cent of the region's private wealth. Wealthy Chinese from Hong Kong, Singapore, Malaysia, Indonesia and Taiwan have bought some of Australia's prime real estate. The most scenic parts of Queensland are in Japanese hands. A government report released in 1998 found, to the horror of white purists, that Australia has become China's biggest investment target abroad. Today the Australian dollar and shares, mainly in mining, tend to rise and fall with demand from China, Australia's largest trading partner.

Tens of thousands of Chinese students are enrolled on Australian campuses that advertise aggressively in Southeast Asia. Many students overstay or find legal loopholes to settle. Demographic predictions claim that within 25 years every fourth Australian would be an Asian, mainly of Chinese origin. Already 40 per cent of annual immigrants are Asians.

In fact the dream of a White Australia evaporated with a United Nations convention promoting the reunion of families. Australia subscribed to this agreement. After the 1989 massacre of pro-democracy demonstrators around Tiananmen Square in Beijing, a weeping Labor party Prime Minister, Bob Hawke, offered asylum to 10,000 young Chinese who alleged political persecution at home. In reality few of those who pleaded for asylum and mourned fallen comrades had taken part in the pro-democracy movement, had any democratic affiliation or cared one hoot about the ideals of those who died and fought in Beijing. The majority simply saw Tiananmen as a god-sent opportunity to obtain residence permits abroad by exploiting global compassion and the media frenzy over trampled democratic rights.

"The 10,000 have now become 80,000 thanks to the family reunion policy," admitted Henry Tsang in 1999, ten years later. Tsang, an ethnic Chinese, is a former deputy lord mayor of Sydney. Today demographic estimates talk of half a million Chinese in Australia.

By the end of the 1990s some estimates claimed that those 10,000 granted asylum by the Hawke government had multiplied to around 300,000, many of them relatives or friends who came on student or visitor's visas and were looked after by those already in the country. Thousands more were smuggled into the country, a Shangri-La for a people short of Lebensraum. The news made headlines only when one group of illegal Chinese, exhausted and near death, was found wandering in the barren northern Kimberleys. These lost Chinese were only the tip of the iceberg, a group of mavericks who had tried to make it on their own. In bygone days the majority of those smuggled into the country were met at remote coastal points and taken care of by a network of "slavers", most of them white Australians in the pay of the taipans.

All that has changed as China boomed. Today the majority of Chinese who arrive in Australia are part of the new rich, the new millionaires of communist China who come on business visas and are granted residency after investing or depositing money in Australian financial institutions. The Chinese are no longer among the boat people arriving from Indonesia on rickety vessels, dropped off by crooked captains along the vast Australian coastline where they often perished.

Today the Chinese fly into Australia.

Already Sydney is tagged as Little Asia, an example of the Asianization denounced by Pauline Hanson and her One Nation party. Hanson advocates an end to all Asian immigration. Her followers are red-necked Australians, throwbacks to colonial days who mourn the premature death of the White Australia policy. A group of these dinky-die Aussies in their traditional akubra hats—the ones made famous by Crocodile Dundee—recently glared at a swarm of Taiwanese arriving at Sydney airport.

"Mate," one of them shouted across the terminal: "They ought to lynch the bloody drongo (idiot) who abolished the White Australia policy."

The sentiment expressed in that remark was not different from what the miners called out to Tom See Poy a hundred years earlier.

Then, as today, Australians were alarmed by the success of the new arrivals. Today the Chinese dig a different gold, in academia, business and commerce. And Australians are bristling: 71 per cent questioned by a newspaper poll in the late 1990s still advocated cutbacks on Asian immigration. At the same time a survey among Chinese found more than half had been abused, threatened or physically assaulted. Singaporean soldiers training in Queensland were pelted with eggs. The Malaysian consulate in Sydney received death threats and the Chinese-born deputy lord mayor of Adelaide had his office thrashed and daubed with racist slogans.

In the 1990s, Australian Race Discrimination Commissioner Zita Antonios said she believed the new wave of racism had been "bubbling under the surface" for some time, stimulated by rising unemployment and an ever more obvious dependence on Asian markets. Helen Sham-Ho, the first ethnic Chinese parliamentarian in New South Wales, put it more bluntly: "We Chinese will always be singled out in Australia because we have black hair and yellow skins."

Alhough the Chinese profess they are here to stay this time, many have kept a stake in the old country. Even Sham-Ho and her husband have a joint venture making potato chips in Beijing. All the 110 Chinese Associations in Sydney maintain commercial links to the mainland, Taiwan or Hong Kong. The majority of these associations are kinship networks of Chinese immigrants from the same villages or region who gather for protection and to do business. China today has a Fifth Column of economic moles in Southeast Asia and Australasia. Sure, these moles are building their own business interests but simultaneously they are expanding official Chinese commercial interests in the region.

The Chinese associations in Sydney are mainly Hakka with names like Ti Loy and Co, War Hing Co-operative, Hung Fook Tong (run like a Freemasons style secret society) and The Chinese Youth League. The League is Beijing-supported and most of its members—surprise, surprise—are the young immigrants who fled "the yoke" of Chinese communism in 1989.

Tom See Poy could not read the racial ranting of the media in his days. He did not speak a word of English. The lack of language skills haunted him for years. Each spare minute he sat down and copied the awkward letters of the Latin alphabet, stringing them together to make words that sounded alien to a Cantonese speaker. His efforts were remarkable since Tom had never learned how to read or write in China.

About the time he arrived in Gold Mountain the papers were filled every day with indignation over the invasion of "the Chows". The weekly *Northern Miner* carried the headline: "THE COMMON ENEMY JOHN CHINAMAN" and the paper's editorial, written in the shock-horror tone of the times, warned its readers:

"Is our civilization to go down under the hoofs of those barbarians or shall we stand up and beat them back?"

The *Queensland Punch* penned a ditty in its December 1880 issue which summed up growing public anger with Chinese immigration and showed Australians had already learned the hard way their Chinese immigrants could be stubborn and troublesome once they gathered in a mob.

The Chinese must go
They're right enough while they're in the minority
When they come here with a teeming majority
What they will do is not easy to say
They'll be our bosses and we'll grow their cabbages.

In those days white bullies found it easy to push around single or two and three Chinese. But once four or five Chinese congregated, their attitude changed, their bearing became aggressive and their pent up frustration ignited into primitive savagery.

Since the era of the Warring States. mass attacks had made the Chinese a frightening foe. In a mob the Chinese feel invincible by the sheer power of their numbers, perhaps a feeling nurtured by the gamblers' instinct that the odds of being killed among such a vast multitude of humanity are in favor of the individual. The U.S.-led United Nations forces in North Korea saw evidence of this death-defiant courage in the Chinese mass attacks on their positions. Vietnamese soldiers who repelled the punitive Chinese expedition in 1979 still talk with awe of the wave of Chinese soldiers they mowed down. But fresh waves kept coming, leaping over the bodies of their fallen comrades.

When U.S. aircraft carriers rushed to the defense of Taiwan in the mid-1990s during a standoff with China, I saw a chilling Peoples Liberation Army (PLA) study. It argued that in case of a nuclear conflict with the United States, some 20 million Chinese could die. But China had the capacity to send a nuclear missile into the U.S. East Coast with a predicted casualty rate of about 10,000 Americans. Public backlash from their death would force Washington to withdraw from the defense of Taiwan. The island could then be reunited with the Motherland without further interference from the Americans.

In the late 1980s and early 1990s foreigners found it easy to browbeat individual Chinese in Beijing. But foreigners were advised by their embassies to beat a hasty retreat as soon as a mob gathered.

In those days the Chinese would run their bicycles into the cars of foreigners and pretend to be seriously wounded. It was usually done near a traffic light when the car was almost stationary. The distraught foreign motorist, aware he was inevitably wrong in China no matter what the circumstances, was only too eager to shell out some cash to avoid problems with the authorities. If the cash was deemed insufficient the victim would howl. This immediately brought a large crowd to the scene and made the foreigner hurriedly delve deeper into his or her pocket.

In 1988 the U.S. embassy instructed its diplomats and their wives to drive on to the embassy compound after an incident, pick up an embassy lawyer and interpreter and then return to the scene. The wife of a diplomat did just that. After being nudged by a kamikaze cyclist—who instantly fell down and pretended to be unconscious—she stepped on the accelerator. To her astonishment the cyclist revived miraculously. With baffling agility, he leapt onto the bonnet of her car. He clung to the windscreen wipers all the way to the embassy compound. He was not about to let this windfall escape.

These apparent shows of solidarity with fellow Chinese believed wounded by foreigners were extremely baffling since the Chinese have a reputation—rightly or wrongly—for a chilling lack of compassion for the plight of others and simply look the other way.

In Tom See Poy's days, the British Empire was in its heyday and belief in white supremacy was a byproduct of its success. In those days the Yellow Man was just as exploitable Down Under as the white man is in China today. Down Under the cultural differences between the white settlers and the Chinese were based on the suspicion the Chums had come to carve out a large chunk of northern Australia for the emperor in Peking. Soon nothing would be left for the whites.

By 1878 anti-Chinese sentiment was running at fever pitch. A front page headline in the *Cairns Post* read:

"Nothing much: Only a dead Chinaman."

The *Queensland Figaro* published a vicious little poem titled *The Yellow Agony*:

> *Shoals of pigtails, almond eyed*
> *Flooding all the countryside*
> *Skimmed off as their country's scum*
> *Odorous of opium*
> *Yellow rascals, cunning, knavish*
> *Bowed in foul, vice-bondage, slavish*
> *They, with Eastern filth embedded*
> *Form one monster, hydra-headed*

Years later, with Chinese immigration down to a trickle and the gold rush over, a *Cairns Post* editorial on October 28, 1897, was more condescending:

> *"Perhaps no class of men evoke less sympathy than the Chinese. Schooled as we are to look upon them as little better than beasts of burden, we sometimes fail to realize that these men are capable of feeling as deeply as we do."*

In his memoirs, a letter to his three sons and two daughters, Tom See Poy makes no mention of race hatred.

Even today the Chinese in the Diaspora never talk about persecutions or pogroms. They do not want to burden their children with nightmares or sentiments of revenge that might interfere with their pragmatic judgments and business decisions. Unlike the Jews, the Chinese see the past as a waste of time. Regurgitating past injustices is only useful if compensation can be obtained. But even then the Chinese carefully weigh the benefits of compensation against the loss in goodwill and future commercial interests.

For most Chinese only the present and the future counts.

In his memoirs, Tom See Poy wrote: "Five years had passed. I now realized that to search for gold was like trying to catch the moon at the bottom of the sea."

His lyrical leap over those five tortuous years encapsulate a philosophy shared by his compatriots whose history of personal endurance and ability to absorb hardships has been eloquently captured in historic records by foreign authors, rarely by the Chinese themselves. Their search for gold, whether in California, Queensland or Victoria, has been symbolic of the relentless Chinese pursuit of wealth. No race is as single-minded, as determined and as dispassionate in its struggle to accumulate money.

And no Chinese person is ever satisfied with an achievement, although it may set up the family for generations to come. Making money is not just a necessity but a way of life, in fact the core reason for one's existence. Nature and human beings are exploited without limits. Protecting the environment is a luxury invented by the already wealthy and not applicable to those striving to catch up. Today's China is depleted of much of its forests and fauna and prone each year to the most horrendous floods and droughts. But the Chinese who migrate abroad practice the same merciless plunder of natural resources in their adopted homes. Rootless and ever ready to move on if the bonanza runs out in one place, the Chinese head for new green pastures.

Watching them gouging through the gold fields a hundred or more years ago was no different from observing them over the last decades cutting down and burning the forests across Asia. Chinese developers have cemented Asia's most scenic spots with ugly all-purpose development projects, depleted water resources for vast plantations carved out of the jungles of Borneo and Sumatra and turned green oases into barren brown deserts. Their rapacious fury has destroyed some of Southeast Asia's vital natural habitats within decades.

In small numbers, locusts do reasonable damage but in swarms they are devastating. One can sympathize with the Cooktown reporter who wrote after a visit to the gold fields: "The Chinese have rooted up every gully and ravine that the white man had only pot-holed, carrying everything before them like a swarm of locusts."

Yet few people who have come in touch with the Chinese have failed to admire the astonishing risks a Chinese person is prepared to take, both to his fortune and life. Women and men can risk the earnings of a year in the throw of a dice, the turn of a card or the spin of a wheel. The billionaire taipans of Southeast Asia staked their fortunes on projects that could have doubled, tripled or quadrupled their assets or sent them bankrupt. Asia's economic bust was mainly due to the gambling and risk-taking of the Chinese in the Diaspora. They reached for the stars and were convinced the bonanza would never end.

Australians have a similar gambling spirit.

A few years before Tom See Poy landed at Cooktown, a message was nailed to the wall of a mining office in Cairns. It stated in bold black letters that gold had been found on the Palmer. This message, disseminated nationwide, encouraged 35,000 men and women to trek overland and by sea to the remote outpost in search of fortune.

By the time Tom arrived, the euphoria had subsided. Horses were no longer shod with gold, nuggets were no longer tossed to dancing girls or wagered on frog and cockroach races held on bar tops. Out in the bush, scores had died of starvation. Natives had fatally speared others.

Tom was that rare mixture who seeks his fortune but maintains a secret fondness for the finer arts in life. He was possessed of a combination of mandarin elegance, merchant astuteness and coolie crudeness so common among wealthy Chinese in the Diaspora. He liked paintings and hoarded the daguerreotype photos coming into vogue in those days.

In his first years—the years he never talked about—he not only taught himself to read and write, a prerequisite for his future ambitions, but also realized the gold fields were a fool's paradise. Rarely did a digger make his fortune from the nuggets and the gold dust he panned. He saw lucky miners strut into Cooktown after months of hard toil in the bush and blow their gold in a few nights of booze, women and gambling. He saw his own countrymen, who were being cruelly exploited by the representatives of the Hong Kong and Guangdong merchants, turn on each other. He knew by the time their bondage had expired the gold would have petered out. Tom must have realized early that the truly wise became wealthy by providing the gold-crazed fools with the basic fuel for all humanity—food.

Two days after his arrival he was told by "the bossman" to shoulder a pole with a basket on each end and join the caravan of porters heading for the gold fields. Inside the baskets were supplies of rice and dried vegetables, fish and spices, all carted by boat from China. The miners would pay for them in sweat and gold.

Walking in twos and threes, more than 200 porters set off from Cooktown on a journey that could take a fortnight. Each time a contingent took off into the humid virgin bush theirs was a journey into the unknown. Accompanying the human train were tough Tongs, the muscles of the merchants. All Tongs were armed with ancient muzzle-loading guns, cutlasses and whips. Each porter had to carry in a wicker basket his own rations, mainly rice, in addition to his cargo. Each man shouldered a load of 150 pounds.

The human train meandered along the bush track carved out by previous expeditions and ox carts. Sometimes the caravan strayed from the track and took short cuts, arduous hikes over untracked terrain, which made their cargo heavier, their footing more insecure. But the Tongs felt this would give the human train an edge over the carriers whose ox-carts were slower and more cumbersome. Fierce competition existed between the Chinese and European suppliers. No tricks were barred.

Some of the men carried cages filled with live chicken and ducks for sale to those miners who had struck it lucky. The men walked at a steady amble until two hours before sunset when they made camp. The terrain was baked brown by the tropical sun. To them it was a country of alien vegetation, sparse grass and hostile natives.

On the fifth day they struck camp by a flat riverbank. The river was dry but for a pond of stagnant water embedded in the center. The chicken and ducks, legs tied to strings, were released to fend for their own fodder. The men spread leaves and grass to make beds for the night, then cooked a ration of rice over campfires. Hungry, tired and a little frightened by their isolation, they stuffed large gobbets of rice down their throats.

Next morning the Tongs ordered them to move out early so the grass along the riverbanks could be burned. In this way, the Tongs destroyed the fodder for the ox teams of the white carriers coming behind them. The fire would slow them down. Smoke soon billowed from the tinder dry plain. About an hour later the Tongs caught up with the main body of the caravan.

The days came and went, most of them taken up by swatting flies, buzzing, crawling and swarming all over the men. The tiny insects entered every exposed orifice, crept, crawled and winged their way up the men's nostrils, into their ears, into their eyes, crazed by the search for mucus to feed on. A favorite target was the corner of the mouth where white saliva always gathered from the heat and the exertion. An older coolie who had made the trip three times advised the men one night to ignore the flies. "The blacks leave them alone," he offered. "They let them sit all over their face and eyes."

The mere mention of blacks sent shivers of apprehension along the backs of the coolies. Cooktown buzzed with tales of spearing and sordid accounts of the cannibals' fondness for Chinese flesh. For most Chinese, superstitious by nature, the black Merkins were the embodiment of all their nightmares. Chinese folk tales are spiced with black monsters and evil black spirits waiting in the dark to pounce. Every man had his own remedy to keep the evil away. Some burned sticks of incense at night, others carried a frog leg and there were those who swore a snake's eye or the leaf of an oleander were the best antidotes.

Twice they came across white miners, their mules loaded with the chamois saddlebags rumored to contain gold. Tom remembered meeting three miners, each holding his breech-load rifle at the ready. One of the miners yelled to the tong boss. "Hey Chinky! Give us a couple of your boys to carry for us? We'll pay you with gold."

The tong boss had no qualms. He pointed at three emaciated coolies and ordered them to drop their loads and go with the white men. One of the coolies loudly protested. The tong boss whacked him across the face with his whip.

One of the miners handed over a small black pouch. The tong boss undid the strings and poured the gold dust in his palm. He seemed satisfied.

"Now tell your fellows to walk about a 100 yards behind us and keep that distance all the way to Cooktown," one of the miners instructed.

It was months before Tom realized the white miners made a habit of hiring a couple of coolies to trail them. If the Merkins attacked, they always went for the unarmed Chinese, an easier, and it was said, tastier target.

About two weeks into the trek an eerie silence had descended on the human pack train. The chatter and banter down the line died gradually until no one had the courage to speak anymore. The Tongs had become tense and vigilant. One or the other would climb a rise from time to time and peer towards the forbidding ridge on the horizon. The Tongs kept checking their guns. Imperceptibly the pack train closed ranks so much in fact that some of the porters stepped on the sandals of those in front of them. This caused some heavy cussing.

By then Tom knew the caravan was approaching the dreaded Devil's Kitchen on Hell Gate's Road, a notorious stretch of ridge and favorite ambush site of the Merkins. All over the Palmer River, Hell's Gate Road had become associated with horror stories told around camp fires and bars. Everyone knew the area was a perfect trap.

As miners wound their way over the ridge, often losing sight of each other, the Merkins pounced on the tail-enders, cut them down with spears or beat them over the head with wooden clubs. The story was, though anthropologists often are in dispute, the natives were not after gold but flesh. Those unfortunates to survive the attacks were reputedly dragged into Devil's Kitchen, a cave deep in the hills. Outside the cave, so it was said, captives were hung by their pigtails from trees after having their legs broken first so they could not run away if they managed to free themselves. Each time the Merkins needed a meal, they would cut down a few Chinese, club them to death and roast them.

Over the years, white diggers had tried to find this hell hole of a cave, not to rescue the hapless Chinese, but to find the gold the captives must have left in the cave. Gold was of no interest to the natives.

Palmerstone police warden Sellheim referred to the dreaded cave in his reports with the comment: "The object was evidently the use of the bodies for food."

No one ever found Hell's Kitchen or Chinese hanging as fodder anywhere. In the end the story became as much folklore as the exploits of Christie Palmerstone, the enigmatic maverick explorer who prowled the river named after him and harbored a particular distaste for the Chinese. According to folklore Palmerstone, a wiry little man with a withered arm, was some kind of hero among the natives. He was never short of gold although no one ever saw him dig for the precious metal. He had an army of Aborigines devoted to him and was said to have robbed and killed dozens of Chinese during raids on their camps, pack trains and digs, a feat that made him a kind of Zorro among white diggers.

As soon as the pack train approached Hell's Gate, the Tongs fired their weapons to scare off any natives who might be waiting in ambush.

Once the cargo had been delivered the new arrivals were allotted to work the claims staked out by the Chinese merchants. Tom, like other freshmen, was detailed to carve the tunnels that would soon scourge the entire river area. This was the most arduous and perilous task. The tunnels were rarely reinforced with wooden stanchions or planks and frequently collapsed on the diggers. If one were lucky, the other Chinese would pull you out. Generally no one bothered to waste time digging for survivors.

The Tongs had only one aim in mind: Find as much gold as possible to increase their own percentage of the profits.

Besides, there were no doctors and an injured man had to be fed and attended. This meant more waste of manpower and less gold.

Reports by police wardens frequently spoke of weak or injured Chinese simply abandoned by the roadside, left to die by pragmatic compatriots who considered it futile to drag a man all the way back to Cooktown. Even if the injured man recovered, he might no longer be able to work in the mines or be any use as porter.

The custom of leaving behind their sick and wounded was seen by the white miners as more evidence of the callous nature of the Chums. One simply did not leave an injured mate behind, according to the unwritten code of conduct prevalent among Europeans Down Under. Even the Aborigines looked after their injured. These rough pioneers, always ready with fists, knives and an atrocious choice of vocabulary, were endowed with a sense of mateship that has remained to this day. In a hostile environment, mates depend on each other and have to be backed up, no matter whether they are right or wrong, sick or wounded.

Tom arrived on the gold fields when finds were dwindling rapidly. Yet the Chinese kept coming in droves. In one long trek, 2,300 of them, released from quarantine on Fitzroy Island, marched from Cooktown across the bush to descend on the gold fields. The mob jumped claims temporarily or permanently abandoned. Emboldened by their numbers, they forced small groups of both white and Chinese miners to leave for new fields. Hardly a day went by without bitter complaints to the authorities.

Neither gold nor supplies could keep pace with the invasion. The Chinese outnumbered the white diggers on most fields 10 to one. On fields they had jumped and staked out for their exclusivity, the numbers sometimes were 100 to none. As the gold diminished, resentment among Europeans rose proportionally.

But the worst was yet to come.

The first sign of trouble was a report from wardens and sent back to Cairns and Brisbane. The inspectors complained that the Chinese had refused to pay the obligatory 10-shilling mining fee. The wardens pointed out that the handful of troopers under their command had no chance to impose the fee or round up the escalating number of defaulters. Sometimes troopers hauled a few Chinese back to the police camp by their pigtails and one ingenious warden devised a long chain to which he handcuffed two dozen Chinese at a time.

The trend to default on the mining fees went not unnoticed. Despite the thousands of new arrivals, colonial authorities became aware revenue from these fees had dropped dramatically. In one case, a warden reported he managed to collect the obligatory fee from only 75 out of the 1,500 Chinese miners in his area. The rest refused, ran away or hid during police raids. At times, the Chinese were so destitute the wardens, who had little compassion for the Celestials, considered it useless to arrest them or confiscate their empty swags. Sellheim complained the authorities could not feed those arrested.

Collecting fees was a minor problem.

The chronic lack of supplies, offered only in return for cash or payment in gold, had turned many Chinese into bandits and marauders. A Cooktown newspaper reported: "Barely a white digger exists who has not been robbed of something by the Chinese. Any parliamentary action that would exclude the Chinese from the colony will be hailed with delight."

The white miners struck back.

One group lynched a Chinese shopkeeper called Ah Joy after they found stolen gold dust in his store, ingeniously hidden away inside two huge German sausages. No one was convicted for the lynching. It was considered a rough but fair type of justice.

The well-armed whites were not an easy prey. Soon the Chinese turned on their own kind as often happens in China during times of famine, floods and drought when gangs of ruffians go on vicious rampages to forage for food and valuables. In China bandit gangs have ransacked and burned villages, murdered the men, raped the women and sold the youngest into slavery. Even the communists failed to eliminate this system of self-help and survival of the fittest and the cruelest.

The trouble on the gold fields started when a gang of Macau Chinese thrashed ten Cantonese during a raid on their camp, then walked off with their supplies, gold and swags. Within days Macau Chinese miners were found with native spears sticking from the chests. But it was not the Merkins who had skewered them.

The peak of the internecine feuds came at the battle of Lukinville.

The shoot-out lasted three days and three nights before the authorities could muster enough troopers to stop the blood bath between Cantonese and Pekingese diggers. The Peking miners had been stealing gold at night from the digs of the Cantonese so the latter prepared an ambush in which 48 of the 50 thieves were clubbed and knifed to death with a savagery that amazed even hard boiled Irish cops. The Cantonese then attacked Lukinville, the camp of the hoards from Peking.

The battle was fought with old muskets. When the ammunition ran out, the Chums went at it with knives, hatchets, clubs, picks and shovels, sticks and fists. Astonished miners who watched the fight came back with tales of no quarter given but also a new admiration for the fighting spirit of the Chinese, a people they had always considered on the timid and cowardly side of a good fight. After all hadn't the Chinks always run off when the Merkins attacked? No one had ever seen one fight the black devils.

Of course, no Chinese ever explained to the miners that one does not fight black monsters, spirits who are part of the supernatural and therefore unbeatable. One's only salvation is escape and the hope the evil black demon will choose someone else as take-away.

In the end a mere 20 troopers brought Lukinville back under control. They disarmed 3,000 Chinese—but not before hundreds had been killed. Many more survived only because the aim of the Chinese marksmen was so atrocious and the ancient muskets were a greater danger to those who fired them than to their targets.

A few weeks later, another 1,000 Chinese fired on a camp of Macau miners while they were at breakfast. No one counted the dead and the dying.

The reports of escalating violence and the size of the Chinese invasion did find its mark back in Brisbane. The colonial authorities passed the Chinese Immigration Regulation Act of 1877. It imposed a poll tax of 10 pounds on Chinese entering the colony. Miners' rights were pumped up from 10 shillings to three pounds and business licenses for Chinese from four to ten pounds.

The Act coincided with the discovery of a new gold field on the Coen River. In fact, it had been a Chinese person who found the first nugget and the first vein. The word spread quickly and 6,000 Chinese packed up at the crowded Palmer and headed for the new El Dorado. Other Chinese and white diggers had already embarked for New Guinea after reports that gold had been struck there in large quantities.

The Coen strike petered out quickly, but probably saved the Palmer from civil war among the Chinese. The Coen was also one of the last strikes. From then on began the long and painful decline of the gold rush and the tragic odyssey of the Chinese to repatriate or find a foothold in the inhospitable nation. They felt they were in a country where natives considered Celestials as food while white colonizers despised them as inferior beings and feared them for their numbers.

As the Chinese began to leave in large numbers, the atmosphere changed.

After years of diatribes against marauding and thieving Chinese, the shopkeepers on the gold fields and in the urban areas sent a petition to the minister of mines in Brisbane, requesting him to remove all anti-Chinese legislation because it was driving the Chinese away from the colony.

The shopkeepers had discovered, to their dismay, and a little late, that the Chinese had become their best customers. Without them they could close shop on the gold fields. Trade with the Chinese had become so important that the Maytown Branch of the Queensland National Bank, right in the heart of the gold fields, accepted a consignment of opium as security for a loan to a Chinese merchant.

Eighty years later Indonesia's socialist founder Sukarno and his tottering regime would face a similar dilemma after a bloody purge of Chinese left the country in economic ruin and without the commercial infrastructure the Chinese had created and controlled.

Cooktown witnessed an unusual spectacle that same year: Shopkeepers from all over the Palmer held a joint rally with the Chinese to protest against anti-Chinese legislation and to request that these measures be rescinded at once. Speakers praised the diligence and contribution of the Chinese to the colony while at the back of the rally the old diggers, well into their cups, cat-called and booed this sudden praise of people who would always remain for them "the locusts of the gold fields."

For the ordinary Australian, the Chinese continued to be a pest best banned. But neither the Coen rush nor the shopkeepers' plea could save the gold fields or the Chinese exodus. Thousands of the unwanted

Celestials trekked back to the coast where those who could still afford it bought fares to China while the rest drifted south into market gardening, sugar plantations, small groceries and the fledgling Chinatowns in cities like Sydney and Melbourne.

One of those who eventually went south was Tom See Poy.

But before that he had already branched out into commerce. Tom's children never found out if the old man had managed to salt away some of the gold he had been forced to mine. Tom never talked about how he obtained the cash to open a sidewalk eatery in Cooktown. All he would say was: "I worked hard and saved my money. I didn't gamble and I never went to the cat houses or the opium dens."

His initial enterprise was a modest venture: He had an open wood brazier on which he boiled Chow Mein and rice. It was quick and cheap and many a miner had just enough coins to buy his dish and stop hunger from gnawing at his insides for a few hours. Tom spoke hardly any English and just kept smiling when the miners insulted him or his stew.

"Hey, you money-grabbing yellow bastard, put some more rice on this grub or I'll tear your bloody cue out!"

The miners soon realized there were no extras, despite their curses and the threats. From habit and to hide their own frustrations, they vented their anger loudly and rudely and without fear of retaliation. For them all Chows were stupid, good enough to cook, that was all. Yeah, they said to each other, that's what all Chows ought to be doing. Instead of trying to take a white man's living away from him, they ought to cook.

In time the cooking Chinaman became an Australian icon. Every farm and station worth its mettle tried to recruit a Celestial chef for its kitchen. The tales of irate "Chinky chefs," always armed with kitchen hatchets, chasing after disrespectful jackeroos is part of Australian folklore in the Outback. And no jackeroo was worth his salt if he couldn't tell a story of how he teased the cook and barely avoided being cleaved asunder by that pig-tailed king of the kitchen.

A few months later, Tom added chunks of kangaroo and possum meat to his fare. By then the miners were bartering their mining tools for food. Tom was smart enough to realize there would always be new Chums to try their luck out in the bush. Once or twice he convinced some of his destitute compatriots to act as his porters on a tong train. As payment, he gave them old mining tools. He split the revenue from the haul with the Tongs.

On other occasions, he helped out at the Chinese grocery stores and quickly learned that small profits over long periods can accumulate large fortunes. He also learned how to "stretch" rice, cooking oil and booze. He was more than ever convinced that the only way to make money from the Mountain of Gold was by catering for the stomachs of people and selling them the tools to work the land.

After a year, he sold his sidewalk brazier and moved into a shanty hut among the sand flies in Chinatown. The hut became his first grocery store. He slept behind the sacks of rice on a mat, with a hole in the wall serving as a toilet. An old Cantonese brought him a bucket of water every day. Tom was too scared to leave the shop, even for a few moments. He was convinced his stock would disappear as soon as his back was turned.

For almost a year he lived in his own prison as the town died around him and crime and desperation took over. His only joy was a young Chinese boy who had learned to read and write. He coaxed him with sweets and sweet words to come now and then and teach him the Latin alphabet.

The boy was smart and Tom thought of a future in which he would need help. His chance came when the boy's father decided to return to China rather than starve to death with the rest of Cooktown. But the man did not have enough cash to buy the steamer ticket. So Tom made up the difference and as security, was left the boy, a common practice in rural China even today. The boy could be redeemed once repayment was made.

Despite his frugal life style, Tom's revenues were dwindling. The gold rush was over, the number of miners still willing to try their luck unable to sustain the traders in Chinatown. On the day the European shopkeepers along the Palmer called for a pro-Chinese rally, Tom realized it was time to move on. He sold his shop and stock within 48 hours to a Cantonese who was prepared to gamble on another strike along the Palmer, a discovery that would give the rush a shot in the arm.

Tom received three gold nuggets and 20 pounds in cash. His stock was worth far more but he also knew it could be worth far less the following week. What annoyed Tom most was the owner insisted the price included the boy. He wouldn't budge.

In the end Tom bought a steamer ticket to Cairns where rumor had it good land was to be had at cheap prices.

Cairns had grown with the Palmer Gold rush in the mid 1870s. Located on an estuary, it provided the main access to the Hodgkinson Gold Field. By 1877, there were 10,000 Chinese in Cairns. A year later most of them were eating grass to stay alive.

The same year eight Chinese tried to land in Cairns from the steamer, Lord Ashley, and were met by an angry mob who tossed them one by one into the sea when the Celestials insisted on their right to immigrate. The eight wet Chinamen clambered back on board to a cacophony of jeers and the Lord Ashley sailed away.

The next group of Chinese immigrants disembarked under police protection. A media report described them as "a group of laborers and one fat business personage."

Tom See Poy disembarked under the media item: "A Group of laborers arrived last night".

He had sneaked into Cairns at night, like a thief to avoid the locals. He had no stomach for a repetition of the Cooktown battle a few years earlier. Besides, he now had money and some gold to protect. He was looking for a new opportunity. Only this time, his expectations were pegged far lower and he was his own boss.

Cairns then had a population of 1,376 Chinese, about 17 per cent of the local residents. Most Chinese had taken up plots of land to cultivate fruit and vegetables and Tom made a few discreet inquiries among them. He was interested in the possibility of opening a grocery shop but was soon discouraged by the reports he received. All Chinese ventures of that nature had run into militant opposition from white businessmen.

On the first night, a toothless fellow Cantonese at the Ling Ling eatery told him the story of Young Wong and his store.

"Wong had already spent two pounds worth of fireworks to drive out the bad spirits from his store," the old man said. "He should have bought four pounds. He had already stocked goods worth 20 pounds when they came, at night, and baled straw against his back wall. The Long Noses poured oil on the straw and lit it. Wong lost everything. He barely escaped with his life. Next morning he hung himself from the drain pipe outside Old Hong's eatery."

On the second day Tom heard a group of Chinese had leased the rights to a 50-acre strip of land along the coast south of Cairns. The land was located on flat country crisscrossed by several rivers. It was prone to floods but the soil was rich river-silt.

The idea of land excited Tom. Every Chinese dreams of owning land into which he can sink his own roots and that of the future dynasty he intends to found. By nightfall he had made contact with one of the group, a fellow named Andy Ping who spoke English well. Ping had organized the land lease deal.

"We'll grow sugar," Ping told him without much ado. "We're a group of about 100. Everyone puts in ten pounds as a stake. "You interested?"

Sugar? Tom could not remember anyone growing sugar. All the sugar on sale at Cooktown had come from the Far East by steamer and usually bore the brand of the East India Company.

"It'll be the first sugar plantation on the coast." Ping was matter of fact.

Tom was in two minds. Any new venture was risky but sugar was a commodity in great demand. Sugar would sell. It could be exported all along the coast at a price lower than the imported variety. The idea was sound. But he needed to know more about its execution.

"We're going to call it the Hop Wah plantation and we all take out equal shares and divide the work. It'll be tough in the beginning because we have to clear the land. But once it's cleared, sugar will grow by itself. We can then clear more land and expand. There's plenty of flatlands, perfect soil for sugarcane, better than in the Far East where I grew up."

Ping sounded like someone who knew what he was doing. He had cut his cue and wore his garb the white man's way. He was a natty dresser and the locals often referred to him as "a regular white man."

Next morning Tom rode an oxcart to the land the Hop Wah plantation had leased. The cart rocked over a rough track, occasionally swamped by rivulets of water. The grass was taller than a man's neck, the weeds thick as a baby's foot. It was wet everywhere. On both sides of the track he saw neat vegetable gardens. From the whiff of human excrement, manure the Chinese call "night-soil," he deduced the owners had to be sons of the Yellow Emperor.

Wedged between the vegetable patches, he spied orchards, oranges, lemons, mangos and bananas, the young trees already offering the first fruits. The bush was thick here and he thought what an arduous task it must have been to clear the wilderness and burn the land before it was ready to bear fruit.

In the fields he saw the bent backs, padded backsides and cone hats of his countrymen. He was even more surprised to see an odd woman here and there, white and black. On a patch of cabbage he saw a Chinese woman wielding a hoe. She wasn't young. But she wasn't old either.

"Women? Are we allowed to marry in Cairns?"

Ping took off his slouch hat and dusted his chamois boots with its rim. He shook his head.

"No son of the emperor is allowed to marry in this country. But mind you no law says we can't live with them. And I tell you, See Poy, some of these white ladies prefer the men of the Middle Kingdom to their own kind. We're always sober, we work hard and we treat them well. We don't beat them up every night. Women in this country are hard to come by so we treat them with care. And you should know," he added, nudging Tom: "We've got two gins on the plantation. If you pay five shillings every month you can have your turn with them, anytime when they're not busy."

The prospect of climbing on everyone's woman did not excite Tom as much as the prospect of a highly marketable crop.

Later on he took one look at the members of the cooperative and realized nearly all of them were lowly coolies good enough to do the rough work of clearing and planting but easily dominated when it came to marketing strategies, management and profit making. He realized that the land, once cleared, was capable of a handsome yield. And there was a good chance to expand as long as someone was willing to clear the bush. Right to the edge of the horizon the coastal plain was flat wetland, soaked during the rainy season but parched and hot in summer. The 50 acres could be turned into 500 and maybe 5,000. All it needed was labor, a few additional ox teams and some brains behind the venture.

Ping himself showed no interest in the daily chores on the farm. He was more interested in hobnobbing with the white folk. Tom saw a golden opportunity to take the farm under his wing as soon as he had gained the trust of his fellow workers. Right now they viewed him with the suspicion reserved for newcomers who had not yet put in his stint of hard labor on the land.

Tom tossed his swag into one of the shanty huts made of leaves and branches and told a surly fellow who stared at him with undisguised suspicion: "I am ready to work."

A week later he was one of them.

Later that week Tom had cursed his rashness in joining the cooperative. He had never imagined clearing land could be such an arduous task, the wilderness could be so resilient and the flies and mosquitoes so numerous. The task of turning the lowlands into a plantation was backbreaking. The men were at work the moment the first ray of light sprouted beyond the dark velvety inland mountain range. They worked with axes, spades, hoes and chains dragged across the ground. Ox teams were too expensive, a dream for the future. The humidity was stifling. No breeze ever penetrated the marshy shrub world. Torsos trickled all day. Beads of perspiration dissolved into meandering brooks. Their faces were always crimson, flushed by the heat and the exertion. Their hands had become callused, some bled and the black woman called Sheila ministered to them with a potion of dark mud and ground leaves. This brought relief for a few hours but by the end of the next day the calluses burst again. Finally the men bandaged their hands with rags.

A snake bit a Hong Kong man named Ah Lim who yelped and yelped as if he was being slowly skewered over a barbecue. Finally one of the men cut deep into the bite with a bush knife and sucked out the poison. Soon after that Ah Lim stopped his yelling and fell into a state of stupor. Now and then he moaned. The men went on with their chores and when they came back in the evening to the spot where they had left Ah Lim, he was dead.

Two of the men dug a shallow hole and tossed the corpse into it. When one of the arms stuck out a gravedigger banged the arm back into the grave with a shovel. Then everyone walked home to the huts.

Steeled by his years on the gold fields, Tom found the clearing work tough but not beyond his capability. On the other hand, he had no intention of spending years in the mangroves preparing for a crop he would rather sell than grow. His mind was made up half way through the second week when a crocodile bit off a man's foot. The reptile came out of the weeds so fast the poor fellow did not notice until he felt the tug on his ankle. The men made a torque to stop him bleeding to death. One way or the other his foot was gone and he would be of no further use on the plantation.

That night, after some argument, the men agreed to give the footless fellow back his money and to send him on his way the next time Andy Ping came to check on their progress.

Ping came two days later. He not only took the wounded man back to town but also took Tom who had convinced him that as a merchant, a former shopkeeper and an expert in salesmanship, he was of far greater use to the Hop Wah cooperative in Cairns than as a slash-and-burn coolie.

Before Ping accepted, the two men had a long philosophical discussion about supply and demand, utility and futility, unused cash and the skill of making money with money. Neither of the two spelled it out or detailed it on paper but by the end of the conversation they agreed: The 50 pounds left over from the initial investments of cooperative members was best utilized by opening a store. The proceeds from the store could meet all the expenses of the workers for the next months. The requirements for cash were minimal: Food and tools for the coolies.

The cooperative members had agreed to forgo wages until the first crop was sold. Then the proceeds would be shared—equally—with two extra shares going to Ping for the expense incurred in procuring the lease.

Tom intended to keep the store deal scrupulously honest. He saw no breach of trust by investing the funds. The money could do more good as investment in a grocery. Right now it was only collecting dust in a bank at two per cent interest.

Ping welcomed the idea. His main aim in life was to reap large profits from as little manual work as possible. On the way to Cairns, he boasted about the beige riding breeches and chamois boots he intended to buy for the fox hunt, an annual social highlight among the Cairns upper class to which Mr Anderson had invited him. The invitation had come in a pink envelope and printed on a white card. Ping saw it as the peak of his social aspirations. The invitation was, so he kept saying, his membership to the white society that systematically spurned the yellow man. Riding with the pack of squatters and their women was the ultimate recognition that he was now one of them.

Poor Ping. The "high society" of Cairns saw this pretentious little Chow as no more than a useful tool in dealing with the rest of the Chums. All the better if he was on their side. With a little pampering he could work for their interests. Besides, who had ever heard of a Chow on horseback riding to the hounds. Everyone would have a good laugh.

"It's a great honor," Ping kept repeating over and over.

"I'm sure it is," replied Tom.

His thoughts had been elsewhere. He was adding and subtracting from the 50 pounds. Mentally he had already figured out what stock he could purchase and what turnover the store would have in the first month, what could be expected in the second and subsequent months. Whichever way he looked at it, the affair was sound. What the hell was this puffed-up Fujianese yapping about? What was this foxhunt? Was it something that could be marketed?

Like most Chinese, Tom See Poy knew only one sport and one hobby in life. Anything else was a waste of time.

■

The store was called Hop Wah Enterprises and weathered the storm of protest by local shopkeepers thanks to Ping. He told his white friends it was a temporary venture to tide the cooperative over until the first sugar crop came in. He also promised Mr Anderson a friendly discount on the cane from the plantation. The squatter was going to crush their cane, if it ever grew, in the multi-purpose mill he had built.

Tom had nothing to do with these arrangements. He stayed away from the squatters, embarrassed by his lack of English and suspicious of the coarse remarks he knew came at his expense. As soon as the store made a little money he started to take English lessons from a Cairns schoolteacher at two shillings an hour. He kept scrupulous track of this personal expense, to be subtracted from his share of the crop. He knew other Chinese were taking free lessons from the Methodist Mission but their progress was slow, hampered by brains unaccustomed to education. A fellow storekeeper named Yu Kee was bribing schoolboys with candy to help him understand the basics of the language.

But Tom was in a hurry. He felt like a fish out of water without the vocabulary to understand what was going on around him. By the time he left Cairns, a wiser man, he had accumulated 106 lessons of English. He wrote and spoke the language with the same meticulous precision that became the hallmark of his bookkeeping.

While the older generation of Chinese found it difficult to absorb the new language, most of them made sure their children had the kind of education ordinary Chinese were not permitted in Imperial China. As soon as the parents had a decent income the children were dispatched to colonial schools. The Chinese became dedicated students, as are the children of most immigrants who are discriminated by fellow students and know they are supported by parents who made big sacrifices to pay for their education.

Within a few years, Chinese students did so well in Cairns and other parts of Australia they kindled the envy of the settlers whose own children were far less motivated. As usual the best way to curb the Chows' aspirations was to legislate against them. In 1904 every headmaster in the colony was empowered to exclude "full blooded Asiatics over the age of fifteen" from higher education.

Tom often wondered how his compatriots managed to have children when marriage was prohibited and Chinese females barred from entry to the colony. Only 18 of the 1,575 Chinese in Cairns were legally married. In the end he figured many Chinese had illegally imported wives disguised as men. Whatever method they used, there seemed to be no shortage of Chinese children. More amazing still, no one seemed to particularly mind. In fact an affluent Chinese person named Kwong Sue-Duc had come down from Darwin with four wives and 26 children and was highly respected for his procreative prowess by the Australians.

Chinese fortunes were running high. At Innisfail, some 50 miles south of Cairns, Tam Sie had started the first banana plantation and soon became known as the "Banana King." He was highly respected and would seal deals with a handshake. His scrupulous business transactions led to coining the phrase: "A Chinaman's word is his bond." The saying is still popular in Innisfail today.

Many colonials saw in the Chinese immigrant the driving force to turn Australia into a wealthy nation. Publicly the Chinese were praised for their thrift, industry and perseverance and often held up as models white workers should emulate. Such praise was not well received by the old style Australian wowsers. A man called Bamford, a Labor minister and MP for Cairns complained bitterly to parliament:

"In one of our northern towns the Chinese give an occasional banquet attended by a great number of the leading citizens. The visitors propose the health of the Chinese and the Chinese return the compliment. And it has now become an axiom in that place that the leading citizens eat with the Chows and sleep with the Japs."

The Chinese made money. Chinese entrepreneurs opened gambling dens and the first Chinese Opera company came to Cairns, assured of sufficient patronage to meet the cost of the long sea journey from Guangdong.

The Hop Wah Enterprise store did well even before the first sugar crop came in with a good yield. Tom had made sure the goods he stored were in demand—rough and ready to wear clothing, boots, tools, seeds and nuts and bolts. He was careful to select a supply that could survive even a depression. He took no chances and rejected Ping's urgings to branch out into ladies' and gentlemen's garments.

"Who would buy knickers from a Chinaman?" Tom had protested.

"You're an old fashioned coot," Ping replied. "Us Chinamen are now part of the colony. We're a solid part with capital and land. The days of the Yellow Menace are over."

He looked splendid in a new suit imported from London and bought on credit from Mr Anderson's "Store for Gentleman". He was now a regular at social events and had negotiated, for a salty fee, most of the land deals under which rich squatters leased rural tracts to the Chinese. Only a month ago he had bought a racehorse. It had run fourth in the Cairns Derby. The nag's name was Elisa in honor of Mr Anderson's daughter. Ping had ambitions.

The demand for sugar escalated with the wealth of the colony. Tom beseeched Ping to negotiate for more land to expand the plantation. A fortune could be made. Labor was no problem. More could be imported one way or the other. With more land and more sugar Hop Wah could build its own mill instead of losing some 35 per cent of the value of their crop to Mr Anderson's haphazard crusher.

Ping rejected the mill initiative for personal reasons. But he saw the advantage of more land and promised to do his best. Thousands of acres of squatters' land lay vacant and with the limited labor available, would remain so for decades to come. The squatters simply did not have the men or the machinery to clear the wilderness.

Everything seemed to be going well until that night.

Tom realized something was wrong when he found Ping rifling

through the accounts. The dapper little Chinaman was disheveled, his beige breeches mud-stained, his collar loose. One glove was missing.

"Get your hands out of my accounts?" Tom snapped.

"How much do we have in the bank?" Ping asked.

"Enough," Tom replied guardedly.

"Listen," Ping whispered, grabbing Tom by the elbow and dragging him across the store. "Things are going bad. There is a law before parliament to ban all Chinese from owning or leasing land. Any land already leased can revert to the owner the minute he wants. We're in trouble."

Tom sat down. Once more the Mountain of Gold had crashed down on him.

"What can we do?" he asked. "What do your friends tell you?"

"Pah!" Ping kicked at an imaginary obstacle. "Anderson told me today to pay back all my debts and Terry Smith sent the stable boy this afternoon to let me know he was taking the horse in lieu of my arrears in training fees. What can we do? Take the money and make a run for it. That's what we can do. We'll head south to Sydney or Melbourne and go under in one of the Chinatowns there. That's what we'll do."

Tom felt a sudden urge to spit into the little fop's face. But, as always, he kept perfect control of his emotions.

"There are 400 pounds in the bank. The money will be split between every member of the cooperative. We can sell the store and the stock and make another 300. It's not much but it's more than what we started with."

Ping stared as if Tom had gone mad.

"Pay the coolies? The silly fools wouldn't know what to do with the money. Even if we give them something back we'll keep the rest. We need a fresh stake. The whites have screwed us again. We cleared the land for them. Now they're taking it back all cleared and laughing at us. I hate this place. I hate these bastards."

A few days later the law was passed. The Chinese were dispossessed and the cleared tracts of land laid the foundation for many a fortune among the white settlers. Some of the Chinese, particularly those who had worked for years on cultivating vegetables and growing orchards, could not cope with the injustice. A fellow called Ah-Lin had a mental breakdown and wrote out dozens of checks. Eighteen local Chinese committed suicide. One hung himself over the door of his landlord. Another was found dead, hanging by his belt from a lamppost after he was dispossessed of land and then accused of being infected with leprosy.

Ping did manage to escape with the lion's share of the proceeds from the sale of the store. He had surreptitiously signed it over to Anderson, mainly to cover his debts. Tom divided the money in the bank evenly between cooperative members. Then, like most of them, he started on the trek south, still in search of the elusive Mountain of Gold.

Once Australia had banned Asiatics from owning land, the Chinese still willing to take a chance could lease it from Europeans who would often repossess it once the Chinese had cleared and cultivated enough of it. Many Chinese sought citizenship, mostly in vain, so that they could buy precious land without fear of having it taken away from them. But citizenship was hard to come by. At the turn of the century, anti-Chinese sentiments ran high once again.

A racist media propagated the idiotic notion that "a Chinkie doesn't feel anything" and the myth that all Chinese smoked opium and carried leprosy. The Chinese were considered worthless, just one grade above the natives and one grade below dogs. The anti-Chinese lobby portrayed the immigrants as a Fifth Column of the Emperor in Peking, a spearhead force paving the way for a Chinese takeover. The idea was promoted in ditties such as this one:

> He is of the people,
> But China rules him all the time.

Since John Chinaman was the common enemy he had to be pegged down and stripped of all civilized attributes. The popular notion that John Chinaman was dirty, had no manners and did not wash was ludicrous in a nation of Anglo-Celtic immigrants notorious for being grubby, disheveled, devoid of good manners and loath to wash. Wrote one hypocritical columnist after a visit to a local hospital:

"Patients naturally object, especially when they have paid, to sitting among Chinese and Aborigines, eating bread they had handled and watching manners which are certainly not attractive."

This kind of attitude made it necessary to separate these lower beings from the civilized traveler. Australian trains had special carriages of inferior quality and destined for aliens of non-European origin. In 1910 a Chinese male was brutally assaulted by a mob of white passengers when he tried to enter a European carriage. Not many attempted such a folly.

Bigotry, hypocrisy and pomposity dominated official thinking and behavior. At a cocktail party in Sydney the Lord Mayor approached Kong Ta, the Imperial consul and in a booming voice announced: "I won't shake the hand of a Chinaman. But I want you to tell your countrymen to stop smoking opium."

Consul Kong Ta bowed politely and replied: "And I'd like you to tell your countrymen to stop importing opium for my countrymen."

Sydney, known as "The Little Mountain of Gold," had attracted the bulk of the Chinese leftovers from the gold rush. Many who could not afford the fare back to China filtered down to the big city in search of an enclave into which they could slip, anonymous but safe among compatriots who spoke a similar language, prepared similar cuisine and provided a common defense against the hostile Anglo-Celtic world outside. These conditions existed in Sydney's Chinatown around an area still known today as Dixon Street.

There, on the fringe of a bustling new metropolis, the Chinese created their state within a state. Tongs supervised districts, ran the trades and policed the area. Late in the 1880s Chinatown had its own Robin Hood, a fellow who robbed rich Chinese merchants and handed their wealth to the poor and those who had arrived penniless from the gold fields. After a 12-month "reign of terror" he was caught and hung. The colony could not afford folk heroes, white or yellow.

As far back as in the 1880s, the Haymarket area of Sydney officially had 63 Chinese shops and restaurants, 23 illegal gambling dens and a daily illegal lottery system known as Pakapoo tickets (Pidgeon tickets). Each morning the Chinese could buy a lotto ticket and a trained canary would pluck the winning number from a cage at night.

Gambling was outlawed and provided an excellent excuse to deport Chinese if the authorities or the citizenry considered their numbers had exceeded the acceptable number. White Australia kept telling itself the Chinese were "a yellow peril" because they bred like rabbits. It seemed a silly charge since Chinese women were all but banned from the country.

Chinatown has changed many times since King Fong came from Fiji in 1946 on an American naval boat. Today, half a century later, everyone knows him as the unofficial mayor of Sydney's Chinatown.

His father was a merchant with $20,000 to his name, a sum large enough to convince the Australian authorities he was a man of substance and therefore should be allowed to officially open an import-export business. In possession of a trading license a Chinaman could live in Australia as an accepted alien. He could also import a wife and have a family.

While Fong Senior went about his "export-import" business, his wife opened a fish shop in Campbell Street. Like many Chinese women, she was far more enterprising than her husband. Her venture soon made more money than the export business.

Fong recalls those early days with some nostalgia:

"In the morning Dad and I would go to the fish market and we watched, amazed, I tell you, how the fish mongers threw away the abalone because they thought it was useless. We Chinese consider abalone an expensive delicacy. But those fishermen didn't know what abalone was. So they tossed them into the gutter together with the guts of the fish.

"No one thought of cooking abalone because it's so tough you need a hammer to pelt it. We Chinese use baking soda to soften it up. We didn't let other people know about that, of course. We also use butcher's hooks to tap into the abalone. This allows the baking soda to be absorbed inside. Then we steam cook it. That softens it up a lot more.

"Of course, we kept all this to ourselves. But we did pick the abalone out of the gutter and prepared it for our own table.

"Some years later Chinese merchants in Sydney started to sell abalone in their shops, not the local stuff but the imported canned stuff from Mexico and California. I still remember the brand was called Calmex. They could import those cans via their Hong Kong agent. It was then that we started to make our own abalone and sell it. And we did make a nice piece of money out of it, mate."

Fong grew up in a post-war Sydney flooded by successive waves of European immigrants who left war-worn and struggling Europe with the hope of a new life Down Under. Demand for victuals doubled, then tripled.

The Fongs opened a grocery shop.

Another of the Fong ventures was a flophouse, a converted Coles Department Store warehouse. The residents were retired Chinese who could not return home because Peking would not have them. These men were without a family to look after them in Australia and lived in the loft of the warehouse.

At night the men pulled up a retractable ladder that served as their staircase in the daytime. The ladder was useful each time the police raided the place in search of illegal aliens and opium. By the time the cops managed to clamber upstairs the opium had vanished and so had the aliens who fled across the roof. The cops never found anything or anyone, though there was hardly a day when the boys did not light up their opium pipes.

In 1960 the flophouse burned down and the Fongs rebuilt it under the weary eye of the local health authorities, who made sure there was a staircase instead of a ladder. The new construction had separate cubicles for each of the old timers.

Every month visiting Chinese seamen would smuggle in porno magazines for the old boys, a substitute for wives. Some of the shops in Chinatown sold calendars under the table with photos of famous Hong Kong movie stars in alluring poses.

Finally, in the mid 1970s, Australia did allow wives and brides to join Chinese-Australian males. The delayed arrival of wives and the late marriages were not a success.

"One of the old boys got married at 83," Fong recalled. "His young wife took him to Hong Kong and he was dead within a week. She got all his money.

"Many of these old boys were the sons of gold miners and I remember at 70 years of age they were still smoking opium with bamboo pipes. We used to go down to Woolloomooloo (a wharf area in Sydney Harbour) and onto Chinese freighters to eat Chinese food. You couldn't import many of the traditional Chinese food items, like sausage or salted fish, so the only way to eat real Chinese food was on board the ships.

"We also went aboard to have a hair wash at the ship's barber. Men and women had a hair wash and then we had dinner. You had to fix it up with a crew member because only a limited number of third class passengers were allowed aboard. First and Second class was reserved for Europeans. These were combined cargo and passenger ships.

"You could get first class as a Chinese in the 1960s if you wore a bow tie and if you were very, very wealthy. We Chinese used to call the third class: 'Traveling in big storage.'

"We went aboard every two weeks. The ships came from Jakarta, Hong Kong and the Philippines. Sometimes a seaman would sneak in an ounce or two of opium and he would bring it to Campbell or Dixon Street to sell. It had to be brought off the ship. Even if the old men were desperate they wouldn't buy it aboard the ship.

"In 1953 the police officially stopped the smoking but you could always get a medical certificate as a certified addict. This allowed you to smoke an ounce a year. Of course all year round they were smoking the same old ounce. Sometimes the old timers would complain but the cops told them: 'That's all you're allowed. You're bloody addicts.'

"Sure the opium was a substitute for family life and sex. An old mate of mine whose father was a judge told me that in the 1920s three Chinese were caught at a King's Cross brothel. The judge told them, 'I didn't think you Chinese needed that.' One of the three accused spoke good English and he got up in court and said: 'You stopped our women from coming here so we've got to do it with your white women. If you want us to stop tell immigration to let our women come here.'

"The judge dismissed the case and asked immigration to do something about it. But immigration said their hands were tied by the White Australia policy.

"All these guys lived alone. They had to take whatever came their way, hookers or Aboriginal women. They got the seamen to bring in lots of pornographic magazines, which they used to enlighten themselves. In the grocery shop we used to sell calendars with Hong Kong movie stars, all pretty ones. They would hang them on the wall next to the photos of their families.

"These old boys were not a very sociable lot. For a start clans separated them and then they didn't speak English. They used to tell me that discrimination wasn't that bad because they couldn't understand 'Ching-Chong-Chinaman' and other insults people and kids were shouting at them. They said in the old days the whites used to be happy if you gave them a few vegetables from your market garden but they'd never let you get near their womenfolk.

"Everyone kept away from politics. Many of us have relatives in both Taiwan and the mainland and we didn't want to speak out against Peking or Taipei. I personally was trained in nationalist ideas by the Kuomintang. But then Australia recognized China. Now we are split 50/50 and most of us don't want to be connected to either side. What we want is to keep a low profile. Today I celebrate Peking's National Day on October 1. I also celebrate Taiwan's National Day and Australia's National Day.

"We didn't know that the Australian security personnel used to videotape us whenever we made a social call at the Peking consulate. We couldn't understand that whenever we went to get our papers to be naturalized the officials would say the papers had been delayed. After the Freedom of Information Act in the 1970s I found out that the papers had been delayed because security thought we were communists since we played Ping-Pong with these communist guys. I didn't know we were under surveillance. All the Chinese gambling clubs were under surveillance. They were watching who went in.

"The consulates on both sides made a lot of propaganda and we were often invited there for dinner. We always accepted. I mean we had free dinners with the communists and with the Taiwan nationalists. I for one always kept a foot in both camps.

"If you were a full blooded Chinese you had a hard time in Australia. You were better off as a half caste. The father of LJ Hooker was a Chinese, his mother was white. He became the country's largest real estate agent but he was born Tin Yaw. He liked football and he liked the hooker's position and he also liked the hookers of America. So he called himself Hooker. But he had to employ white men to sell his real estate. He couldn't do it himself: Nobody would trust him. A Chinese selling Australian land? It's not on, mate.

"Chinatown has changed a lot. The old residents of Chinatown now live in the posh Sydney suburbs of Rose Bay and Double Bay. They don't live upstairs in their shops anymore like we did in the 1960s and '70s.

"In my days I went from school to grocery store and I was lucky: My father let me go to school. Most of the other kids had to work in the family business as soon as they could walk. It was only after I'd left school that Dad allowed me Sunday mornings off.

"As a teenager I kept getting terrible headaches. So my father sent me to Hong Kong to be cured and learn about import-export. I was getting better in Hong Kong on a herb cure when I received a telegram that he had passed away while on holiday in Melbourne. It was his first holiday ever. And it killed him. He had a brain hemorrhage. He was 54 and I was 20.

"For the next 35 years I had to look after the business. We were wholesalers by then. We supplied ships and other stores. But we were still not Australians by the year 1959. I was registered as a student and when I left High School I had to register as a shop assistant.

"As a merchant however I had one concession: I could import a wife with a special license. Wasn't that funny: You could actually apply for a license to import a spouse?

"So I went back to Hong Kong for a wife. I was wearing an akubra hat and a long Gowings overcoat and people said: 'Hey there goes the young man from that new Gold Mountain, Sydney. He must be well off.'

"They had plenty of girls on file. I had a look at them. Some were very nice but I was more interested in business at the age of 20. I had no experience with girls since I had always been forced to be in the company of men. There was one girl I played tennis with who came from the same village at Chungshan (now Zhong Shan) where my father was born. My mother had told me to marry only a girl from the same village. It was the same village next to Macao where Dr Sun Yat Sen was born.

"While I was in Hong Kong my aunt showed me 42 photos of girls and said I could have any of them. I took one of them out a few times. She had applied three times to migrate to Australia but was knocked back because her father didn't have enough money. I thought she was all right. I spoke to immigration and they said: If you want her then you better apply for her because once you become an Australian citizen you're not supposed to be importing a spouse, you're supposed to marry a local. I said: Mate there ain't enough local Chinese girls. Bad luck, the fellow said, then you better marry a white girl.

"For one year I mourned my father's death. For 12 months I didn't go out to any social function. After 12 months I could bring her in. I also had to pay 20 per cent death duty on my father. That knocked me back a lot. I sponsored her and then married her. I had to report the marriage to immigration. My mates said you dumb drongo. You got an import quota, why didn't you bring another few sheilas in?

"It was so difficult in those days. My cousins had been sponsored as immigrants by our shop. But they had to wait 15 years before their wives could join them. And they waited. And they did bring them in. As for the old timers, the sons from the mining days: Out of 25 men left, three brought their wives over once it was authorized. Two years later all three came to our shop and complained they couldn't live with their wives after 45 years of separation. 'I don't know her anymore,' they would say. 'she's a different woman.' But I advised them to go back to their wives because immigration and social security made it necessary to stay married. If they had split up they would have lost their social security and the wife's right to remain in Australia.

"So they stayed together. Now and then I saw them. They didn't talk to each other at all. She was used to a village style life, he to his free ways. Once she started telling him to clean up, the arguments began. Isn't it funny? For nearly 50 years they couldn't be together and then when they could, they wanted to be separated again. In the end they just hated each other."

Not far from the railway line at Innisfail in northern Queensland, Herbert See Poy had a small whitewashed room in the Old People's Home. Visitors have to sit on the cot. Other residents walk by a few feet away along a fenced porch. The room is neat, crammed and lonely. This is the final refuge for the last surviving son of Tom See Poy, the man who built the multi-million dollar See Poy Emporium, a store that became synonymous with Chinese thrift and perseverance.

"And now it's all gone," Herbert said.

There was no regret in his voice. For Herbert, as for most Chinese, fortunes are made and lost. Tears are rarely shed for misfortunes.

He wore denim shorts and an immaculate white shirt, starched just like those his father wore all his life. At 80 years of age he looked back without regret on a time when he sat behind domes of dockets in a dusty office at the back of the huge department store. In those days he dreamed about sun-baking with the locals or fishing from one of those fancy new speedboats that had become popular among Australians.

All three of Tom's sons and his two daughters worked in the store, not for a wage but for the good of the family.

"We never had any fun," Herbert mused. "Father made us work from morning to night. We started on the store floor in charge of cleaning. Then we graduated to counter salesman in the various departments like groceries, textiles, hardware and finally machinery. Once you had done your stint in each of these places, you graduated to the office, sales and accounts. Finally you became a manager of one of the departments. We did it all.

"It was the third generation that broke this tradition. Like us they didn't want to be store-keepers but wanted to be jazz musicians, jackaroos, doctors, engineers and even beach bums. They wanted fast cars, speedboats and the good life of the others. They didn't want to sit behind a desk adding up figures but they wanted to sit on the beach with a beautiful Sheila.

"We understood how they felt. So we let them have their ways.

"In the end nobody was minding the store anymore."

Herbert sighs.

"We, the second generation, didn't have the courage to break away when we were young. But we had other ambitions. We wanted so much to be accepted as Australians. We would have given anything to be accepted. All three of us boys volunteered for the army in World War II. But the army turned us down."

Awkwardly he pulls a battered leather suitcase from under his cot, finds the key and opens it. For a while he rummages through a pile of papers and finally comes up with a rumpled telegram.

"Guess what their excuse was for turning me down from the army? Read it!"

"DEAR SIR: YOUR APPLICATION HAS BEEN REJECTED. REASON: INSUFFICIENT EUROPEAN ORIGIN."

"Now, how'd you like that? We were all born in Australia, weren't we? Do you have to be of European origin to fight in a war?"

Herbert returned to his chair where he sits ramrod straight, still clutching the telegram that shaped his life.

"My brother Gilbert managed to work in an ammunition factory. That wasn't so bad because he felt he was contributing something to the war effort.

"My brother Johnson had good connections so he managed to be made a guard in an internment camp. The place was full of Italian and German immigrants. These poor buggers got grabbed by the authorities and treated as potential traitors the minute the war broke out. One of the fellows Johnson guarded was Mario Banana. He was an Italian who was our store manager and a really good bloke. God, Johnson was so embarrassed."

After the sugar plantation reverted to its white owner, Tom See Poy had moved south to Innisfail, in those days a small agricultural hamlet on a river estuary just 79 kms south of Cairns. Tom opened a small store in the hamlet and watched with some rancor as Innisfail grew into a wealthy city at the center of Australia's richest sugar-growing region. In a fair playing field he would have been part of the sugar boom.

In its early days, as it still is today, Innisfail was mainly populated by hearty southern Italians often treated not much better than the Chinese. Their backbreaking efforts cleared the rugged land and prepared it for sugarcane. Many of the older generation still complain today of bad backs and crooked ligaments from the days when men with bush knives, axes and shovels cleared the land before tractors and bulldozers took over those chores.

Their efforts were not appreciated in those early days when ignorant men with virtually no education but heads filled with prejudice and bigotry ran Australia. In 1902 Hume Black, a Member of Parliament, told the House: "I have no particular hankering after Italians. If we could only induce some European farmers, men of our own color, to come here."

Side by side with the Italians the Innisfail Chinese grew bananas on leased land and prospered for a while. Many of them, like Tom, stayed on after the White Australia Policy in 1901. Others moved inland to Atherton which became a Chinese enclave. Its population was so staunchly Sun Yat Sen Republican they burned the Imperial Dragon flag in 1911 at a ceremony during which everyone cut their long cues. Even the Chinese in Innisfail had raised 200 guineas to help the revolutionary cause. There wasn't any love for the emperor.

Among the Italians Tom and his first store flourished. The Italians wanted to work and own the land and Tom wanted to supply their needs. The symbiosis worked well. He had no intention of giving in to the entreaties of his relatives back in China who sent him message after message urging him to come home, to bring his money and to start a business.

Tom wrote back: "I'm running with the wind and tide. Why leave everything here?"

The family must have realized the only way to maintain a link with the man in Mountain of Gold was through marriage. Tom needed a wife and before desperation could drive him into the arms of a white woman, the family selected a spouse for him. She was a slim muffin-faced village girl with large eyes and a serious expression. Neither Tom nor the family ever talked about how they managed to bring her to Australia, though most likely she came disguised as a boy.

She brought with her a trousseau of white linen, incense, kitchen gods and bundles of medicinal herbs. Her main dowry however was a healthy body. She bore Tom five children.

As the humble See Poy grocery store grew into a mega-store and Tom's marriage bore fruits, the family in China pestered him to cement the ties to the old country by sending at least one of his children to China for a traditional education. The choice fell on Herbert.

"I was the youngest," he said. "So Dad sent me to Canton for six years to learn Cantonese and Mandarin. I didn't learn very much and I've forgotten most of it. But I did see Sun Yat Sen who came to our school to make a speech about the Republic. He was very impressive and I immediately became a fervent Republican.

"Before I went back home, the family found me a Chinese wife. She was a restless little thing and perhaps they had given her the wrong impression about how we lived in Innisfail. She thought we were rich but we lived rather modestly. You could never tell Dad was a millionaire. She didn't like being ordered around by Mum and she didn't like our traditional ways.

"One day she ran away and I heard she'd gone to Sydney to become an exotic dancer in some of the nightspots there. I never saw her again.

"After that I took up with one of the white store girls, a sugarcane cutter's daughter. She got pregnant, so we got married. She turned out to be a good wife and I'm sorry she's dead now."

In 1933, Tom See Poy, owner and founder of the See Poy emporium, the largest department store in Australia's North, died of cancer. He was 74 years old and his emporium was famous throughout the country.

The many years of hard toil had taken their toll.

He had been ill for some time.

"In the end he allowed us to take him down to Sydney on the

steamship Canberra. There the best doctor we could find operated on him. It cost a heap of money and I'll never forget it. The doctor, he was a Sir something or other, came out of the surgery and said: 'Mrs See Poy the operation has been a complete success. Unfortunately the patient did not survive.' "

Unlike other elderly Chinese, Tom had never shown any inclination to return to his village to die and be buried with his ancestors. Although he could afford the best berth on a steamer, he stubbornly refused to visit Ny Chuen. He reasoned, with some justification, that obscure relatives he had never seen or heard of would expect him to finance their pet projects, leave generous gifts or help their sons emigrate. The municipality would pester him to build a school, the clergy to build a temple.

Tom had no time for beggars or relatives. His dream of returning in silken robes had dissolved with the mirage of the Gold Mountain. He firmly believed home was where a man's fortune was made. Besides, who would look after the store and make sure everything was ship shape? He might come back and find the kids had run the place into the ground. Then what?

From all accounts he had received, Ny Chuen was still as poor and as backward as on the day he had left it. And Tom had no ambition to die in China or be commemorated on a temple slab. His ideas were anomalous among the Chinese in the Diaspora.

In January 1991 I was flying from Sydney to Beijing on a CAAC jumbo jet, China's National carrier. The plane was crowded with elderly Chinese. Departure was delayed when a pool of fuel formed below the plane's belly. Firemen in fireproof suits hosed the kerosene away while we all hoped no one would fool around with matches.

A Chinese steward with a wiggly walk had offered me a seat in the business section after I found my coach seat occupied by an aged Chinese male with a parched face who, so I figured, was either fast asleep or in a coma. His wife, equally ancient, was crouched on the floor massaging her husband's bare feet.

The steward had watched my discomfiture and had rushed down the aisle. With his white-gloved finger, he lifted the old man's right eyelid gingerly and diagnosed: "Dead".

Then he steered me towards the business class section.

"It happens all the time," he whispered. "They leave their return too late."

"Shouldn't he be off-loaded?" I whispered back.

The steward shook his head vigorously. "No. Customs would be upset. His family would be upset. His spirit would be angry. He has to be buried in China."

We flew across Australia and into the South China Sea with the corpse slouched in my seat. Now and then his wife, a dulcet little lady with a gammy leg, came to the galley to scrounge for more ice, which she wrapped in a towel and pressed against the dead man's feet. She was keeping the corpse fresh.

Somewhere over Indonesia, lunch was served. The dead man's wife, I learned later, ate with gusto. Her husband's death had not diminished her appetite. But she did not touch the food tray a methodical hostess had placed before the dead man.

During the flight, the steward with the wiggle had explained in graphic details how flights from Australia had become flying coffins for elderly Chinese people anxious to expire in China. Unable or unwilling to leave their wealth behind, these homesick men and women often made the trip with death already by their side.

"Some are brought aboard in wheelchairs," the steward whispered, "perhaps already dead," he added with a knowing wink: "But we are told they are only asleep."

CAAC never turned back any of those moribund geriatrics.

Our flight had barely crossed the coast of China into Guangdong when we heard a little yell of surprise from my allotted seat. The old lady was standing up, her face lit with joy. The dead man had smiled, she announced. And then he had died again. But this time he had died in China, as it must be for the sake of the spirit and the peace of the ancestors.

That was her story and the story she would tell the family.

During his last month, realizing he was ill, Tom See Poy had scoffed at similar superstitions just as he had done all his life. He had no time for people who insisted a spirit could not find peace or union with the ancestors unless the corpse expires in China. He was more worried about what would happen to his store, the monument to his life.

In fact the emporium, one of Australia's first department stores in a rural area, limped on for a few decades until the third generation began to delve too deeply into its coffers. Expensive cars, yachts, women and wine whittled away at the solid financial foundations Tom had created. The grandchildren were no longer interested in running a store, only in harvesting the gains of the enterprise, without exerting much effort. A few decades ago, Coles Department Stores bought the emporium, pulled down the building and constructed a modern supermarket on the site.

Today there is not even a plaque to commemorate Tom's proud achievement.

Before he died a few years ago I visited Herbert See Poy in his neat little room at the Old People's Home. He was leafing through his father's memoirs, bound in book form. The writings exhort Tom's children to be thrifty, honest and good citizen, never to forget their Chinese roots and never to forget their duty to look after their elders.

Alone in his Spartan habitat, Herbert stared out onto a lawn speckled with little beds of daffodils and red roses. In his father's days no Chinese family would have parked their patriarch or any other member of the household in an Old People's Home. Sending them to such places was the Anglo-Celtic way, not the way of the Chinese.

"I guess we didn't read Dad's book very carefully," Herbert said.

GLOSSARY

Batavia: Old Dutch name for today's Jakarta

Billy: Cooking kettle

Celestials: The name given to sons of the 'Celestial Empire' (China)

Chow: Colloquial name for a Chinese person and food

Coolie: Manual laborer from Asia, particularly China and India

Chum: Colloquial term for Chinese and co-worker

Drongos: Australian slang for slow-witted person

Gin: A (now) offensive term for an Australian Aboriginal woman

Jackeroo: Young man or apprentice working on an Australian sheep or cattle station

Kang: Large bed kept warm in winter by coal fire underneath

Merkins: Fierce Aboriginal tribe

Mu: Chinese measurement. One mu is about 0.16 acres.

Nanyang: The island regions of the South China Sea

Sheila: Colloquial term for a woman

Strewth: British and Australian slang expression of surprise or dismay

Taipan: Rich entrepreneur

Tongs: Thuggish armed guards

Wowser: Someone who is annoyingly puritanical

Tucker: Food

CHAPTER 3

THE PHILIPPINES: THE CHINESE TAKE-AWAY

Chinese pig
Saliva drops from your lip
Your place is under the house

— FILIPINO CHILDREN'S DITTY

No one expected Yusan Dichaves to remember the four men malingering near a branch of the Metrobank in Binondo. The quartet could have passed for native Filipinos debating the easiest way to convey their cargo through the narrow, cluttered alleys of the maze that makes up Chinatown. Her chauffeur had parked the white pickup across a driveway marked "Keep Clear" and she remembered later she had some trouble extracting herself from the car. The two small boys, Kevin, 5, and Kirby, 3, stamped their feet and yelled their heads off. The boys tugged at her blouse. Both wanted Mum to take them into the bank. Like most Chinese sons, a species known in popular jargon as "Little Emperors," the boys were spoiled, precocious and used to having their way. It took her some time to wrench their small fists from her clothing.

The bank was crowded.

Christmas was five days away and Chinatown was busier, more congested and more littered than during the rest of the year. Even the calashes, drawn by shaggy emaciated ponies, crawled at a snail's pace, their large wagon wheels at times rolling over the black plastic garbage bags piled along gutters. More garbage floated on the stagnant, stinky canal below the hump-backed bridge. The bridge-pillars at each end bore a "Welcome" calligraphy. Ongpin Street, the Fifth Avenue of Chinatown, bid visitors good fortune and good health. The calligraphy is Chinatown's only visible concession to art and décor. The rest of Chinatown is austere business: Hole-in-the-wall shops, herb-scented drugstores, small teahouses, restaurants, groceries and dealers in hardware, timber and automotive parts. Customers can find anything in this maze: From an ounce of gold to a valve ring; from a truck wheel to a safety pin; from Sichuan peppers to Fujian birdseeds. In a back alley, invisible to those not in the know, hides a Taoist temple, an in-built wardrobe more to tradition than faith. Access is gained through a garage. No space is wasted in Chinatown, not even for the next world.

On the day Mrs Dichaves went to the bank, the garbage collectors were on strike.

Strikes are routine prior to Christmas. The whole of the Philippines goes on strike: Airline crews, bus conductors, factory workers, bank tellers, ferry operators, police and, most of all, garbage collectors. In their heart of hearts the strikers do not expect their bosses or the government to give in to their demands because everyone knows these strikes are part of the annual ritual to extend the Christmas holidays. Still, many of the strikers do believe, deep down in their credulous hearts, that come one Christmas or another a miracle will occur and their demands will be met. Filipinos believe in miracles just as they do in the infallibility of the Holy Father in Rome. Each year the entire nation, with infant faith, expects Santa Claus to shower them with gifts and money. When this doesn't happen, people shrug their shoulders and promise themselves and each other: "Next Christmas."

The people of the Philippines wait for Christmas with the expectation of children not yet aware the beard is false and the reindeers are cutouts. By the end of October, shop fronts and the facades of homes begin sporting tinsel, sprigs, Father Christmas cardboard posters and cherubic angels, all of this illuminated by multi-colored light bulbs. Christmas carols blare through shopping malls, through slum towns, even the airport. Filipino taxi drivers, a fraternity of legalized thieves, retain change with an endearing grin and the excuse: "It's Christmas, sir! Thank you."

When presented with the correct amount the drivers have the gall to demand, with an air of indignation: "What about my Christmas?"

People never heard from the rest of the year, press Christmas cards upon strangers, slip them under the door, offer them in elevators and on street corners, wishing everyone with the most endearing smile and one hand already half extended: "A merry Christmas".

Everyone expects generosity at Christmas.

Adults and children are on the prowl for a handout, an easy buck, a small act of extortion justified by the festive spirit of the season and the poverty of the extortionist. The rich are expected to shed some of their wealth—or rather, mere morsels—to the poor. At that time of the year, the Chinese are the best target and both officials and crooks make Chinatown particularly vulnerable around Yuletide.

Yet Chinatown is never on strike and never decorated with Christmas tinsel. It has no time for beggars or alms-seekers and treats the natives like tourists. Those who live or own shops in Chinatown speak Hokkien, Teochew, Cantonese, Hakka and Hainanese. Rarely do they converse in Tagalog, certainly not in Spanish as does the Filipino aristocracy and seldom in English, as does the modern generation.

The Chinese in the Philippines have never been a homogeneous immigrant community: Their loyalties and connections depended on dialects, sub-dialects, clans and family links. Only at the end of the line were they all linked to ancestral origins in China. Clan connections remained at the root of all business deals right into the 1980s and 1990s. The lucrative partnership of Malaysia's Robert Kuok and Indonesia's Liem Sioe Liong was based on common ancestral origin in the north of Fujian. Both speak the same sub dialect. Although these tycoons no longer live in Chinatowns, their roots and their connections have remained there.

Mrs Dichaves, a slender and attractive woman, spent more time in the bank than she had expected or wished to. At 11.30 in the mid-morning rush, the queue remained long and at one point she thought it might have been preferable to have left the children at home or at the automotive store with their father. The store was only half a mile away.

Outside, the four men moved closer to the bank. One of them peered inside and saw that the lady would be delayed. Perhaps they should have acted earlier. This malingering in the street made them nervous and conspicuous.

One of the men strolled across the street towards a pick-up van. The chauffeur was reading the *Manila Inquirer*. The nanny had her hands full with the two boys wrestling in the back seat. If the snatch went as planned, the kids would hardly be conscious Mummy had gone. Sure, the brats might yell if they saw Mum being dragged into a car. If she struggled, Oscar would give her the full dose of chloroform.

What if the kids yelled? Well, Chinese kids always yell in Chinatown. It's considered good training for their lungs in a society where those who yell loudest are listened to the most. Nobody would take notice of two Chinese brats exercising their lungs.

The man crossed the street again. An herbalist later remembered that the foursome held an animated discussion. The result probably changed their plan. No doubt the original idea had been to snatch the woman. Statistics proved women were the primary targets. Women gave little trouble. The shock of being manhandled usually silenced them. Sometimes they even fainted and had to be carried into the getaway vehicle. Fathers and husbands paid fast and well to guarantee their safety and ensure their speedy release "undamaged".

Sexual abuse of the victim had been a common byproduct of a snatch. Guards were bored when negotiations went on for weeks. The woman was usually young, with fair skin and a clean, perfumed smell, a far cry from the cheap soap of the dusky native girls with whom the guards usually trafficked in a country whose people consider complexion to be a sign of breeding. Who among the guards ever had the chance to hump a little princess like that? And who could resist the temptation to find out what such a woman was like below the belly of a man? By all the saints: It wasn't easy to resist such temptation.

Besides, these haughty bitches deserved it, didn't they? How many of these China dolls ever married a native? There was justice in letting them find out how it was to be humped by a local. Normally these snooty women with their chauffeur-driven cars and their fat wallets wouldn't even give you a smile. You were simply native trash to them. The bitches had it coming.

Such was the attitude in the Manila underworld and among the

Armed Forces of the Philippines which supplied a lot of the retired or cashiered soldiers for the snatches.

In the most notorious case, an entire kidnap gang had their way with the teenage granddaughter of an elderly Chinese taipan even though he paid the salty ransom. What the natives had never understood was that the Chinese had a genetic dislike for damaged goods for which they paid good money. Besides, the old man's honor was at stake. So retribution was a matter of pride and prestige.

The taipan then spread money like confetti to identify the culprits.

In a country where no one can keep a secret, especially when it is pried loose with cash, he soon had the names of all the gang members, including those who abused his granddaughter and those who had stood by. He then spent another fortune to import a squad of professional hitmen from Taiwan. The pros picked off all 13 members of the gang, one by one. The kidnap mastermind, a colonel in the armed forces, was gunned down outside his home in Ordaneta village in Makati.

The executions went a long way towards restoring the taipan's face, though his granddaughter remains under psychiatric treatment. It also sent a warning to the gangs about unwritten rules and the fact someone with money does have the means to fight back if pushed too far.

After the corpses were found and word of mouth perpetuated the story, the number of kidnap-rapes—though not the number of snatches—declined dramatically.

When Mrs Dichaves came out of the bank 25 minutes later, the white pickup had disappeared. She waited. And she waited. The chauffeur might have driven around the block to avoid paying the fine, usually a bribe to the parking attendant. For five minutes she was not unduly worried. Then she panicked.

Every Filipino-Chinese has butterflies in the stomach the moment a loved one inexplicably vanishes or is late for an appointment. Over recent years hardly a family clan has been spared the nightmare of a snatch and no one remembers when a victim was last rescued. Who would rescue them?

The Chinese never inform the police or for that matter any outsiders. And if anyone expresses doubts about the wisdom of keeping silent he is told the story of how one released kidnap victim walked into the police station to see the head of the Anti-Kidnap Squad. But right there in the inspector's office, was one of his kidnappers lounging in a chair and with his feet up on the desk.

The kidnap victim walked out without saying a word. He sold his business, packed his bags and transferred his family to Hong Kong.

The police constantly complain that their hands are tied by Chinese omerta. Not even half the abductions are reported and certainly never before the ransoms are paid and the victims are safe.

Chinatown has no faith in the authorities, with good reason.

In March 1998, Brigadier General Benjamin Libarnes, the head of the Presidential Task Force on Intelligence, publicly admitted that 114 soldiers and police on active duty were members of kidnap syndicates. The general was soon transferred elsewhere and there was no further news of what happened to the 114 he had mentioned. Kidnapping is big business in the Philippines and many illustrious pockets are lined with ransom.

The axe rarely falls on a rogue cop.

In the 1990s former police chief Cezar Nazareno was accused of a series of misdemeanors, including racketeering, running kidnap gangs and misappropriating public funds. In one notorious incident, his wife appeared on television wearing a precious gem and a gold bracelet which some people alleged had been part of the ransom payment for 15-year-old Mark Anthony Lee, the godson of former president Joseph Estrada.

Nazareno fled to the United States but returned when the dust had settled, to a nation with short memory and an infinite capacity to forgive and forget, an attribute often ascribed to Catholicism. But in reality, it was less a virtue than an imperative.

For years the ex police chief was seen sipping cocktails in the lobby of the five-star Peninsula Hotel in Makati, the financial hub of the Philippines. He wore the heavy gold bracelet and ostentatious gold chain that became his hallmark and the trademark of thugs in the Philippines. Nazareno will never face trial because, so those in the know-how whisper: "He knows too much." Besides who would be man enough to testify against someone with his connections?

In the end the Chinese only trust their own ability to negotiate an acceptable ransom. Those who can afford the expense call in a professional anti-terrorism expert, most of them mercenaries trained in the United States. Two or three of these experts have set up shop in Manila, a profitable market since an average 214 ethnic Chinese a year were reported abducted between 1993 and 2002, a figure probably far higher since the majority of Chinese do not report a kidnapping.

(The number of kidnappings declined between 2006 and 2008 after a successful crack-down on gangs by security forces and the death penalty in 2005 for eight kidnappers. But the snatch industry picked up again in 2010 prior to general elections. Many candidates standing for elections apparently obtain campaign contributions from kidnap-for-ransom operations.)

The Chinese Take-Away has been described as a Filipino cottage industry. For very little money and equally little risk a gang can make millions of pesos. So organized and lucrative is this industry that the ransom amount is unofficially fixed, although it fluctuates, just like the inflation rate. A case can be over within hours if executed professionally. The money is handed to a member of the gang who often accompanies the family delegate to the bank and takes delivery of the ransom right there and then. A few hours later the victim is released.

Washington SyCip, the head of one of Southeast Asia's most renowned accountancy firms, once accompanied a nervous female acquaintance to the Metrobank together with a member of the kidnap gang who had snatched her husband. SyCip recalled the gang member was perfectly at ease, showed no sign of nervousness and took delivery of the ransom right there in the bank.

In 1997 the going ransom for a Chinese was fixed at $40,000. Any Chinese family which exceeded that ceiling faced severe criticism and ostracism from the community for inflating the fee. Yet over the next decade this amount more than doubled.

Of course, cases do not always go by the book. Amateur kidnappers have reneged on releasing their prey or asked for more. Killer gangs have murdered their victim right after a snatch to avoid the expense and risk of storing them in a safe house during negotiations. On other occasions, the victims are sold to a second gang after an initial ransom is paid. The new gang then tries to squeeze more money from the family.

Then there are the Shake-Down Gangs, the poor man's alternative.

These desperadoes snatch small Chinese children in crowded shopping malls while their nannies or mothers are distracted. Mothers pay whatever money they carry in their purse to the courteous, well-dressed lady who usually approaches them with the bad news. In general the kids are held or entertained just around the corner and handed back within minutes. Quickie snatches are over before anyone has time to think or raise the alarm and few are ever reported outside the Chinese community.

The Philippine police in 1998 proudly announced they had files on 24 kidnap syndicates. Why they never arrested the members of those syndicates remains a mystery.

Apart from the big 24 there are the amateur snatchers who live with their own grand illusions in a country of illusions. The amateurs demand fabulous sums and generally botch their operations to the detriment of the established kidnap syndicates. When the syndicates track down the amateur meddlers they usually transform them into corpses.

"The boys have gone! My God! The boys have gone!"

In his office, listening to the distraught voice of his wife, Jepson Dichaves knew he had to call his banker—and Teresita—in that order.

When Teresita Ang See received the call for help, she knew the caller would plunge her once again into the nightmare of a family's torment. A small lively woman, she has become the unofficial spokeswoman of a community that does not speak out. Hers is the voice heard week after week, denouncing what has become routine in the Philippines. She is the first to receive the anguished phone calls with the question: "What shall we do now?" Her stubborn voice keeps denouncing the phenomenon—a habit that has made her unpopular with the authorities and within her own community.

In her clattered office on the fringes of Chinatown, the shelves are crowded with background material, photos, testimonials and studies of the Chinese Diaspora in the Philippines. She is permanently busy accumulating evidence against the inertia of administrations. Governments consider her a scourge or a fanatic. Her own community is divided between those who shun her and those who, secretly, applaud her. The syndicates have more than once threatened to kill her.

Teresita was born in the Philippines. Her father came from Fujian in the early 1930s and worked with his brother in a Chinese restaurant in Binondo.

"He used to finish work at 1 am after cleaning up and had to get up at 4 am again to go to the market. He and his brother had paid a lump sum for immigration papers that identified them as merchants, not laborers. Merchants or sons of merchants could come to the Philippines. Three of my father's brothers were already here and had accumulated some capital. The eldest was left behind in China. We were a prominent family in China. Our house had 24 rooms. The whole clan lived there. My father was the youngest son and after he married my mother in the Philippines, he took her to his village in China for six years. My mother is a Filipina but in the village she learned fluent Fujianese and became Sinicized. My parents returned before the Second World War and I was born in Binondo where everyone those days spoke Chinese.

"I was the fifth of eleven children. My father had a flour dealership and my eldest uncle became one of the biggest partners in Liberty Flour Mill. Since my uncle had no Filipino citizenship the mill was in my mother's name. She held the ownership papers and the titles. My uncle imported U.S. flour and yeast and made a lot of money. But since my father was the youngest it was only the elder brother who enjoyed the wealth. In the 1960s my uncle had a huge house in Makati while we lived in very difficult circumstances. The money did not come all the way down to us. It was worse after my father died still a young man. At the time mother was pregnant with my youngest brother.

"We had a very tough time, one of the reasons why I am so independent. I sent myself to college by tutoring children. I had nine students and I tutored most of them until well after midnight every day in order to put myself through college. I had a scholarship so I had to attain a certain grade to maintain that scholarship. On paper my mother owned the flour mill but she only lent her name and she had to work hard all her life. She now lives in the States with two of my sisters and I have one brother in Canada and four sisters in the States. My husband was an anthropologist and he died in 1986. I never felt the necessity of remarrying. We had two children."

Teresita is the typical product of a large traditional Chinese family. Most of the offspring are guided into profitable ventures but one or two are destined to become scholars, a profession that boosts family prestige.

Like elsewhere in the Nanyang, the Filipino Chinese are divided between integrationists and traditionalists. Some wealthy Chinese families integrated so successfully that their Chinese roots became almost obscure. Many Filipinos were shocked when President Corazon Aquino visited China and made a pilgrimage to her grandfather's village. Most people had been unaware of her Chinese roots. The venerated independence hero Jose Rizal was of Chinese origin. So was the late Cardinal Jaime Sin, the powerful Catholic primate of the Philippines who lent his support to Aquino's People's Revolution.

"The Manila Chinese are still very traditional while the Cebu Chinese are more integrationist," says Teresita Ang See. "In the late 1960s the Chinese in Cebu were giving lectures on integration which infuriated the Manila Chinese who were then talking about throwing the Cebu cousins out of the country. It was not until the 1980s that integration was no longer considered a taboo subject. But among the older Chinese here, it is still considered a revolutionary idea.

"It's different now," she continues. "The younger people joined civic clubs, Rotary Clubs, Lions Clubs, while the older ones pay lip service to integration and gave up talking about going home. Home is here in the Philippines and people have realized there is no more going back. Besides, many have also lost a lot of money in investments in China. They don't know how to do business in China anymore. The Chinese in China are outsmarting them.

"Today, among the third and fourth generation, there is no longer this strong sentimental attachment to China. Still, intermarriage with the locals is not encouraged especially after Chinese women were allowed to come to the Philippines at the end of World War II.

"Until very recently, wealthy Chinese still kept two families, one in China, one in the Philippines. My uncle had two families. Sometimes they would bring their Chinese families out to the Philippines and that created a lot of problems, a lot of quarrels. My uncle's family is still quarreling about who owns the Hong Kong property and who owns the Philippine property.

"Then there is the problem of the new generation. The kids don't want to go into commerce. The older generation wanted to earn money fast and once earned, sent it back to their villages. In the Philippines, trading was the only venue open to Chinese peasants because they weren't allowed to own land. Before 1975, the Chinese couldn't have citizenship. Even if you were an architect, you could not practice your profession and might end up selling hardware. But now people are free to practice any profession.

"We Chinese in the Philippines have enormous economic power but we don't know how to use it. We are the biggest political fund contributors but we don't make demands. Traditionally, the Filipino Chinese always support the administration. They never criticize the government. They don't go to their congressmen whom they have financially supported. They will even deny that their child has been kidnapped. They don't talk about it. They keep their mouths shut, tightly shut.

"So I am always the one that is in the limelight because they will not talk. At every gathering I attend, there is no other topic of conversation than the kidnapping. Wherever you go, the Chinese always talk about kidnapping. But no one will talk about it publicly."

Like anywhere else in the Nanyang, the Chinese are notorious for their internal squabbles in the Philippines. Their Chinese Federation was founded in 1904 but in 1964 a rival General Chamber of Commerce was created. In its heyday the Federation had 150 associated chambers from all over the Philippines. Each chamber had associated guilds: The plumbers guild, the electric shop guild, the carpenters guild and so on. It was like a Chinese Trade Union Federation but the decisions and deliberations only concerned Chinese issues.

Today the Federation of Filipino Chinese Chambers of Commerce and Industries has become the umbrella for all these local associations. The Federation members own two thirds of the country's private wealth. Its 500 delegates from all over the islands and 155 executive directors constitute a powerful lobby.

But the leaders are old men. The average age is 60. They are cautious and traditional. The younger Chinese do not want to be members of this Old Boys' Club and only three young entrepreneurs joined the Federation.

Both the young and the old entrepreneurs are victims. The kidnap syndicates have neither respect for hierarchy nor seniority: They snatched the daughter of federation president Jimmy Tan and the sister of the vice president—she managed to escape when the getaway car punctured a tire. The brother of another vice president was also abducted. Not one federation executive can say his immediate family has been spared. Yet not one of them will talk about or publicly denounce the snatch industry.

The silence of her fellow Chinese enrages Teresita: "These people won't talk because they are afraid the criminals will focus on them even more if they disclose details and the government will interfere with their economic interests if they make embarrassing statements. But look at me! I talk about it all the time and I'm still alive."

In the Philippines, it is easy to harass anyone with the law. Filipino laws are as numerous as the sand corns on island beaches and any number of laws and regulations can be invoked to persecute political or personal opponents and tie them up in lawsuits that can go on for decades.

The Chinese owners of Labelle Shipping Line, an inter-island service, found themselves in all kinds of legal tangles after its owners apparently failed to make adequate contributions to a political cause. Chinese born columnist Herman P. Laurel was jailed on charges that he had faked his certificate as a naturally born Filipino—after he criticized the Fidel Ramos administration.

"In this country good cops are told, 'Back off' when they get close to a kidnap case," says Teresita. "The courts acquitted two officials implicated to their necks in the Red Scorpion kidnap syndicate. They cleared them for lack of evidence after the archives burned down during the investigation."

■

By the time Jepson Dichaves had calmed his wife on the phone, the white pickup was heading down the Southern Highway. It drove at a leisurely pace. The occupants were certain no police alert would be out for the vehicle. The boys' father would never tell the police, either from habit or because he was afraid that if the cops did locate the pickup, there was a good chance his sons would be killed in the shootout. It had happened before.

At that time of day the highway was more congested than usual. The traffic, bumper to bumper, toxic with black diesel belching from jeepneys, crawled in fits and starts. In the backseat, the two boys hugged their nanny, Nimfa Celiz, a quiet 23-year-old from the island of Iloilo who had developed the patience of Job to deal with the two lively kids.

The moment the two men wrenched open the doors, the boys had started to yell. A few cuffs had quickly silenced them. The children were not used to being hit. The shock ensured their silence.

"Move over," the driver had been told. He didn't argue with a gun pointed at his chest. One of the kidnappers took the wheel and the other two sat in the backseat with the nanny and the children. The fourth man was following behind in his own car.

"You'll all be fine if you don't make trouble," the man at the wheel said. "Understood?"

"Don't do this," Nimfa pleaded. "They're just little kids."

"Shut up and keep the brats quiet," the man beside her said, poking a finger in her ribs, "we're not after you, honey, we only want the kids."

The pickup had to wait nearly five minutes at a traffic light. When the light went green the driver barked at the chauffeur: "Get out! Quick! And keep your mouth shut if you want to see those kids alive again."

The chauffeur opened the passenger door and leapt out in a hurry. The last he saw was the pickup crossing the intersection, then coming to a halt behind banked up traffic. A policeman with a walkie-talkie stood at the control panel of the traffic lights. It never occurred to the chauffeur to seek the policeman's help.

One of the men had climbed from the back seat into the passenger seat. The other, the one with the poking finger, now turned towards the nanny: "Listen girlie. You get out at the next lights. Now tell your boss we'll be in touch with him. The kids are safe and we won't harm them if he pays. But he has to pay quickly. We are not patient people. Understand?"

Nimfa Celiz was one of those nannies whose maternal instincts are generously extended to their charges. Hers was the kind of devotion that has made Filipina maids the most coveted in Asia, especially by the Chinese who are known as tough taskmasters, bad payers and exploiters of domestic servants but do appreciate a good and loyal worker.

"I won't leave the boys," she blurted, clutching her two charges tighter. The boys had been clinging to her neck. "You'll do as you're told," the kidnapper barked.

"I'll stay with them!" There was determination in her voice right from the beginning.

The kidnapper's hand plunged into her long black hair. He yanked her face so close she could see the white flickers in his eyes. "What's the matter with you, girlie? You want to die for the lousy wage these Chinks are paying you? What you earn in one month, girlie, I spend in one day. Now get out if you know what's good for you."

"I'm not leaving the boys."

The man swiped her face with the back of his hand.

"Wait! Wait! Wait!" his companion in the passenger seat urged. "Here, girlie" he added, reaching into his pocket: "Here's 200 pesos. Take a taxi. It's enough to get you all the way to Baguio."

Nimfa shook her head: "Let me stay with the boys, please," she pleaded: "I can control them. They won't be any problem for you. I can make sure they keep quiet. Please!"

The man on the backseat yanked her head by its hair against his nose: "Listen you stupid bitch. I'm going to throw you out the door. Now! See?"

"Wait! Wait!" the driver interrupted. "She has a good point, Oscar. Do you want to look after these brats? Do you want to spoon-feed them, clean their dirty little asses, dress them and listen to their whining? Come on, she's got a point. Besides," he added, "it might get lonely and she ain't that bad to look at, is she?"

"Yeah," the hair snatcher drawled. And the three men laughed.

Just as quickly the man called Oscar became serious again: "What's Ernie gonna say about this? Hey, compadre? We've already got the kids instead of the bitch. And now we're gonna bring in another bitch."

"Ernie be ok," the driver said. "He'll see my point. She'll look after the brats. Right?"

It took more than an hour before the pickup turned into the driveway of number 12-A Main Avenue near the Melville Market in Paraque.

By Manila standards it was a luxury, duplex villa. Its owner, Carlina Alejo, had rented it out for a week to a businessman named Ernesto Ramos Uyboco. She had signed a receipt for 48,000 pesos (US$1,900). The amount was a small fortune for a week's rental.

The men pushed the two boys and the nanny into the maid's room on the ground floor.

"One word out of you lot and Rrrrr," one of the kidnappers warned, running a finger across his throat.

The room was dirty, without water, furniture or utensils. A small window opened into an inner courtyard. An empty bucket in a corner was intended as a toilet. A single grubby straw mat had been rolled up on the floor. The doorknob was missing. The door could be opened only from the outside.

Ernesto Ramon Uyboco was a weasel.

For years he had been the "pointer" for the infamous Red Scorpion syndicate, an investigator who assesses the financial standing of potential Chinese kidnap victims and reports on their daily movements. Usually the syndicate gave him a name to investigate. Sometimes he would toss in his own choice.

The syndicate demanded a comprehensive report before any decision was made. Most important was a family's financial holdings and whether there had been new cash flow from the sale of property or holdings in recent weeks or months. A fresh cash flow could shoot a family right to the top of the priority list.

Equally important was a family's connections. This ascertained if friends and business partners could help in raising the ransom. If a family had first rate connections its credit rating in the snatch industry was high.

Only the last consideration concerned security and the movement of the various family members. Many of the affluent Chinese had hired bodyguards or armed security officers for senior family members, mostly the patriarch or matriarch. The gangs were aware of this. However other prominent family members remained vulnerable and the gang knew Chinese families were closely knit and unlikely to jettison even a distant kidnapped relative.

It was Uyboco's task to find out how vulnerable and "snatchable" various family members were. This meant detailed daily movements, pointing out, if possible, convenient spots and timetables for a snatch. At times he virtually wrote the script for these kidnap dramas, yet their directors, the gang bosses, often changed the course of events, the target and the timetables, leaving Uyboco always guessing and never wise to their choices.

His dossiers were handed over, either written or verbally, to the syndicate for a nominal fee. The syndicate boss decided if, when and how, the snatch was to be executed. The pointer was excluded from this decision. He was only paid for the information.

It peeved Uyboco that he was never privy to the deliberations and the reasons why one or the other of his targets had been chosen. He usually provided a number of possibilities from the one family targeted. At times he was interrogated by syndicate members on details and observations. Sometimes he had to draw maps or summarize his report in writing. Still, the syndicate did not always act immediately or at all. On a number of occasions he was surprised to find the gang had snatched a target months after he had pointed it out or left another "good target" untouched.

Obviously the syndicate also did its own research.

He had started as a freelance pointer, selling his know-how about the Chinese to anyone willing to pay. After a year or so the Red Scorpion syndicate had decided to employ him exclusively.

Less than a month earlier he had run afoul of the gang.

It was nothing definite, simply a gut feeling that they no longer trusted him. The rift happened after a victim he "pointed" out was snatched by a rival gang. He knew his employers suspected him but had no proof that he had sold the same dossier to the others. No one had complained or questioned him but there had not been a single phone call or contract, or outstanding pay. Outsiders did not question the decisions of the syndicate. And despite his intimate connections, Uyboco had remained an outsider.

But prior to Christmas, the freeze-out was bad, bad news. After all he had expenses and expectations to meet. He had promised his family a Christmas treat, a holiday in Hong Kong. One did not renege on a Christmas promise, not to one's family. And he had obligations to contacts, valuable contacts, people who expected Christmas gratuities for the tidbits of information passed on throughout the year. These people were his bread and butter. Without them he would be a blind pointer.

In desperation Uyboco decided to branch out on his own and organize his private Christmas collection.

Like most Filipinos, he nurtured a love-hate relationship with the Chinese. For years he had stalked Chinatown in a futile quest to learn how the Chinese became rich. Although he took little jobs here and there he remained an outsider, to his great chagrin. Outside Chinatown, among his own, he would tell anyone willing to listen that the yellow race had enriched itself on the sweat and blood of good, honest Filipinos. In the process the yellow devils had become arrogant. Worse, he would say, they behaved as if being Chinese was something special, something more refined, more educated and more civilized than the natives. The Chinese treated Filipinos worse than dogs. And yet they were not even Filipinos. In the end, he would say: "Whose country is this?"

In all the years of wheedling his way around Chinatown, Uyboco had not managed to acquire a Chinese mistress, even though he was a man of modest means and could have set her up, just like a Filipina, in a small flat. Having a Chinese mistress was nearly as prestigious as bedding an American woman, the ultimate achievement of Filipino machos, just as going to America is the ultimate dream of almost every non-affluent Filipino adult. Marrying a bona fide gringo is the fairytale-come-true for most village girls.

The natives are notorious for philandering and creating "second families". The excuse is the ban on divorce, a prerogative the Catholic Church in the Philippines has maintained as its most potent weapon. Without divorce, couples have to make their own arrangements. Most Filipino politicians, including presidents, have kept mistresses who have given them at least one "love child". The custom is tacitly accepted in an already promiscuous society with an infinite number of pretty country girls. Most of these girls are eager for a taste of urban life under the patronage of a sugar daddy. Mistresses give men the chance to prove to other males their rampant virility. A Filipino exhibits his mistress in public like a warranty of his manhood.

Mistrust of the Chinese was common. For generations Filipinos had envied them their wealth and bickered about Chinese aloofness and lack of patriotism.

Anti-Chinese sentiments go back a long way.

When the Spaniards arrived in 1590, their sailors found 150 Chinese already around Manila Bay and eager to trade. Like colonizers all over Southeast Asia, the Spaniards soon discovered the Chinese were indispensable to development. They encouraged more to come to Manila. These Chinese were good workers, excellent administrators and quick to grasp a commercial opportunity. In comparison, the natives were a happy-go-lucky lot with a zest for the easy life, scant ambitions and none too dependable when it came to work.

Within a decade of the arrival of the Spanish colonizers the Chinese population in Manila had grown to 25,000 and by 1603 the new Lords of the Philippines found themselves badly outnumbered by the Chinese. The Spanish panicked. During a night of the Long Knives and under the pretext of stifling an imminent Chinese revolt, the Spaniards carried out a brutal massacre. A mere 500 managed to slip away to China. Another 500 survivors were rounded up and herded each night, from sunset to sunrise, into a walled-in compound known as the Parian.

But the Chinese have the tenacity of the cockroach: They survive on little and thrive in adversity. Only 14 years after the great massacre, Chinese chronicler Zhang Xie wrote:

"They stayed together in the Parian to make their living and their numbers gradually rose to several tens of thousands. One hears that some cut their queues (pigtails) and produced sons and grandsons, married local women and established families there."

During the next two centuries the Spaniards would find periodic excuses to butcher some of their Chinese subjects whenever their numbers gave rise to anxiety. The excuse was always the same: The Chinese had rebelled against Spanish rule. But the real reason, as it still remains today around the globe, was to confiscate some of the riches the Chinese had accumulated.

In those early colonial days the Celestials, trading silk for silver, sent back to China all their profits: Large quantities of silver ingots from the silver mines of the Philippines.

Not that much has changed since then. Instead of ingots many Filipino Chinese invested their profits in their motherland once Deng Xioaping spread the welcome mat. Simultaneously, more Chinese arrived in the Philippines.

In the old days the sons of the Yellow Emperor were smuggled into the country or admitted on short-term coolie contracts. In the post-Mao era the newly affluent Chinese, their associates or envoys simply buy their way into the Philippines, not on rickety coastal tramps or fishing boats but through the nation's main airport.

At Manila's Benigno Aquino International Airport, Chinese "businessmen" arrived in the 1990s without documents. Special handlers met them at the plane's staircase and escorted them through immigration as "business delegations". For just $4,000, a mainland Chinese could buy a Filipino resident permit and an ID. These documents gave them not only a permanent legal status in the Philippines but allowed them to go back to China any time and be classified on the mainland as Overseas Chinese, a special category which enjoyed tax exemptions and preferential treatment in the booming decade.

Unlike these modern mini-tycoons, the original Chinese arrived in the Philippines as coolies contracted to work in sugar and coconut plantations. In time they became farmers, storekeepers and finally financiers and industrialists, driven from one trade to another not so much by ambition but by periodic bans on their chosen livelihood as Filipino governments tried to curb, in vain, the locust-like grazing of economic opportunities by the Chinese.

The 1935 Philippine constitution excluded the Chinese from owning land, developing natural resources and operating public utilities. Nearly a million Chinese left the land and sought livelihood in urban areas. Soon they dominated the market place. But in 1939 an ordinance banned them from owning market stalls. The same ordinance reserved for Filipinos the right to trade in rice and corn, the country's two main commodities. As a result of the ban the Chinese invaded the retail trade. But in the 1950s the Nationalization Act outlawed the Chinese sari-sari stores, the hole-in-the-wall mini groceries and ordered all retail trade reserved for Filipinos. This time the more affluent turned to manufacturing, the textile industry, money lending, banking and accountancy. The less affluent left the country.

Today's Chinese live in the golden era of the Chinese in the Nanyang. Attitudes are more liberal now, discrimination is outlawed and materialism has become Asia's new religion. The closely-knit Chinese community has flourished. Its members pioneered regional industrialization and networked their way into most major projects. The majority of private conglomerates are owned by rich Chinese today or by the descendants of Chinese who integrated with wealthy native families through marriages. These "integrated" Chinese have, on occasion, managed to hide their origins for generations and are the loudest to proclaim there are no racist sentiments in Southeast Asia today.

"We do not have racism in the Philippines," banker Bon Juan Go told me once. He is an executive of the Chinese-owned Metrobank, the country's largest. "It is only economic envy that discriminates against Chinese," he explained. "We are being kidnapped not because we are Chinese but because we are rich."

Filipinos disagree.

The country's finest English-language novelist, Francisco Sionil Jose, a man in his 80s whose books chronicle Philippine history and native peculiarities, is candid on the feelings of his compatriots:

"Filipinos believe the Chinese are clannish and send their profits to China and Taiwan instead of investing them in the Philippines where the profits are made. The Chinese won't let their children marry natives and the stigma of their past as cruel money-lenders and wholesalers in rural areas still clings to them like bad body odor.

"Twenty years ago the Chinese were demure and anxious to hide their wealth. Today they have been Filipinized: Ostentatious, showing off their cars, their new furniture and most of all their new houses. The Chinese have become showy: Look at their weddings and funerals and look at the Chinese cemetery.

"In the old days the Chinese were junk dealers, iron mongers and newspaper collectors but today the Chinese own most of our newspapers while Filipinos collect the junk. A Filipino shopkeeper wants to make profits in pesos, the Chinese is content to make profits in centavos. Yes, we Filipinos are envious.

"When the first Vietnamese boat people arrived in Manila Bay I wanted to help them but a friend dissuaded me: 'These people are all ethnic Chinese. Let the Chinese take care of them.' This is the attitude that persists today: Let these people be kidnapped. They're only Chinese."

Puerto Princesa is the capital of the island of Palawan, one of Asia's last Wild West style frontiers. The northern part, south of El Nido, is a lush greenbelt containing the only remaining tropical rain forest in the Philippine archipelago. Until a few years ago, Palawan was a drowsy backwater of tin roof huts, dirt roads and hamlets. People cultivated rice in flat, naturally flooded paddies and harvested coconuts. The local sari-sari store kept a case of warm San Miguel beer on the shelf. A basketball hoop provided the entertainment. Village society was divided between the rich who owned a pig and the poor who owned a chook.

In the 1980s, before the Chinese arrived, Palawan had the lowest population density among the main Philippine islands. Once every two days the national carrier sent a flight down to Puerto Princesa. It was rarely more than half full.

The Chinese landed on Palawan as Boat People in the late 1980s.

Their search for new homes had been "encouraged" by Hanoi's ethnic cleansing campaign. Half a million ethnic Chinese in Vietnam ventured onto the ocean aboard rickety fishing boats, embarking on a cruel odyssey. Thousands became the victims of pirates, were raped, robbed and tossed into the ocean to die. Others navigated around the South China Sea in search of abode. The early Boat People headed for Hong Kong, the Shangri-La of their dreams, a colony of Chinese with British laws and Western opportunities. Hong Kong did not want these fellow Chinese. The authorities herded the refugees into cramped camps. Malaysia, with one third of its population Chinese, did not want them either. Police and troops used clubs to beat the refugees back into the sea. Singapore, 95 per cent Chinese, had no stomach for the runaways. It too turned them back.

In the search of a better future and a friendly country, the boats sailed as far as Australia. The Philippines, poor and with limited opportunities, was never a choice for a people seeking not only a home but a commercial opportunity.

Running out of ports, fuel and welcomes, the boats began to land on Palawan, the long narrow island that sticks out in the South China Sea like a lido for the rest of the Philippines. Filipinos are Asia's most hospitable people, a genetic positive inherited from their ancestors. The Vietnamese were given shelter in an army camp on the western outskirts of Puerto Princesa adjacent to the airport. The camp was wedged between the ocean and the airport runway and guarded round the clock by troops. It was finally closed in 1998 when Manila granted temporary resident status to some 2,000 remaining inmates who had no chance of being accepted by a third country for immigration. The residency permit enraged the rest of Southeast Asia where governments insisted all Boat People unable to obtain third country residence must be repatriated to Vietnam. But the Filipinos have always generously opened their country to outsiders, one reason why the Spanish and later the American colonial masters (who simply bought the Philippines from Spain) found the place so attractive. Yet these masters looked down their noses at the child-like friendliness of the natives although all of them generously sampled the charms of Filipino women, among Asia's most attractive—and fertile.

"I wished the Japanese rather than the Spaniards and the Americans would have colonized us," says author Sionil Jose, "because then we would be a developed self-confident country today. First the Japs would not have tolerated the oligarchies that have ruined my country. The Japs believe in their own superiority so much they could not have tolerated colonial subjects who believe they are superior. Second, the Japanese would have exploited our labor force and natural resources. As a result they would have given us an industrial infrastructure and a good communications system. Third, we would not have had this hate-love relationship with our colonial masters. We would have hated the Japanese guts and that would have made us far better and less wishy-washy as a nation.

"Instead we have become a nation of braggers. A Filipino always brags about his achievements, beginning his bragging with the phrase "modesty aside". Once you hear this phrase a whopper follows. It is because people are not confident in themselves: they need status symbols to prop up their confidence."

Years before the government of Fidel Ramos opened the gates and allowed the last ethnic Chinese from Vietnam free movement within the Philippines, the inmates at the Puerto Princesa camp had already managed to create their own industrial network inside and outside their confinement. Many had bought their way out.

The camp bakery with its French baguettes changed the eating habits of Palawan. The camp restaurant with its cheap but tasty dishes and Vietnamese soups was crowded for lunch and for dinner. The vegetables, grown between the army Nissan huts, the open drainage and sewage pipes, were items coveted by every local housewife and restaurant owner. The camp laundry was popular, the clothing hand washed, sun dried and smoothened with coal-fueled irons in a town suffering from daily electric blackouts.

By law these Boat People were restricted to the fenced camp confines. Armed guards were stationed at a boom gate. Yet a good number of the Vietnamese bribed their way out during the day and worked on farms, often for half the wages of the locals. With their earnings the Vietnamese opened cheap eateries in town, using Filipino "partners" to obtain permits. While still camp inmates, a handful of these new-rich Vietnamese-Chinese entrepreneurs owned motorcycles and Korean pickup vans, the kind of vehicles most natives of Palawan could only dream about.

Today Puerto Princesa is one of the most flourishing provincial towns in the Philippines. Palawan has become the country's boom province. On the eastern outskirts, off the road to Roxas, the Vietnamese, with the help of the Catholic Church and charitable organizations, have built a model village, far more modern, far better organized and more functional than anything similar in town. Taiwanese investors, aware their ethnic kins had established a bridgehead on Palawan, invested heavily on the island. China, which has cast a covetous eye on Palawan and its rich marine life for decades, has sent fishing trawlers ever closer to the island and established marine structures on atolls in the nearby disputed Spratly Islands.

Less than a year after the Boat People camp was closed, much of the new wealth of Puerto Princesa came to be dominated by Vietnamese-Chinese enterprises, from dealerships to hardware stores, tailor shops, eateries and good-time bars.

For centuries the little town, ramshackle, poor and backward, had drowsed in the tropics until the Chinese from Saigon gave it a stimulus that has now attracted hefty Taiwanese and South Korean investments as well as perhaps some unwanted attention from a China aware the capital Puerto Princesa is also headquarters of the Philippine's Southern Defense, a dreadfully understaffed and under-armed outfit which can barely muster a few planes to patrol the Spratlys or launch the odd superannuated patrol boat, prone to break down.

Uyboco's acquaintances recall he was fascinated by the commercial acumen of the Chinese and frequented Chinatown initially to spy out the secrets of their success. He expected the Chinese knack for making money to rub off on him. Instead he found the Chinese a reticent community, by nature suspicious of outsiders and unwilling to part with any commercial savvy, even to their own kind. Most of the Chinese success was due to hard, dedicated work and not due to any magic formulas.

In his quest to ally himself with the Chinese, Uyboco took several jobs as a laborer. But his attempts to ingratiate himself with the boss soon came up against the harsh way the Chinese deal with their hired help, their reluctance to pay more than minimal wages, their insistence on punctuality, overtime without pay and free days only over Chinese New Year.

In a country with a plethora of holidays, strikes and religious feasts, Uyboco began to refer to his Chinese bosses as "slave drivers". He talked darkly of a day of reckoning. This attitude was reflected in his work. He was fired from several jobs. This only further fueled his hatred and his obsession to teach the Chinese a lesson.

Drifting around the bars of Manila frequented by petty crooks, Uyboco fell in with a gang of small time hoodlums in search of easy money. Eventually he came in contact with the syndicates which realized his knowledge of Chinatown might be useful to pinpoint potential kidnap targets.

Soon he appeared in white shirts and neatly pleated slacks, carried a leather briefcase and shaved every morning. He passed himself off on his visiting cards as the sales representative of a bogus company looking for wholesale bargains. His new status won him the instant respect and deference of Chinese entrepreneurs. Even the most careful Chinese tended to let down their guard at the prospect of a lucrative deal.

Uyboco was a slick talker and had retained good contacts among Filipino native workers in Chinatown. He pried on their hatred for their bosses and their harsh conditions of employment even though most were candid enough to admit that but for the Chinese they would have had no jobs or income at all. Most significant however, Uyboco had made friends with two bank employees who could supply him, in return for cash, with the account extracts of certain companies and names.

And that is how he started his career as a pointer.

A man of inflated self-confidence, Uyboco had no doubt he could carry off a snatch as successfully as the syndicates. He had been around long enough to learn the modus operandi and gauge the risks. A snatch would allow him access to the entire ransom rather than the mere morsel his employers usually tossed him for his services.

He was so confident that he had purchased first class return tickets to Hong Kong for his entire family for Christmas and figured five days, probably less, would be enough time to conclude the transaction. After stashing away the ransom and changing part of it into Hong Kong dollars he would go straight to the airport accompanied by his family.

The former syndicate pointer had reason to be self-assured. His son had a gun dealership. Weapons for the snatch would be no problem. His best pal, retired Colonel Wilfredo Macias, owned a security agency in which Uyboco had invested. The agency was not doing well. Many of the guards, mostly former policemen or soldiers, were without a job and only too happy to make a fat Christmas bonus from a snatch everyone knew carried a minimum of risk and a maximum of gain.

Uyboco had worked it out meticulously. He deliberately overpaid the rent on the safe house to ensure the old lady would not head for the police if the snatch became public, an eventuality he seriously doubted. The high rental for such a dump would make the authorities awfully suspicious about her role in the affair.

Every detail had been taken care of, until he rang the safe house and was told that instead of an attractive wife he had two small boys on his hands.

"You blundering idiots!" he yelled. "Can't you fools follow orders?"

He slammed down the phone and tugged at the airline tickets in his pocket. The buffoons! He had selected Dichaves not because he was extremely wealthy but because of his good-looking wife. The guy would have paid up in no time and a pretty neat sum too, way above the going rate. He knew from experience husbands and fathers had nightmares at the thought of their women in the hands of Kidnap Anonymous.

But kids! Jesus! Kids!

You didn't kill kids, you couldn't rape kids, you could only cut off their finger or an ear and even that would cause a public furor. It simply wasn't done. Kids made headlines, but not a wife. A man could never live down the stigma of everyone knowing his wife had been in the hands of kidnappers for days. The Chinese were chauvinistic and anxious about saving face. No Chinese wanted others to know his private treasure may have been opened by alien hands.

"Jesus!" he said aloud. "Those damn idiots."

Jepson Dichaves was not a rich man although he had a branch of his automotive dealership in Singapore and was doing well financially. But he was not the old fashioned Chinese who takes what is coming to him and pretends a kidnapping is part of the permanent overheads, like the political contributions, the kickbacks to the cops and the payoffs to the customs officials. Such were the penalty-levies for being Chinese in an alien environment.

The stocky dealer in his late 30s had no doubt about his permanent roots in the Philippines. And he was not the type to take an injustice lying down.

Uyboco had done his psychological homework badly.

Jepson was born as Jepson Chua, son of a family of immigrants from Fujian. His wife too was from a Fujianese clan. Like many Chinese born in the Philippines, he changed his name to give it a Spanish sound. Filipinos with social aspirations always invent a Spanish bloodline. It gives them a claim to membership in a pseudo-white society that still considers the white race a superior species and desperately tries to parrot first Spanish, then American culture.

Jepson had no such ambitions. But he saw the commercial benefits that could be accrued by being named Dichaves.

The Chua family had done well in Chinatown and Jepson still ran his rather modest-looking dealership from the maze but lived in a new house in the best residential part of the metropolis. His family was now buried at the Chinese Cemetery at Santa Cruz, a monument to the wealth and welfare of the community and its age-old respect for ancestors.

Those ragged immigrants who began life in the Philippines in hovels today rest in a splendid city for the dead, inside marble-walled mausoleums, some with air conditioning, most of them with mail boxes and nearly all of them with flushing toilets.

Armed security guards protect the dead against thieves and squatters who may take advantage of their physical absence and move in from the slums of tin roof and cardboard huts that surround the necropolis, perhaps Manila's most exclusive residential area.

It is not the living but the spirits of tens of thousands of Chinese who dwell here in homes few could afford when still alive.

On All Saints Day, on New Year Day and the Chinese Day of the Dead the villas teem with thousands of ethnic Chinese who bring with them large parcels of the favorite dishes and drinks enjoyed by their venerable ancestors while still alive.

As a sign of respect and to ensure prosperity for the dearly departed, the visitors burn stacks of paper money and imitation gold bars. The offerings are not unselfish: The spirits believed to reside in these marble mausoleums are expected to provide guidance for the business deals of their descendants and endow their clans with wisdom and prudence to survive any crisis.

"We really need the old ones to tell us what to do," said Herbert

Choy, a construction tycoon visiting the tomb of his parents. "Most of us have heavy investments in China. Should we pull out, should we ease off or go on investing?"

At the Chinese cemetery, the dead rest in magnificent sarcophaguses, many made of Carrara marble imported from Italy. Their remains sit at the center of towering halls as large as churches or at least the size of chapels or tabernacles. Spiral stairways lead to the upper floors. Double glazed windows keep out the heat. Electricity provides light from chandeliers. There is running water. Armed guards with walkie-talkies patrol, all year round, day and night.

Mao Zedong banned ancestor worship in communist China as decadent and unworthy of socialist man. But it continued to flourish in Southeast Asia where Chinese minorities remained fiercely loyal to their Confucian, Buddhist and Taoist traditions.

The Chinese arrived in the Philippines long before the Spaniards. The sons of the Yellow Emperor were not only attracted by trading prospects but an ancient belief in the existence of "The Isles of the Immortals" where one could eat food in abundance and find eternal youth.

The necropolis is proof the migrants did not find the immortality they sought, though the fertile soil of their new home offered plentiful harvests.

Many Chinese have become Catholics but they still burn incense and eat with their ancestors on Ching Ming, the traditional Tomb Sweeping Day in April and also on All Saints Day on November 1, the day the Christian calendar sets aside for honoring the dead. Some Chinese say mass on those occasions.

The necropolis on the northern outskirts of Manila houses some 20,000 family mausoleums. Thousands of shoe-sized boxes in wall drawers hold the cremated remains of less affluent Chinese. Many of the visitors bring their Filipino maids to help with the cleaning, the gardening and the meals on the table: Fried chicken, boiled rice, pancit (rice noodles), rice cakes, oranges, apples and pears imported from China. All of them include the dead person's favorite dishes.

The maids or the drivers feed the flames in a cauldron where paper money and paper gold bars stamped with the ancestor's personal Chinese seal go up in flames. After some prayers and a respectful pause to allow the spirit of the departed to gorge on the banquet, everyone sits down and eats.

"No use wasting it," say the living with typical Chinese pragmatism.

Incense and thick red candles, embroidered with gold leaf, burn in the mausoleums. Children fly kites outside and the adults eat, drink and discuss business, often pretending that the dearly departed is still among them. If the dear one has recently expired, his family may bring him a helicopter, an airplane, a motor car and maybe a computer, all in miniature and burned before the altar, to ensure the venerable one has the same comforts his family now enjoys.

On the bustling streets of this Necropolis, Filipino vendors with special licenses from the Chinese Association offer soft drinks and food for those who did not bring enough. One vendor advertises: "Take two Pizzas and pay for one!" Street urchins scamper from tomb to tomb scraping the melted candle wax from altars into plastic bags. At the cemetery gates women squatting behind spring scales offer 20 cents a kilo for the wax which they remake into more candles.

Once darkness descends the worshippers fold up the marquises, set up in the gardens of the tombs. They head home through an ocean of candles lit by superstitious Filipinos who say the spirits of the dead play awful tricks on the living during All Saints nights.

Jepson Dichaves had no time to consult his ancestors on the day his children were kidnapped. He is a practical man, part of a new generation who see the trappings of the old culture as a social obligation rather than a conviction. His reaction was: The time had come to call in a few outstanding favors and make use of friendships cultivated over the years.

He rushed to an emergency meeting with his good acquaintances, Generals Panfilo Lachson and Jewel Carson. After he had left, the telephone rang in his office. Jepson's secretary picked it up.

"Tell your boss we want 26 million pesos ($1 million US) for his kids. It's 13 million for each boy. And tell him we want it quickly."

Yusan, sitting in a chair nearby and trembling with tension and foreboding, saw the horrified look on the secretary's face and snatched the phone from her:

"Look," she yelled: "I can give you half a million pesos right away if you give me back my children."

"You're joking!" replied the male voice: "If it's only 500,000 we don't need to talk anymore."

The line went dead and Yusan collapsed. Twenty minutes later she was still hyperventilating in an ambulance on the way to hospital.

Teresita knew the life of the two boys depended on a carefully studied plan that would neither upset the kidnappers nor close the door on negotiations to lower the ransom to an acceptable figure.

She had advised the family to expect an initial demand for a shockingly high ransom. She still remembered her first case when the kidnappers demanded an astronomical $30 million for a Chinese builder, a sum that nearly gave his wife a heart attack. In the end the ransom was bargained down to $650,000.

Her main argument remained the dictum: "Don't give up. Remember these people want money not corpses."

The next step was to prepare the families for the inevitable threats over the telephone: "We will kill him!" or: "We'll cut off his finger and send you the rest of the body piece by piece."

From the initial ransom demand she could determine if she was dealing with amateurs and inflated hopes of a fortune or with professionals whose agenda was to conclude the affair quickly and within a reasonable ransom parameter.

Of course, Teresita knew, the kidnappers also probed to find out if they were dealing with a panicky or a level-headed family. A panicky family always paid more.

She recalled that in the first case she handled, the kidnappers knew a lot about the man they had kidnapped. "They knew he had just bought property and expanded the warehouse. She was certain the information was coming from inside his office. There was an informant. She told his wife that since the kidnappers knew so much she might not be able to get away with a low ransom.

"We started with 100,000 pesos against 30 million and worked our way slowly down to a million pesos which they adamantly refused. Then we moved it up by 100,000 until it reached 1.6 million.

"That's all I have," she told them.

The kidnappers called every day and every day she said: "That's all I have." Finally she told them: 'Ask my husband who else I can call.' In this way we would know if the husband was located close by or being kept at a distant safe house. It can take one day for them to come back with an answer or it can take just an hour.

"They got back in a few hours with advice from the husband to try some people he knew. Ironically the husband had told the kidnappers his wife would be able to collect about three million. And the husband was mad at his wife for not getting the money together which he knew was there. Meanwhile the wife and I were just trying to pay as little as possible. We were really sure they were ready to accept one million but stalled because he had told them he had three million.

"We stayed firm. At midnight she told them she had 1.6 million. They said no. She said: "I have another 100,000 in checks I can cash. She said she could get probably a few more 100,000s and get close to two million. But they refused to give in.

"At two o'clock in the morning they called her and said whatever you have now, cash, jewelry, just bring it."

"The payoff was at 3.30 in the morning. It was a very sophisticated payoff: the kidnappers had checkpoints. She was asked to bring two cellular phones with extra batteries. She was also ordered to let cars following her pass by and was constantly informed where to turn right or left. They had checkpoints all along the route which means she was being watched. She was asked to slow down. Finally she was told to drop the payoff. Her husband was released at nine o'clock in the morning.

"I was worried. Often, if they're not satisfied with the amount of ransom they'll kidnap the wife as she drops the ransom and release the husband to get more money for her release."

Paranoia is a prominent by-product on both sides, among kidnappers and the family of the victims. At times family members were so scared of being pursued or watched by invisible agents of the kidnap syndicates they made elaborate arrangements to meet Teresita at weird rendezvous, a bank, a kindergarten or even a hotel toilet.

"Once I was attending a congressional hearing. My beeper kept going off. I had to walk out and leave a note for the Speaker. I left my car at a bank and they picked me up and asked me to deal with the kidnappers who had their children. The kids had sent a note saying 'Pay faster'. I got involved in that case and then the kidnappers sent a note saying 'sent away the one helping you'. The gang had five people, three children, the wife and the driver and they wanted 50 million pesos ($2 million) but we got them down to 10 million pesos.

"Both sides panic when it lasts too long. If you insist that's all you can afford, they don't push you. But you always pray. You never know if you haven't pushed them too far. The only thing you know is whether you're dealing with professionals or amateurs. The professionals don't harm their victims. Amateurs are more likely to kill their hostages.

"One way or the other the family always wants to give in sooner than you think they should. I am always the one who insists to hold on, to bargain, because if you don't you only encourage them and there will be more and more abductions. I always argue if you give one gang more, all of them will want more.

"These gangs are highly sophisticated today. Nearly all of them have their own fleet of cars, their set of cell phones, radio transmitters and an arsenal of modern weapons. Each year they are getting bigger and better equipped.

"Its easy to frighten the Chinese community. We were really terrorized when Myron Ramos Ui and Kenneth Go were killed—after their parents had paid the ransom. What scared us most was that they had been brutally tortured first. The torture was a warning for the presidential anti-crime squad to get off their backs. In fact we had a report later that the crime squad had tried to muzzle in and get a part of the ransom. There had been a shoot-out. No one was killed and the boys were still to be released. But the anti-crime squad insisted on their cut. So the kidnappers tortured and killed the kids, as a warning.

"That was in September 1992 when kidnapping was escalating and the ransom was 1.25 million pesos per person. The entire Go family left for Singapore after their son's murder and the Chinese community threatened to call off classes. But the government pre-empted the school strike and closed down all schools claiming a typhoon was coming. It never did, of course, but the authorities didn't want the publicity of the strike.

"On January 7, 1993, just a few months later, 15-year-old Charlene Sy was killed during a bungled rescue attempt. There were three getaway cars, new Fords while the agent chasing them was using his own 1978 model. He was about to lose them when the kidnappers got held up on a traffic light. In the shoot-out, all the kidnappers were killed but so was the girl.

She was being used as a shield. A bullet went through her temple, fired, apparently by one of the kidnappers who just executed her when he saw there was no way out. The police said their operatives hadn't been aware Charlene was in the car.

"The family refused to have an autopsy and the Chinese community created the Movement for the Restoration of Peace and Order with the slogan: 'After Charlene who is next?' We demonstrated. We had a placard whose text embarrassed and enraged President Ramos. It said: "Mr President you should know who they are?"

"In the end 53 police officials were relieved of their duties. But many of them were actually promoted, one became a presidential adviser on immigration and is one of the real crooks in immigration. Among those fired was the Chief of Police, General Cesar Nazareno. He ran out of the country after two cases were filed against him. Now he is free on bail and has sold his house for $1 million. Yet he still owns a row of condominiums. On his salary, tell me, how could he afford even one condo?

"No one ever asked where he got the money?"

The next call came just after 6 p.m. the same night. Uyboco tried to sound curt, businesslike. Since children were involved in the case, he argued, no one desired harm should come to them. And in view of this humanitarian consideration he was ready, but just this once, to take merely 10 million pesos. But it must be now.

Jepson Dichaves looked at the burly man standing next to him. He was the expert, recommended by the two generals as a specialist trained in anti-terrorism tactics and negotiations with hijackers and kidnappers. The two referred to him simply as "The Major". He was an American. Ex Special Forces. No one ever told Jepson where "Mike" came from or his professional background. His services did not come cheap.

From the start "Mike" insisted the 500,000 pesos figure would be the basis of negotiations. But with each call, Jepson would pretend he had managed to rake up another 50,000 or perhaps, depending on the reaction, even another 100,000.

"Don't give in," the Major warned. "Once you say yes, there is no going back."

Both Major "Mike" and Teresita had figured out they were dealing with amateurs. Professionals would never ask for 26 million and then slice off 16 million within six hours. Both were preoccupied: The case could turn nasty, amateurs had high expectations and their illusions were unrealistic, their impatience and disappointment could have fatal consequences. Amateurs, usually from the rank of simple Filipinos, believed each Chinese was a walking gold mine. Once tapped, the mine was worth a fortune.

While the two experts analyzed their options and the psychology of the abductors, Jepson worried over the fate of the maid. Nimfa had been an excellent maid. She was utterly devoted to the two boys and she was a placid, patient young woman.

The kidnappers had not asked a single peso for her as ransom.

She was the only person who could identify them. The boys were too young. She might also recall details that could lead police to the gang. No doubt she was a liability. Jepson was afraid the kidnappers had already decided to kill her. Perhaps she was already dead. How could he ascertain whether she was alive and well? How could he be sure these amateurs had not killed all three of their victims and were stringing him along for any old ransom they could extract?

Only one factor was in Jepson's favor: Christmas was only two days away and the banks would be closed for at least four days. He assumed the kidnappers wanted the pay-off before Christmas and were willing to make concessions. Christmas without money was hell in the Philippines, especially if a bonanza was at an arm's length.

The Major agreed the bank closure was the ace up their sleeves.

But Uyboco had his own twist to the deal: Twenty-four hours later he lowered the ransom to five million pesos but told Jepson to make a choice between his two sons. The five million would only obtain the release of one boy before Christmas. The other child would remain until Jepson had raised the second five million.

The Major slowly shook his head and held up two fingers.

"No deal," Jepson said. "I want both boys together. Listen," he added. "I can throw another 100,000 into the pot. But that's all I managed to raise."

There was a pause at the other end.

"Not good enough," the voice finally replied.

The phone went dead.

In the Philippines, like in the rest of Southeast Asia, the Chinese thrived on the lack of infrastructure and government agencies in rural areas. Over generations they had created their own alternative network for basic rural services: Chinese shops supplied local needs; Chinese money lenders offered credit in return for land as collateral; Chinese wholesalers bought crops and guaranteed farmers minimum prices for exclusivity; Chinese trucks and ships transported goods and crops.

Native governments, spurred by popular discontent and nationalist sentiments, periodically curbed the Chinese expansion into their economies by imposing discriminatory laws on their commercial activities. At one point 80 per cent of workers at any Philippine firm had to be native Filipinos. Lawyers, engineers and other professionals had to be native.

The restrictions on the Chinese in the Philippines, Indonesia, Thailand and Malaysia were ample proof of the success, if not the commercial superiority, of the Chinese Diaspora. The bizarre and often infantile methods to curtail Chinese commercial zest were proof of the native inability to compete on equal terms with the Bamboo Network. The Chinese had to be constantly and heavily handicapped to level the playing field.

This method of control was successful until the economic boom swept aside restrictions and made the Chinese the commercial partners of an ever more greedy political hierarchy. The Chinese paid for the privilege by giving their native partners hefty stakes in their profits.

It was during this golden era that the Diaspora gained an unseemly and disproportionate share of wealth, enraging ordinary people who were unaware how the system functioned, that the sudden wealth of the Chinese was the making of crooked officials and politicians who shared in the Chinese riches.

In hindsight, certainly after the boom went bust, many of these politicos regretted their alliance with the ethnic Chinese. Few had realized to what extend the Chinese overseas network had dominated the region's economies, had gobbled up most viable commercial assets and set up a network dominating Southeast Asia and its economies.

Even Suharto, towards the end of his three-decade long regime, complained that the Chinese had fleeced his country and its resources and taken the profits abroad rather than reinvesting them in the local economy. Suharto, of course, made no mention of how he and his family had also stashed their fortunes away in hard currency or investments abroad the moment they realized the trend. Worse, the dictator did not curb the export of profits.

Conspiracy theorists among Sinologists argue that the Chinese have been subconsciously preparing for generations for this one great opportunity to make their fortunes. The theory is weak since the Chinese in the Nanyang have rarely planned ahead but seized opportunities as they presented themselves. Being opportunists by nature and handicapped in the past by the restrictions imposed by their host nations, the Chinese were obviously best prepared to benefit when these restrictions were removed. The Bamboo Network was far superior to anything the natives or the competition could offer. The Chinese took the boom by the horns and rode it to death.

The natives had found it difficult to compete against the Chinese networking, one of the reasons for the constant pogroms and repressive measures, a scenario similar to Europe where Jewish communities and Jewish networking also dominated large sectors of the economy. This kindled the envy and the wrath of non-Jewish competitors and resulted in periodic persecutions of Jews in nearly all European countries.

Anthropologist Theresa C. Carino summed it up thus: "Under Spanish regimes, periodic expulsions, massacres and strict immigration laws kept the Chinese population sizeable enough to serve the Spaniards but not large enough to be an economic or political threat."

A royal decree in 1608 restricted the Chinese to life in the Parian, an enclosed fortified area in Manila. The penalty for being outside this area after dark was death. The number of Chinese in the Parian was limited to 6,000 but often exceeded that quota. If the Chinese became too populous the Spaniards would find an excuse to purge them.

Subsequent colonizers, the British, the Dutch and the Americans followed to some extent the Spanish recipe in dealing with their Chinese. After the United States bought the Philippines from Spain—a purchase backed by a show of U.S. force off Manila Bay—Washington passed the Chinese Exclusion Act to prevent the Chinese in Manila from using the Philippines as a gateway to America.

Without support from the motherland, the Chinese had no choice but to tolerate these curbs on their mobility and commercial activities. It was only after the Japanese invasion of China in 1937 that a Pan-Chinese Salvation Movement catalyzed into some kind of Overseas Chinese Organization. Chinese merchants, notorious for never turning down a deal, boycotted Japanese goods. Even more astonishing was the sudden patriotism of the overseas Chinese who contributed vast sums to China's war chest. At the same time, Chinese war refugees found shelter among Chinese communities in a rare show of solidarity. Some 7,000 refugees, mainly women and children, received hospitality in Manila alone.

Yet when the war ended and Mao declared a People's Republic, with obvious limitations on foreign trade and investment, the Diaspora quickly switched its loyalty en masse to Chiang Kai-shek's Kuomintang on Taiwan. The Kuomintang might not have survived without overseas Chinese support and funds.

However the overseas communities were divided: Many idealistic young Chinese, mainly from the have-not or academic sectors, returned to Beijing to help Mao build socialism. Their return was exploited by Maoist propaganda. Yet the communists in Beijing, so I gathered in the 1990s, would have preferred investments and donations rather than people they never really trusted.

In the Philippines, post-War discriminations pursued the Chinese initially. Nationalization laws in the 1950s specified that Filipinos had to constitute 80 per cent of the employees of any company. Engineers, lawyers, doctors, accountants had to be Filipinos.

By the late 1960s young professional Filipino-Chinese were tired of the discriminatory acts and a group of college educated graduates created the Pagkakaisa in 1970, an organization demanding citizenship on the basis of Jus Solis—by right of birth in the Philippines.

Their aspirations bore fruit, thanks to Richard Nixon who went to China. His overture encouraged Ferdinand Marcos, always a loyal U.S. ally, to normalize relations with Beijing. More importantly, he allowed 60 per cent of the Chinese in his country to acquire citizenship in 1975, but only after all of them had renounced Chinese nationality.

The dictator's decision to solve the "Chinese dilemma" by granting citizenship became a clarion call for other Chinese in Southeast Asia, all navigating in the nebulous penumbra of dual statehood. An astute businessman settled with an extravagant wife, Marcos, like other strongmen in the region, realized his Chinese minority could be useful for Philippine commercial interests abroad. Others soon followed his lead. Citizenship became no problem for those who could afford it or could accrue commercial benefits for their hosts. For the ordinary Chinese, the vendors, hole-in-the-wall store proprietors and market peddlers, citizenship remained as unattainable as it had always been.

Washington SyCip is a member of the privileged class of Filipino Chinese. He is known throughout Southeast Asia as "the Wise Owl". Now approaching 90, he is the founder and chairman of SGV&Co, perhaps the most respected ethnic Chinese accountancy firm. He deals mainly in inter-regional investments, a man who knows more about the Bamboo Network's cash flow and operations than anyone else in Asia. His own life story is symptomatic of the ups and down of the ethnic Chinese and he chuckles when he talks about kidnappings:

"Many rich Chinese started their own fortunes by kidnappings. It was a traditional form of extracting money from someone who owed money. Everyone has been involved in kidnap dramas in this country. At the beginning kidnapping was an illegal Chinese way to make money. My own grandfather was kidnapped in Shanghai for ransom. If you didn't have money and you wanted money quickly what could you do? Rob a bank? There are a lot of guards at the bank so it was better to kidnap someone who didn't have security. There was much less risk in kidnapping than in robbing a bank.

"Many Chinese came to the Philippines to carry out a kidnap operation, especially Chinese from Taiwan. The problem with the Philippines is that the law enforcers are also the law violators.

"A few triad groups from Taiwan became so successful here they regionalized their kidnap operations."

Washington, like Jepson Dichaves, is one of those super confident ethnic Chinese, mavericks in the community, who are apt to break with tradition if it goes against the grain of their beliefs. He set himself three targets in life: He was not going to follow the Chinese practice of nepotism. He would not create a family business and he insisted his clients should pay proper taxes.

A small, fragile man, he learned about Chinese commerce the hard way at the age of five when he gave away his toy telephone in return for three days of rent of a toy car owned by his brother. Even at that tender age he realized it had been a lousy deal.

At the outbreak of World War II he joined the Second Philippine Regiment attached to the U.S. Army. But his high IQ and language skills were considered too precious for cannon fodder. He was trained as a cryptographer and helped break the Japanese code in the China-Burma-India war. Soon he became a leading decoder.

After the war and once his company flourished in the Philippines, Washington SyCip's went regional as far back as the 1960s. In those days nearly all the leading businessmen in Southeast Asia were ethnic Chinese.

"These ethnic Chinese saw the advantage of regional union. Besides overseas Chinese always have some relative somewhere and it was much easier for them to do business than for the natives. When an ethnic Chinese is successful, he doesn't try to get into politics. Now a Malay, for example, as soon as he has made money, wants to play the game of politics. The ethnic Chinese knows politics is constantly changing. So if they tie themselves up with one politician what are they going to do when the next guy comes in? That's why they tend to be nice to everyone.

"For a Chinese, business is like sitting on a poker table and the Chinese loves to gamble, win or lose, as long as he is at that table. The Malay, the moment he wins, wants to spend it all on his family, take a trip to Europe, buy a bit more jewelry. The Chinese do love jewelry but that comes at a much later stage when they are already extremely successful. The Chinese will tell his wife: 'You go on a trip to America but I want to stay.'

"There is a similarity with the Jews, the Jews in Europe before the Second World War. The American will say when you come over to the States, I'll buy you lunch. The Chinese is not interested in lunch. But the Jew will say, when you come over bring your son and I'll get him to meet my daughter.

"America has an enormous asset these days since most Asian leaders sooner or later send their children to U.S. graduate schools. These kids come back dressed like Americans, love American music and American habits. To my mind if I were an American I'd feel so much more confident. For every four Asian students in America there is only one in Europe, including the U.K."

In his penthouse office, SyCip sees the Bamboo Network as an ethnic brotherhood with strict rules, not unlike a benevolent Mafia. Deals, he says, are made by a simple phone call on the strength of mutual trust. Anyone who reneges is ostracized from any future deal.

"The decision process is very quick. There is a project: A guy rings up and says: You want ten per cent of this? There is no project study, no long meetings. The answer is yes or no."

Initially the Bamboo Network was restricted to family members in different parts of Southeast Asia. Then it included people from the same region, speaking the same dialect, with the same ethnic background. Today it has extended even further.

"The large Chinese groups don't care anymore where its members come from. The big corporations have gone beyond that. At one time the immigrants came from the poor provinces, 75 per cent from Fujian, 25 per cent from Guangdong. Those from Fujian went into certain trades: Construction and hardware. The Cantonese bought hotels, groceries and supermarkets. You had an informal line: All groceries were Cantonese, so the wholesalers and the retailers were all Cantonese.

"In Hong Kong you have shipping and textiles concerns owned by people who came from Shanghai after the communist take-over. Those in shipping set up textile mills in South America.

"In New York you saw initially Cantonese, then when the communists came to power they were mainly Shanghainese. The Cantonese came from poor families and opened laundries and restaurants. The Shanghainese came from rich families and went into banking and textiles. It was unlikely these two groups would meet socially. The bankers would be meeting with other Shanghainese rather than the immigrant Cantonese families.

"But today many Shanghainese own restaurants. It's all a matter today where they can make money. Business interests have become so diversified you have to cross ethnic borders."

Initially the tycoons dealt only with people from their own villages or regions or with relatives. But during the last decade these restrictions vanished, replaced by personal contacts, success—and greed.

"If a fellow had previous success, then everyone wanted to be in on his next deal. But if your first project fails, you're dead. On the other hand, if you brought off five successful projects and one fails, that's fine.

The main distinction between ethnic Chinese and non-Chinese is that the Chinese are willing to take a gamble: They are not seguristas.

"When Cory (Aquino) came to the presidency, many ethnic Chinese felt times had changed and they started to buy land. They moved faster than the others. The price of land did go up a lot and many fortunes were made. The Filipino families which had the land and sold it later regretted it and this caused a lot of envy and anti-Chinese feelings. It didn't help either that Cory went first to the village of her ancestors when she visited China."

"But that's typical Chinese. Once we have done well, we want to do something for our village where people have suffered in the past. It's like the Jews in New York. They like to buy Israeli bonds, really not expecting to be paid back or make a profit. They simply want to do something."

Washington SyCip is convinced the close-knit Chinese society and networking in Southeast Asia is the direct consequence of discrimination. Laws forced the Chinese to adopt local names in order to qualify for public positions such as on the board of a bank. Many changed their religion and became Christians in the Philippines or Muslims in Indonesia.

"But it's hard for a Chinese to become a Muslim: Not eating pork is too much for any Chinese to sacrifice. And the obligation to make the haj to Mecca is difficult too: Can you imagine a Chinese wrapped in a bed sheet walking in the hot sun? We Chinese don't take religion serious, basically we're agnostics."

Despite the boom that went bust in Southeast Asia, the man who looks after the accounts of many corporations envisages a future dominated by China. Back in the late 1990s, he had already told me Beijing would replace Washington as the region's de facto leader and the change would herald another golden era for the Diaspora:

"At this point, the U.S. can still do what it wants because it has the huge advantage that everyone wants to get into the U.S. market. But China is learning every day from the U.S. that her strength is the size of the market. The Americans can tell anyone: 'We've got you: Don't you call us sons of bitches or you can't come into our market.' That's what the U.S. has done for years. The size of its market has enabled it to demand anything and everyone has to accept it.

"The U.S. did not criticize Taiwan about its violations of human rights or its dictatorship. Had Taiwan been faced with the same criticism when its income level was the same as China's is today, there would be no prosperous Taiwan today. Had the U.S. criticized South Korea on human rights or dictatorship when it was at the same income level as China is today, there would be no South Korea today.

"After Tiananmen, the West boycotted China but the Overseas Chinese realized, once order had been restored, that the hotels were cheap, the investment opportunities great and from their point of view orderliness is the main issue for the development of any country, not democracy.

"I tell my Western friends: You favored a boycott of China at that time but today the same system is in power and yet you are rushing in to invest. So who made the better decision after Tiananmen: The Overseas Chinese or you?"

Uyboco had tickets for his whole family to go to Hong Kong for Christmas. The tickets weighed heavily on his mind. So did the expectations of his associates. All had plans for Christmas. He could not disappoint them if he wanted to keep their services for future operations. Loyalty in the underworld is based on patronage and largesse and Uyboco knew Filipinos do not forgive unfulfilled promises made before Christmas.

During the whole day he had tried to think of a way to pressure Dichaves into parting with at least five million pesos after the businessman had sharply turned down his offer to release one of the boys before Christmas, the other after Christmas.

He finally picked up the phone: "Five million for both, my last offer. Take it or leave it. But I warn you if you don't take it, I'm moving the boys to the provinces for a long spell. It may be months before you hear from us again. Perhaps never."

He waited. The silence on the other end made him tap his foot on the floor of the telephone cell. A youth in a ragged T-shirt waiting outside the booth was pointing at his watch. Uyboco turned his back on him.

"I'm sorry," the voice of Dichaves finally came down the line: "I can't possibly raise that much money. You have to understand I'm in bad financial straits these days, contrary to what you may believe, I ...

"Drop the bullshit!" Uyboco snapped. "You want the kids alive or don't you? It's as simple as that now. Make up your mind. Now."

Dichaves did not reply. He was consulting with the Mayor who had listened in on an extension. The Mayor shook his head. Dichaves made the cut-throat sign with one hand. The Mayor shook his head again.

"I want my kids alive. I really do. But I can't bleed water from a stone. Believe me, I've exhausted all my credit among friends. I can't raise any more. What else can I say. I want my kids. I love my kids, but I can't raise any more."

"What happens now is on your head," Uyboco snapped.

Then he hung up.

On December 22, a few minutes after midday, Dichaves drove his station wagon south towards the Magallanes Market. On the passenger seat the 1.5 million pesos in ransom were stashed in a blue and red sports bag.

Traffic was heavy as it always is in Manila at any hour. He was edgy and anxious, torn between righteous indignation and anxiety over the course of action he had taken. What if it went wrong? He would blame himself for the rest of his life. How could he be sure no one in the system would snitch? That he was not the victim of yet another set up? Was it really worth risking the lives of his two boys and the nanny to justify his own sense of justice? How would he face his wife if the operation failed?

As the car crawled south along a river of moving metal and belching exhausts he kept a wary eye on either side, staring at the faces of motorists for a nod, a pointed finger, any signal to indicate: "Follow me". He was told somewhere along the route someone would make contact.

The curt voice of the kidnapper on the telephone had been short and precise: "Bring the one and a half million now, right away and alone. Take the main road south to the Magallanes Market. You will be contacted on the way. Don't tell anyone and leave right away."

He had made two quick telephone calls and transferred the cash from the safe into the sports bag. The thought struck him the whole affair had now slipped out of his control and he was only a pawn in a game played with his money while the lives of his boys were at stake.

The knock at the driver's window jerked his head around. The man was suddenly there, mushrooming from three lanes of stalled traffic. He was a short fellow with a flat face and bushy eyebrows. Two flapping fingers signaled: Wind down the window. Without a word, the man tossed a walkie-talkie into the car and was gone, just another crazy pedestrian meandering across the highway, undaunted by the concrete barrier in the center.

Dichaves picked up the set and placed it next to the sports bag. It was an olive green army set, a simple battery gadget with a one-button system even an idiot could activate. How apt, he thought: For years kidnap victims and ransom deliverers had observed the use of army communications by gang members.

The set crackled for what seemed an eternity. After ten minutes his body started to shake with agitation. What if? What if it didn't work? Behind him a rust bucket of a car tooted its three tone horn. He stepped on the gas pedal to fill the gap in the traffic.

When the set finally came alive the volume surprised him.

"Turn right at the next traffic lights," the set ordered.

Twice more he received similar instructions until the voice ordered him: "Turn left into the parking lot in front of you... Good! Now take the vacant spot next to the Red Chrysler on your right... Good! Now sit and wait."

Obviously the gang was making sure no one had followed him. One of them must be very close by. His skin began to crawl.

About five minutes passed. His palms were now wet and his brain was screaming for something to happen.

"Now take the money and put it in the trunk. Leave the trunk unlocked and walk away. Take the handset with you and keep walking for 15 minutes. Do exactly as you are told or you'll be going to a funeral."

The mechanics of the operation were never made fully public. From an expert's point of view, the operation had a 50/50 chance. Far too many people had become involved and a leak along the chain was an almost foregone conclusion. The gang, it was determined later, knew outsiders had been called in.

But kidnap gangs are arrogant in the Philippines and often complete the commercial transaction of a snatch under the very noses of security forces. Rarely do they abort or reschedule. In the worst cases a gang might have to share the ransom with the cops who had come to take it away from them. A number of shoot-outs between kidnappers and police turned out to be battles over how the ransom should be divided or reaction to attempts by one side to cheat the other. Apart from these internal mishaps, kidnappings had become almost routine in the Philippines and statistics show over 95 per cent of the victims walk away physically unharmed though often with lasting psychological problems.

The ransom is rarely recovered.

The two helicopters began circling over the drop-off area a few minutes before Dichaves had turned into the parking lot. Their presence would have warned any professional gang. Even a novice should have deduced something was wrong or might be wrong. But Uyboco was so confident, and so firm in his belief that a cowed Chinese community did not have the nerve to cooperate with police, that he simply ignored every negative signal.

It was his undoing.

In Manila, two main organizations officially fought the snatch phenomenon in the 1990s: One was the Anti-Kidnap squad of the Metropolitan Police, the other the then vice president Josef Estrada's "Presidential Anti Crime Commission" or PACC. The latter was created by President Fidel Ramos to combat a runaway crime wave and, as some wags had it, to give Estrada something to do. Both organizations garnered their clues from bank contacts, rumors and anonymous tip-offs that a particular Chinese family had been "hit". The crime busters followed the trail of the money. Those on the take determined their cut by mutual agreement with the crooks before the cash was ever delivered.

The many hands on the pot made the snatch trade prolific. By the time the loot was split, the next grab was already in its embryo stage or born. The appetite for easy money was insatiable. Supply and demand remained constant and quite frequently the Chinese Take-Away became a simple fund-raising operation. Its proceeds financed elections, private militias and deficits in company and public budgets.

Statistics prove that prior to every Filipino election, local or general, the number of kidnappings go up dramatically.

Four factors favored the operation to rescue the Dichaves boys and capture the kidnappers. One was the proximity to Christmas, two the fact that Uyboco's gang were amateurs with no previous experience, no contacts in the security forces and no plan to pay off "outsiders". The third factor was a bonus: vice-president Estrada had taken a personal interest in the case. But the final factor was probably the most important: A gaggle of amateurs was muscling in on the professionals. This upset not only the established kidnap syndicates but also their police pals. Uyboco and his gang had no friends on the inside.

The modus operandi of the rescue operation remains somewhat vague. There was no blueprint, no consultation between the two security forces or contact once the money changed hands. Each side improvised as the operation progressed. Both PACC and General Lucson's men were involved. Who did what and when was subsequently covered by folklore and media imagination.

What is certain is that General Lucson was throwing the annual Christmas bash for his "boys" when he was called to the phone and told by Dichaves the handover was taking place somewhere near the Magallanes Market. The general's "boys" were in civvies, about 100 of them. They moved in private vehicles, well armed and tanked up on Christmas punch.

As they took up positions in the market area, the vice-president's personal helicopter was circling overhead.

Estrada, the paunchy former matinee idol of Filipino action movies, had managed to transfer his reputation as a gun-toting modern Robin Hood from the silver screen to real life. As the head of PACC, he was often photographed with an assault rifle and purportedly leading the final attack on crooks. Bad guys came out of hiding to surrender to him, overawed by the hero of more than 100 films and his reputation that a villain had no chance to escape once Erap—the Tagalog word for pal, pare read backwards—was on his trail. Filipinos venerate idols and those who promise to take from the rich and give to the poor. The same promise allowed Ferdinand and Imelda Marcos to plunder the country for decades and remain beloved by millions.

Estrada made the same promise during the campaign to succeed Ramos as president. Ramos, who had had no intention of seeing the popular but bumbling action hero succeed him, saw his error too late. He removed Erap as head of the PACC two years before the presidential election.

In May 1998, Filipinos elected Estrada—a self-confessed womanizer, high school dropout and suburban mayor—to the presidency of the Philippines with a landslide majority.

While still vice-president, Erap had set his sights on the top job and he was not going to miss an opportunity to participate in the reflected glory of the rescue of two kidnapped children. He dispatched his helicopter.

Uyboco opened the trunk of the car and took out the sports bag and transferred it to the trunk of his own red Ford. He drove out of the parking lot slowly, turning left. Before he entered the highway, he zigzagged through a maze of small streets, checking in the rear-view mirror to see if he was being followed. He was not.

Two thousand feet above, the officers in the helicopter had picked Uyboco up with their binoculars the moment he approached the car containing the ransom. The eye in the sky followed him through the side streets and out onto the highway.

Meanwhile Dichaves was stumbling through pot-holed sidewalks in the general direction of the market. He was soon drenched with perspiration, not from the sun but his own anxiety. The handset was clutched to his chest, its static crackle a reminder the lifeline to the kidnappers still existed. He knew whatever message came across the ether would be their last. And he prayed, silently: "Dear God, let them be alive."

When it came, he almost missed the message because Uyboco was nearing the fringe of the set's communications perimeter. All Dichaves heard through the crackle was: "Gasoline station... meters... ahead... ."

He started to run towards the Caltex sign in the distance.

Nimfa held the two boys in each hand. The three stood under the sun on the footpath outside the petrol station, rooted to the spot like cemented statues, just as they had been told to do.

"Daddy! Daddy!" the boys cried as they flew into his arms.

Over their shoulders he saw Nimfa, the real heroine of the drama, brush away tears.

The epilogue is virtually unique in the annals of the Chinese Take-Away.

The police operation turned into a celebrated success story and yet the ensuing legal battle to convict the two main protagonists has become a prime example of the intrinsic inability and ineffectiveness of the legal system of the Philippines and the hardships and financial deprivations it imposes on plaintiffs.

The two Dichaves boys were snatched on December 19, 1993.

The case had no loop-holes, the evidence was overwhelming, including film taken from the helicopter, recordings of voice messages and finger prints and receipts from the safe house. Uyboco was captured in possession of the ransom. For the prosecution it should have been a cinch.

But by 1999, neither Uyboco nor Colonel Macias had faced trial.

With the ransom in his trunk, Uyboco drove straight home to pick up his family and head for the airport. He was so self-assured he had used his own car to pick up the ransom which made it easy for the officers in the helicopter to obtain his home address. As he approached his villa in the luxury residential zone of Das Marinas Village, he was startled by the number of police vehicles waiting there and made a run towards the boom gate at the Village entrance where he was apprehended at gun point.

Colonel Macias was waiting at the villa for his share and offered no resistance. Only two other minor gang members were ever arrested.

Both Uyboco and Macias were refused bail.

For the next six years, the lawyer for the two men filed one restraining order after another in the Court of Appeal. Each order costs 300,000 pesos, which the court earns once it accepts the petition for what in reality amounts to a postponement.

The defendants' lawyer is an ethnic Chinese named Lolito Go, notorious for having spent 15 million pesos on restraining orders. Known as the champion of delay, he has obtained 51 restraining orders, each of them accepted by a court apparently more interested in filling its own coffers than in the progress of justice.

Dichaves still owns his spare parts store in Chinatown. For years he complained his business could have done better if he could have spent less time making appearances in court that only ended with another postponement. The court attendance kept him away from his work and his overseas ventures.

In the beginning the Department of Justice assigned a state lawyer to plead the family's case in court.

"But the guy assigned to us came to me after a few days with an Armelite rifle and asked me to pawn it for him. I gave him 10,000 pesos and immediately got my own lawyer," Dichaves said.

He added: "We have a new prosecutor now. His name is Nino Mariano and he seems very honest. I tried to give him 20,000 pesos for Christmas as a present but he refused to take it. I think we might go ahead now.

"Estrada has made a lot of noise about the delay but it hasn't done much good. I really wanted to drop it but Teresita convinced me to keep on fighting. Without her and Estrada I would not have bothered. Many times I cannot go abroad to Singapore where we have an office because of the case. It's hard to leave because there is always a hearing and I have to be there.

"Fighting this case in court has cost me twice as much as the ransom I paid for the boys and the nanny. Perhaps now you understand why the Chinese in the Philippines just pay up and shut up."

POSTSCRIPT

Nine years after the kidnapping, Uyboco was finally sentenced to life in prison. The other mastermind of the kidnapping, Colonel Wilfredo Macias, died in jail in 2001. Estrada became the 13th president of the Philippines but was removed from office in 2001 by an orchestrated People's Revolt headed by his own vice-president Gloria Macapagal Arroyo. He was later charged with corruption. Estrada spent seven years in detention, mainly house arrest, but was pardoned by presidential decree. His supporters want him to contest the 2010 presidential election.

Teresita Ang-See is still running the Citizens Actions Against Crimes (CAAC) committee which documents and denounces the kidnappings of ethnic Chinese. The kidnap rate briefly dropped after 2005 when eight kidnappers were sentenced to death by lethal injection. But since 2008 it has picked up and currently, in 2010, is running high with 49 people, including eight foreigners, kidnapped in the first three months of the year, one third of them ethnic Chinese. The 'snatch' industry always reaches new records in a general election year (like 2010) when gangs need cash to donate to the campaign of their favorite candidates. The Philippine Center for Investigative Journalism said in a recent report: "Manila is still the Kidnap Capital of Asia. Kidnapping is a virtual cottage industry in which a little capital and apparently equally little risk can mean millions of pesos in profits."

Between 1993 and 2002 alone, 2,142 kidnappings were reported, an average 214 a year. Both police and the Chinese community admit however that only a small percentage of the snatches are reported.

"No foreign novelist touches the Philippines because in my country fantasy still has to catch up with reality."
— FRANCISCO SIONIL JOSE, *Novelist*

GLOSSARY

....

Calash: A two-wheel horse-drawn carriage
Celestials: See Chapters 1 and 2
Coolies: See Chapters 1 and 2
Nanyang: See Chapters 1 and 2
Sari-sari store: Cabin-like mini-grocery store
Segurista: Someone not taking risks

CHAPTER 4

MALAYSIA: COLD WAR

In the summer of 1934, a middle-aged man stepped out of a rickshaw on Beach Road in downtown Singapore. He glanced around, perhaps checking for a familiar face. Satisfied, he fished from his breast pocket a bank note and handed it to the rickshaw driver. As the coolie trotted off, keeping an eye on the pavement to see if any pedestrian required a ride, his last passenger began to stroll along the pavement towards the Raffles Hotel. The man twirled a silver-knobbed cane with the jaunty air of an adventurer. He was small, fragile and elegantly dressed. Thick eyebrows arched across a broad forehead as if drawn by a pencil and his black hair was glossy, lacquered in the fashionable style of the time. Large round eyes gave him a Eurasian appearance though his skin, high cheekbones and flat nose pointed to an Indochinese bloodline. A square chin left his features with a harsh finish, sharply contrasting with the rest of an almost melancholic face. The man's dark suit, vest, black tie and high white collar would raise eyebrows today in a tropical city like Singapore. But in those days such attire, more suitable for London, was compulsory for anyone, especially for Asians, entering the hallowed halls of Raffles Hotel where, until a few months earlier, no Asian had been allowed to set foot. After the hotel went bankrupt during the Great Depression, the new owners, more anxious to earn money than cater to colonial class distinctions and inbred racism, relaxed the strict no-Asians-or-dogs ban. Asians, if properly attired and accompanied by a white male, could now enter—and the rule about dogs had never been strictly implemented. After all, a Duchess' lapdog was not a mere canine. And an Asian attired like a European was not common riff-raff.

From below his towering yellow and brown turban, the uniformed Sikh at the hotel entrance examined the visitor with the lofty look of Sikhs on guard. The visitor handed him a card. The guard, towering over the frail man with the cane, stared at the card then waved to a bellboy. "Try the Long Bar," he told the boy, handing him the name card. The Sikh stood aside to allow the visitor to wait in the hall, where it was decidedly cooler. Five minutes later a tall, broad-shouldered Englishman with a face as if chiseled out of granite and dressed in the comfortable tropical uniform of a police officer approached the Asian. The two shook hands and vanished into a quiet alcove off the main hall.

■

In those days Singapore was already a bustling multi-cultural city, an Asian Babylon with 26 languages spoken by a workforce of immigrants mainly from China, but also from India and Indonesia. Situated just north of the equator, Singapore had become the hub of a Malayan colony where rubber and tin made fortunes for British planters and mining companies, where trade had not only made Europeans but also many Chinese rich. The port was constantly besieged by freighters, while thousands of sampans and junks moored and moved on the Singapore River, a waterway snaking though a city of stately Victorian mansions and columned government buildings.

People flocked to this new city—founded by Sir Stamford Raffles as a British trading post in 1887—to make money, enough to climb a rung or two on the social ladder when they returned home. But the majority remained and became wealthy and status conscious, core residents of a once nomadic Singapore population now increasingly sedentary. Chinese immigrants dominated the demography of this free wheeling city, albeit tightly policed. By the 1930s the Chinese had founded Clan Associations— huay kuan—small fiefdoms within the city, a kind of brotherhood capable of turning militant if the situation so required. These associations now issued all-important marriage certificates that would allow spouses wedded in Singapore to be accepted as legitimate by family clans back in

China. This was a vital requisite to solve inheritance quarrels in immigrant societies where men often had one family back home and another abroad.

Like elsewhere in South-East Asia when opportunities surfaced, the wave of migration came mainly from the southern provinces of China. Hokkien, Teochew, Cantonese and Hakka-speaking villagers migrated to try their luck and, as happens even today, they were followed by their children, parents, relatives and friends. The need for cheap labor for plantations and mines as well as the building boom in Singapore and Kuala Lumpur readily absorbed the newcomers, at least while they were needed.

Five hours after the Englishman had met his visitor, three Morris vans filled with policemen dressed in civvies meandered through the throng of bullock carts, rickshaws, horse-drawn carriages and motorcars crowding the main venues of the city. The motorcade headed towards an insignificant shop house about a mile and a half from Raffles Hotel. Inside the van, the officers gave the men final instructions: One van was to drive around the back of the shop house to cut off an escape. The other two were to park some distance away. The men were to amble leisurely in small groups of no more than three, towards the front of the shop house, chatting with each other as if on a stroll. When all had gathered near the entrance of the building, the operation would start with the shout "Harry" by the chief officer. In the back of the van, the senior policemen once again passed around the drawing with the exact location: One flight of stairs leading up from the shop house entrance, then turn left on top of the landing. The first two men were to kick down the first door on the right and burst into the room. The others would follow, brandishing handguns. If anyone tried to escape or resist, the order was to shoot.

Shop houses can be a maze of rooms, some functioning as living quarters, others as shops, or storerooms, sometimes as opium dens or brothels. So the detailed map the informant had given the policeman at Raffles Hotel was a blessing. He had clearly marked the room where the meeting was being held. The informant had even drawn the square table around which the five executive members of the Singapore Town Committee of the Communist Party of Malaya would hold their meeting. And he had identified each man by name, all of them Chinese.

The raid went swimmingly as per the records of senior police. In one fell swoop, the authorities had dismantled the entire cupola of the fledgling communist movement. The communists, buoyed by the events in Russia and now China, had emerged two years earlier to stir things up among wharf workers who were paid a pittance for their backbreaking labor. Their pamphlets and speeches did not bother the authorities, until the first strikes occurred. This cost the transport companies and shipping lines money and upset the clockwork rhythm of the city. Worst of all the strikes challenged the Empire's rule of law. Suddenly a complacent colonial administration, which had dismissed the new socialist fanatics as a storm in a teacup, realized the communists not only demanded workers rights and higher wages, but called for a government by the proletariat—the rabble, the coolies, the indentured Indian laborers. Such an exhortation was synonymous with rebellion. Singapore's colonial rulers had no intention to allow a Russian-style popular uprising or wait for the mob to storm and torch the austere governor's palace propped above the city.

In retrospect, the raid on the shop house influenced the future of Malaya for the next 45 years and tested, for the first time, the efficiency of "Our Man in Singapore," the super spy the Home Office in London had groomed to infiltrate this new communist threat to British colonial rule.

The police crashed into the room. The five communist cadres, the executive committee of the yet to be publicly proclaimed Communist Party of Malaya, gaped at the pistols pointed at their heads. Two of them cursed loudly. Then the five were quickly hauled away in the vans.

Within days all five were deported to China, the fate the colonial administration had decreed for any Chinese identified as a communist activist or sympathizer. Being deported would have been a minor punishment but then the unfortunate deportee was handed to a China still controlled by Chiang Kai-shek's Kuomintang. For the Nationalists, a communist was a traitor. The deportee would be charged with treason and sentenced to death. The British were wily: Rather than dirty their own hands and cause popular outrage by executing "communist troublemakers", the authorities simply pushed captured communists into the waiting arms of the Chinese Nationalists who did the killing for them. The British media would occasionally complain about the barbarity of such executions but it suited the colonial administration since reports of the executions intimidated citizens who may have been tempted to flirt with the Maoist version of communism. As an empire publicly priding itself on its enlightened rule,

Britain did not want to be accused of being callous or barbaric by executing people for their ideological beliefs. The killing was done in China, not on British territory.

The elimination of the communist party hierarchy gave the lower ranks an opportunity to advance up the party ladder. Among those who progressed to a more prominent position in the party nomenclature was Our Man in Singapore.

■

At most other times, Ong Boon Hua would have followed in his father's footsteps as a shopkeeper of bicycle accessories. Born and brought up in a typical shop house in Sitiawan, Perak, together with ten siblings, he might have built a commercial empire based on bicycles, mopeds, even motorbikes and motorcars. Intelligent and ruthlessly single-minded, he might have turned into another Chinese taipan, one of those movers-and-shakers who run Southeast Asia today.

As the son of a an émigré from China and a second generation Malay-Chinese mother, young Ong offered no hint of a future that was to stamp an indelible mark on the Malaysian peninsula, cause the violent deaths of thousands during a four-decade long civil war and the conviction among Southeast Asians that Beijing and its communist doctrine controlled the Chinese Diaspora. In Ong's case, that conviction proved to be true as he metamorphosed from an idealistic youth into a communist guerrilla leader, a hero for some, a scourge for most, menace for every capitalist in the region and a loyal follower of directives from China.

As a boy, Ong sang in a Methodist church choir. He was offered a scholarship in a Catholic College, which he turned down because he felt the Catholic faith was "too severe". He preferred his mother's far gentler and less dogmatic Buddhism. At home he spoke two Chinese dialects. He learned Malay and English at school and from his father, a Chinese patriot with a political mind, he learned that China was destined to play a leading role in world affairs. Intellectually armed in this way, his teenage years were quickly shaped by the momentous events of the 1930s that pushed young men in the Chinese Diaspora relentlessly towards a political choice. In general, émigré societies concentrate on material gains, rarely on politics or 'isms. The Chinese buy politicians. Only the third or fourth generation of émigrés tends to branch out into politics once assured of a solid financial foundation.

As the Japanese conquests unfolded in Asia, the teenager, like most ethnic Chinese youths, was torn between loyalty to Mao Zedong and Chiang Kai-shek. In the end it was Mao's writings that won him over to communist ideals. Maoism was closer to the indignation he felt over the subservient role assigned to the Chinese in a colonial Malaya ruled by Britain and lorded over by white planters, men smoking pipes and gulping gin and tonics at swanky Planters' Clubs marked "Europeans Only". These colonial rulers posted blatantly racist placards on public parks and gardens advising: "No dogs or Chinese". He saw these men bullying their Chinese servants in the belief that being harsh was the best way to control the Chinese and prevent them rioting just as they had done in other parts of colonized Asia once their numbers had multiplied.

The white colonizers felt they had a valid concern in a Malaya where the ethnic Chinese population was 2.6 million strong in colonial days, superseding the 2.4 million native Malays and the 600,000 Indians. This demographic majority would be inverted to favor the Malay population after independence and the passage of the Bumiputra laws, which granted preferential treatment to ethnic Malays in scholarships, civil service, business licenses and reservation of land. This policy enraged the ethnic Chinese and led to the expulsion of Singapore from the Malaysian Federation. Singapore was a Chinese dominated port city. Today it is a Chinese City Republic.

Young Ong often peered over the fence into colonial clubs where white ladies in chiffon gowns strolled below white parasols through blooming flower gardens while their husbands played bridge or rummy on the terrace or tennis on the manicured grass courts. Sometimes he and his friends were caught peeping by the turbaned guard who chased them a few yards, more out of duty than conviction.

The boy might have lived the rest of his life under this condescending British administration, accepting the inbred arrogance of the colonial masters and their ridiculous belief that nothing and no one was superior to the English or their way of life. But destiny intervened. The Japanese invaded China. The invasion converted ethnic Chinese everywhere into instant enemies of Japan, raised their sense of patriotism and their willingness to contribute to the Chinese war chest. Fired by patriotism,

Ong became a student leader at the age of 14, showing for the first time his talent to inflame and lead others. He was active in raising funds for China's liberation. Had he been older he would have volunteered, like other young men, for military service in China. Yet he was soon to have his own chance to take up arms when in December 1941 General Tomoyuki Yamashita's 25th Japanese Army crashed into the Malayan peninsula with lightning speed and scant opposition. The British hurriedly withdrew, promising to fight another day, allowing the Japanese to annex Malaya's rich tin mines and rubber estates for the Empire of the Rising Sun.

Soon after the Japanese conquest, Ong Boon Hua metamorphosed into an ogre for his new colonial masters and a revered resistance fighter for the Chinese and native Malays, a mysterious, faceless figure known only by the nom de guerre Chin Peng.

■

In those days Malay Chinese had two choices if they felt patriotic: Side with Chiang Kai-shek's Kuomintang or Nationalist Party or Mao's Communists. The choice often depended on social status. The working class, the lumpen-proletariat and many intellectuals had a natural predilection for the kind of people's power that Mao's grandiose proletarian dictatorship offered. It was a style of communism celebrated by propaganda emanating from the Soviet Union, which prior to World War II, was still regarded as a bastion of workers' rights and aspirations. News of the gulags and the horrors of Stalin's purges had not yet percolated to the rest of the world. But in Malaya, the colonial administration, the upper class and well-to-do shopkeepers already viewed communism with growing trepidation, as a challenge to their status and a threat to their property. The foremost among those "colonial" Chinese were the Straits-born ones, nearly all of them staunchly pro-British and imitating the colonial masters in dress, speech and manners, not unlike the first generation of African independence leaders who were educated in Britain and did their utmost to copy British colonial lifestyle and colonial exploitation once the white masters had turned their colonies over to black disciples educated with a white man's mindset. In Malaya, the Japanese occupation was anathema to the Straits-born Chinese whose only desire was to be rid of the "yellow devils" and bring back the British and their own privileged lifestyle. Yet for the Communists and the majority of Malays, all determined to fight the invaders, the goal was not to bring back the British but to rout the Japanese and then declare independence. All sides, whether communist, capitalist, pro-Mao or pro-Chiang, loathed the invaders but saw in the invasion an opportunity to realize their dreams.

Many years later, when he was older and wiser, Chin Peng admitted he made a fatal error when the Communist Party advocated a post-Japanese government that would be a "dictatorship of the proletariat". In his autobiography, My Side of History, published in 2003, he admits he should have united all of Malaya, communists, capitalists and Malays under the unifying battle cry of independence.

He should have figured that under independence his own Red Army had a good chance, just like the Maoists, to convert Malaya into a communist nation, by force if necessary. Like Mao he firmly believed power comes from the barrel of a gun and not the ballot box. In his envisaged proletarian dictatorship all plantation land was to be confiscated, state-owned and worked as cooperatives, just like in Maoist China, his model.

(Diverse opinions inside the party about land distribution led to a split and a purge later when one of the party's most senior cadres, Siew Lau, the Malacca Strait Security chief, proclaimed all land would be distributed to the landless and those who had worked it as serfs. For this heresy the cadre, his wife and two bodyguards were executed in 1950, a signal that, just like in China, the party in Malaya would not tolerate dissent by reactionaries even if it meant this would cause desertions and splits.)

The Japanese invasion of Manchuria and Tokyo's subsequent annexation of three northeastern Chinese provinces in 1931 had already generated strong patriotic feelings throughout the Chinese Diaspora, certainly among fledgling communist sympathizers in Malaya. As a teenager, Ong (as he was known then) was already drawn to communism, especially Mao's fateful booklet On Protracted War. The booklet became a kind of gospel and beacon for him during the next five decades. As Chin Peng, he gave a whole new meaning to "protracted war" and faith in a credo.

Towards the end of his life he wrote:

"Conversion to communism is as strong as a religious conversion. It provides a faith and belief in a system which, at least to the convert, appears as the incontrovertible true path to what is right and fair among human beings... ."

Before the Japanese arrived in Malaya, communism had captured the imagination of the poorer members of society and worried the British administration. The British realized that leftist ideals—self-determination, social justice and an end to colonialism—were poisoning society against them. Maoism was being propagated by the youthful and dynamic communists. Never half-hearted in their reaction to the possibility of rebellion, the British proscribed communism, accusing its adherents of organizing strikes for better wages as well as inciting anti-British activities, charges that were true. Further, Malayan communists openly supported the Maoists in China while the British preferred to covertly court Chiang's Kuomintang, whose brutal but effective style of government was more in tune with the mercenary profiteering of British colonialism and empire-building than the Maoist idea of handing the country over to peasants.

Young and idealistic Ong was horrified by the callous nature of the suppression. Ethnic Chinese suspected of being communists or caught in a demonstration were simply deported to China even if they were born in Malaya. Once in China, they were usually executed as traitors by the Kuomintang. In no time the colonial authorities had cleansed Malaya of some 5,000 senior "trouble-makers" plus their families, totaling about 20,000 Malay Chinese being pushed into China. Families were broken up, the parents exiled, the children left with relatives. This brutal method was not only employed against Chinese protesters but also against Indian indentured labor which, once unemployed, was simply shipped back to India as deck cargo on freighters, irrespective of whether they had children or spouses born in Malaya. The seed of violent anti-British hatred was planted in those days and would grow and pursue the British until their withdrawal from the colony in 1957.

■

The defense of Malaya was certainly not one of Britain's finest hours. The lightning-fast advance of General Yamashita with an inferior number of troops found the colonial forces ill-prepared and, as has happened so often in British history, poorly led by bumbling officers more at home in social clubs than on the battle field. The British ignominiously withdrew, leaving Singapore and their rich Malaya colony to the forces and mercy of the children of the Rising Sun who promptly subjected captured soldiers, sailors and civilians to brutal treatment at Singapore's Changi Prison or on the Burma Railroad.

By this time, Ong had moved quickly through the ranks of the student movement and the China Relief Fund, which elected him as secretary general at the tender age of 15. The fund's chief supporter was Singapore entrepreneur and multi-millionaire Tan Kah Kee. In 1938 Ong had become a member of the newly founded and illegal Communist Party of Malaya (CPM). He was then 14 but told the party he was 16. Three years later he was already a member of the executive committee, the decision-making inner circle. By the time war broke out he was in charge of a small but growing guerrilla army, which raided Japanese supply lines and positions but often had to purify its own ranks of traitors or turncoats, those who allegedly collaborated with the Japanese. These periodic purges prompted critics of the CPM to complain after the war—with some justification—that the communists had killed more of their own than they had killed Japanese soldiers.

The Chinese are pragmatic. Many saw in the new conquerors the opportunity to become "useful" in advancing their personal fortunes. After all, in neighboring Indonesia, the Chinese had for generations been useful to the Dutch, virtually running the Indonesian colony's day-to-day affairs for the colonizers. Seizing opportunities is a basic instinct in an over-populated China, where each citizen is conscious that chances of financial, social or academic progress are limited by the enormous number active in pursuing them.

Although many collaborators were at heart loyal to China and had embraced communism, or at least party membership, they could not resist doing business with the Japanese—and sometimes selling information in return for concessions from the new colonial bosses. On the other hand, the young, fanatical and rigidly Maoist guerrillas could neither understand nor pardon anyone who betrayed their sacrosanct credo and with it the party and its ambitions to take over Malaya. The number of collaborators executed or assassinated runs into many hundreds and seemed to have taken up most of the guerrilla operations before London decided the communist fighters could be better harnessed in the war against the Japanese. In fact the communists could help to ensure that one day the Union Jack would flutter again over Malaya.

War often brings together strange bedfellows. The British contacted the CPM—principally an ethnic Chinese organization, which the British had proscribed—and offered to supply its guerrilla army with weapons, ammunition, money and training. In return the CPM would collaborate with British Special Forces dropped behind enemy lines and would accept British agents working with the guerrillas. This unholy alliance was sealed on December 31, 1943. The text of the understanding was written on a page torn from a school notebook.

One of the senior members of the Communist Party delegation present at the signing ceremony was Ong, now operating under the codename Chin Peng. He was 19 years old. He would remark later on the irony of this alliance when overnight the much maligned communists—hitherto persecuted, executed, exiled and demonized daily as heartless killers—were promoted to brave allies... .

"... We were fine fellows and no one thought killing the Japanese made us murderers..." Chin wrote in his memoirs, but wistfully added: "I was aware of Britain's determination to reinstall her colonial supremacy once the Pacific War was over. We were then the only functioning resistance movement. I had no illusion about bonding with the British. I knew my old imperialist masters would soon be my enemies again. For both sides it was a deal with the devil... ."

The overall assumption of the British was presumptuous and utterly in character with their imperial arrogance: They felt it would be perfectly reasonable for Malayans to accept that Britain, a white man's nation, must reclaim Malaya as its colony with native help. In fact the same native population, which was discriminated against for decades as inferior creatures, must now fight the Japanese and possibly die for a return to British rule. After all, Malaya was part of Britain's empire.

The communists accepted the deal because it would provide them with weapons, money and training and bring into their ranks young non-communists eager to fight the Japanese. Once under Maoist tutelage, these youngsters, who streamed in from universities and colleges, could be easily indoctrinated. In fact the guerrilla army was soon swelled by thousands of idealistic youths who felt they were fighting for Malayan independence rather than a return of the British. But the majority of these new recruits soon drifted away, worn out by the unexpected hardships and deprivations of jungle living as well as the rigid and dogmatic training in Maoist doctrine and guerrilla warfare.

Chin Peng and the party hierarchy made it clear to their new British allies that the communists would retain command over operations although they accepted the presence of British "advisers". Years later the CIA used the ploy in conflict zones such as South Korea, Vietnam and South America where such advisers trained either the rebels, the resistance or government forces, depending on which side was pro-American. The British, accustomed to having their way in the colonies, figured they could lure the communists into the British camp after the war by offering them lucrative commissions and other baits—plus medals for their bravery.

■

In the early days of British-communist collaboration, Chin Peng's work was cloak and dagger stuff. Already considered a seasoned jungle fighter, he would be rowed offshore to a rendezvous with a British submarine to take delivery of one or two "advisers". Using his local knowledge and contacts, he ferried these military men through the jungle to his guerrilla camp.

The cooperation between the communist guerrillas and the British military developed gradually, nurtured by their common desire to see the departure of the Japanese from Malaya. Yet no one believed the British High Command intended to use the guerrillas beyond the recapture of the colony. In fact British officers training and arming the guerrillas had already been told they must ensure the military capability of the communists remained limited to the point where they would not become a threat once colonial rule was restored. Ideally, so the unwritten instruction went, the military capacity of the communists should be exhausted by the time Malaya was retaken. The tacit hope was: The more communists died in the recovery of the colony the better for posterity. Worse, the bilateral accord of mutual cooperation, which Chin Peng had witnessed, stipulated that after the Japanese were routed, the guerrillas must hand back all weapons "borrowed" from the British. The idea was, as Friedrich Schiller wrote so succinctly: 'The Moor has done his duty, the Moor can go!"

If all this sounds naïve, even infantile, one has to remember that the British hierarchy, with some exceptions, had for some time underestimated the mood in their colonies. London forgot that a war victory was certain to galvanize native clamor for liberty from the colonial yoke and a demand for self-rule. Worse, with its military capacity mauled by the sacrifices of World War II, it was obvious the old style empire was well and truly moribund and was being rapidly replaced by a new kind of Americanized colonization. This new method was far more economical than the cumbersome "invade-occupy-administer" system of the British. It was also far more lucrative. One simply paid off the country's leaders to gain access to its resources and markets. It was grandly called "bilateral cooperation" and the mass media, always the lackeys of those in power, doted on occasions when flamboyantly dressed and be-medaled foreign dignitaries and U.S. officials signed documents of mutual understanding that was no more than mutual exploitation, with the American share many times greater than the relatively paltry deposits transferred into the Swiss bank accounts of native chieftains. The system was reminiscent of the Conquest of the Far West when Red Indian chiefs with feathered heads signed away their land for a few medals and a sack of glass baubles.

The Americans were masters of this new "Empire of Bilateral Exploitation".

On the other side of the Atlantic, London still struggled with the old system, one based on military might and old fashioned intelligence, the kind of suave, well-dressed Oxford-Cambridge-educated Mister Fix-It later globalized by the James Bond movies or glorified by legends such as that of Lawrence of Arabia.

■

The British have always been fascinated by good, old fashioned spying. Perhaps that's why so many high-ranking British spymasters ended up spying for and eventually defecting to Moscow. Yet in the voluminous annals of espionage, rarely can one find a double agent as successful or as ruthless as the person British spy chiefs dubbed Our Man in Singapore.

Spies fall into four main types: Those who spy for money, those who spy to save their lives, those who follow ideological dreams and those who want to promote their personal ambitions. Our Man in Singapore combined all four categories even though Major Satoru Onishi of the Japanese military intelligence outfit, Kempeitai, would tell his judges after the war that Our

Man in Singapore's main motivation was "to save his own neck, even at the expense of his comrades".

The Major was sentenced to life for his part in the wartime atrocities in Malaya. He spoke of his informant with the disdain of a soldier who loathes traitors, informers and those disloyal to the cause. At his trial, he unmasked the shady, subservient character he had ordered to appear twice a week at Kempeitai headquarters in Singapore to report on the location and movement of guerrilla forces and the whereabouts of senior communist cadres. He described this man as short, slim and with Eurasian in looks, someone who spoke softly and with an accent both in English and Mandarin. The informer used at least three aliases known to the Japanese. The Major said the man admitted he was born in Vietnam. His French was immaculate but not so his claim of having studied in Soviet Russia, or his boast that he had been part of the Communist Shanghai Committee and had accompanied Ho Chi Minh to Saigon to organize the communist movement in 1920. These claims were false, the Major bluntly told his interrogators. However he had not questioned them because the man's information was so precise and consistent that he was not about to jeopardize a source of information that ensured the guerrillas represented no real threat to the Japanese during the three years of their occupation.

Onishi was surprisingly forthcoming with information about a man whose spying activities had won the Major not only medals but promotion. From his interrogations it became apparent that the informer had been active in the Viet Minh movement but was captured by French intelligence and probably turned into a double agent. Most likely he was sent by either the Viet Minh or by French intelligence to Singapore, where, furnished with credentials from the Vietnamese communists, he obtained work on the wharves, notorious for being a communist hotbed, and was soon engaged in union activities. He became a prominent activist in the fledgling communist movement after the five leading members of the movement were mysteriously arrested in a swoop by the British in 1934 and expelled to China. There was no doubt the informer had worked for the British, and possibly the French, as soon as he arrived in Singapore. More astonishingly, he also provided information, some of it valuable, to the Viet Minh in Saigon. And as soon as the Japanese arrived, he was on their payroll too. In other words Our Man in Singapore was flying all flags, playing all sides against each other and for his own benefit.

He had joined the nascent CPM, betraying its members and its activities in measured doses of information to the British. The Japanese Major told his interrogators he was sure that once the Union Flag resumed flying over Malaysia, the informer had offered his services again to the British. This assumption was later confirmed as was the Major's cynical conclusion that the informant used both the Japanese and the British to eliminate those members in the CPM who might have exposed him or challenge his role in the party.

The Major, who would be released after serving only five years of his life sentence, admitted, somewhat ruefully, that his Man in Singapore had not told him everything. In fact, he had carefully siphoned his information to give the Japanese what was useful to further his own ambitions and remove obstacles in the pursuit of these ambitions. This realization, too late, seemed to have visibly peeved the Major who felt he had been used by the informant and had failed in his mission to obtain the entire picture or the man's real identity and motives within the communist party. Major Onishi admitted he deserved to be imprisoned, not for war crimes but for failure in his duty.

∎

Some people, or organizations, never fully recover from a betrayal. It haunts their future like a shadow. It can warp their perception of others and turn trust into permanent suspicion. It can make people and organizations over-react to any indication, insinuation or even unsubstantiated rumors of treason. Worse, in time it can convert an organization into an introvert self consuming itself, gnawing at its own entrails in the frenetic search for a mole, more moles and finally an entire network of moles—all within itself.

The CPM, almost entirely made up of ethnic Chinese, soon became aware there was a traitor in its midst. In the search to find the traitor, the party and its regional branches launched one purge after another, each more extreme than the last. As a result, many innocent party members became classified as deserters or traitors and the party split into splinter groups. Members went over to the less sanguine side or to the enemy to escape being assassinated or executed by their comrades on mere suspicion or someone's denunciation. In their crazed endeavor to root out the traitor or traitors, the party passed a regulation that those who had betrayed the party would be spared execution if they named other traitors. More enticing still, the traitors-turned-informers-on-their-own-people would only have to spend three years in re-education camps and then would be allowed to re-enter party ranks. This policy, known as "repentance" would be successfully employed by the Italian authorities to dismantle the urban communist guerrilla groups of the 1980s. Needless to say, many of the accused, innocent or not, quickly pointed the finger at more innocents to save their own neck. In Perak province alone, more than 150 "traitors" were executed, most of them denounced by other "traitors". Party purges, rather than the fight against the Japanese, became a major preoccupation and the most divisive cause of party solidarity and efficiency. These destructive inner-party purges would continue even after the British retook Malaya. Often the purges coincided with the periodic purges in Mao's China, the role model of the CPM.

All these misfortunes were mainly the result of the betrayal of one man who remained faceless.

■

The chink in the armor of the CPM, just as in the Chinese party, was the rigid adherence to party discipline and the virtual deification of party leadership and supreme "leader". The revered secretary general or chairman had to be obeyed and venerated no matter what idiocy he ordered or committed. This idolatry was copied from the Chinese communists and their disastrous loyalty to an often erratic and unrealistic Mao, perhaps a legacy of imperial days when the Chinese emperor was God on earth and deemed infallible. If Mao's grandiose and impractical projects often resulted in the deaths of tens of millions of Chinese in famines, purges and campaigns to weed out ideological renegades, the undisputable loyalty to party leaders in Malaya would cause similar disasters and loss of life, of course, on a proportionally smaller scale.

The awareness that a rotten apple was inside the party basket began soon after Our Man in Singapore arrived on the Malayan peninsula in 1932. In Singapore city alone, between 1932 and 1935, police carried out 432 raids against suspected communist households and arrested 226 suspects. Most of those arrested were unceremoniously deported to China, without legal recourse. The majority of those arrested were denounced from inside the movement.

As experienced leaders were captured, they had to be replaced by less experienced men from the middle ranks. In this way, some recruits who had either good connections or friends in the upper party echelon enjoyed meteoric promotions. Among those promoted gradually was the traitor. Of course, the majority of the new cadres were young, some of them barely out of their teens, fired with the enthusiasm of youth and loyal to the few older officials, especially the sacrosanct figure of the party chairman. By 1938 when the movement finally founded the official CPM, only a few of its original members had survived. Among them was a middle-aged man known as Lai Te. A smooth talker, ingratiating and apparently well informed about world affairs, he was elected as the first party chairman, or secretary general, of the CPM. One of the party's first directives was that he had to be protected and had to remain concealed at all cost in order to forestall the fate that befell other senior cadres who had been picked up so easily by British intelligence. Lai Te was given the credentials and the appearance of a bona fide businessman engaged in import and export. He lived in relative luxury and quickly married a woman cadre of the newly formed party who bore him a child nine months later. Lai Te became the most ardent supporter of secrecy and insisted his person must never be exposed to the lower ranks and his identity must remain a faceless mystery. Only his name must be on everyone's lips. Given the past history of arrests, the young party members, many of them naïve and credulous, thoroughly agreed with their chairman's penchant for secrecy. So began the system of cumbersome party communications that sometimes left regional branches incommunicado for months and their senior cadres running their own private wars.

Ong had joined the party in the founding year by telling the party selection committee that he was not 14 years old but 16. In conformity with the new party rules for anonymity, he assumed the code name Chin Peng. Like nearly all the new recruits, he was fiercely devoted and loyal to the chairman, whose knowledge of international affairs and inside information on Comintern (Third Communist International) deliberations and decisions, left Chin and his comrades in awe. The number of arrests waned in the following months, a sure sign—or so the comrades told each other—that the new security precautions instituted by their chairman were bearing fruit. Despite his tender age, Chin Peng soon became active in organizing armed resistance to the colonial masters who, the party doctrine specified, had to be expelled from Malaya to make way for a dictatorship of the proletariat. His youthful devotion won Lai Te's confidence and when the first guerrilla groups were created, Chin Peng was deputed to lead the one in Perak. Like most youngsters inflamed by an ideal, he showed exceptional bravery in those first forays against the British and their commercial interests.

Handicapped by cumbersome communications, their lack of weapons and the constant fear of betrayal, the guerrilla operations were minor incidents and posed no major worry to the British. All this however would change dramatically once the Japanese invaded and the British, hurriedly and ignominiously, withdrew from the peninsula.

■

With the Japanese arrival came also the paranoia of betrayal. Soon the witch hunts for traitors and collaborators eroded the efficiency of a guerrilla movement, which had been inflated in numbers by patriotism and youthful idealism even among native Malays who previously had little to do with a party made up almost entirely of ethnic Chinese. The Japanese occupation forces were conscious of these ethnic and religious differences between the two main communities and knew how to capitalize on the rift between Muslim Malays and mainly Buddhist or Taoist Chinese. Their most successful operation to stoke this communal conflict was launched soon after they occupied the country. A group of armed Japanese soldiers dressed up as Chinese guerrillas invaded a Johore mosque where they calmly slaughtered a pig. This contrived act of sacrilege precipitated one of the first serious race riots pitting the Chinese against the Malays, further stoking the rivalry between natives and immigrants. Racial and religious tension would hang over the Malayan peninsula like a Damocles sword for decades to come. It still surfaces today when unscrupulous politicians or officials fuel the simmering fire of hatred and mutual recriminations for their own benefits. The ethnic rivalry would lead to the secession of mainly Chinese Singapore from the Malaysian Federation in 1965.

The Japanese, thus, effectively raised tensions between the two communities. Yet their main success in eliminating armed resistance was far more destructive, thanks to the invaluable information of Our Man in Singapore, who had switched his services from the British to the Japanese.

In the summer of 1942, CPM Chairman Lai Te caused bewilderment among his followers by calling for a restructuring of Malaya's industrial base. This was virtually a call on workers to return to their jobs in the tin mines and rubber factories, which had been idle since the Japanese invasion. For the guerrillas on the frontline this made no sense since any revitalized industrial activity could only benefit the Japanese. As a good communist Lai Te explained that by rekindling the country's industrial base, workers would be able to earn an income and this would alleviate the current suffering and poverty among the labor force and gain the party popularity. It seemed to make sense.

In order to discuss this revitalization of industry and other burning issues such as communications, Lai Te convened a meeting of the 40 senior cadres of the party. In his memoirs Chin Peng said the reunion was to take place on September 1, 1942, in the Batu Cave region of Selangor not far from the village of Sungai Dua, also known among the Chinese as the village of Shi Shan Jiao. Four women guerrillas were given cooking duty and a ten-man detachment from the Selangor unit provided security. The cadres were to show up a day early and discuss preliminary issues that would then be presented at a plenum attended by the Chairman.

The meeting was immediately betrayed to Japanese military intelligence. Given an opportunity to eliminate the entire party nomenclature in one stroke, the Japanese went about their task stealthily but with considerable planning. Little by little, over days, they infiltrated into the Batu Cave area soldiers dressed in civvies, as if they were on R&R leave. Military intelligence even imported prostitutes to carouse with the troops and add to the impression by local observers working for the guerrillas that the Japanese were creating a holiday camp.

The mask of convivial soldiers on recreational leave dropped shortly after midnight on August 31 when the Japanese troops, gathered over days, suddenly went on a war footing and surrounded the camp site where the meeting was to be held a few hours later. The attack, however, lost its surprise element when a vigilant guerrilla guard gave the alarm and immediately began firing at the invaders, alerting his companions, many of them asleep. Few cadres were armed since they had been sluiced through villages and towns and possible body checks to arrive at the meeting. But those who had brought or procured weapons gave the Japanese an unexpectedly hard time as the soldiers advanced on their huts.

During the fierce firefight, the entire guerilla security unit of ten men was wiped out by the advancing enemy. The senior cadres of the party tried to slip away but more then 20 of the 40 invited cadres were killed, some fighting on bravely even after they were wounded, in order to cover the escape of others. Those who did break through, including Chin Peng, quickly separated to seek refuge in friendly Chinese villages. The Japanese also suffered heavy casualties, among them a Lieutenant Colonel, a Major and a Captain.

There was one consolation for the guerillas: Their beloved Chairman Lai Te had escaped unscathed. His car had broken down well before he reached the caves. Despite heavy losses, providence had been on their side.

Of course, no one doubted that the meeting had been betrayed by a senior cadre and suspicion quickly fell on a delegate who had not arrived at the meeting. It was soon—and conveniently—discovered that the man had been arrested by the Japanese, tortured and later executed. As far as the party hierarchy was concerned, he had obviously talked under torture and given away the location of the meeting. The reality was different: In this subtle way, the traitor and his masters had struck a major blow against the resistance and at the same time averted suspicion falling on the real culprit by arresting and executing a scapegoat. It was a fiendish plot. But it would be the beginning of many.

The next meeting of the remaining politburo was held in an abandoned rubber plantation deep in the jungle. This time Chin Peng took personal charge of security. He writes that he made separate arrangements for the arrival of senior cadres so that each would only know his point of rendezvous but not the exact location of the plenum. And yet to everyone's chagrin, the participants had to escape helter-skelter even before they arrived at the meeting when Japanese troops raided a nearby village and captured two delegates from Perak. One of the two was executed when he refused to divulge information, even under torture. The second delegate saved his life by turning informant for the Kempeitai. The rest of the communist party hierarchy, including ideologue Cai Ke-ming and chairman Lai Te either managed to escape unharmed or were told to turn back before arriving. The entire party nomenclature scattered like scared chickens in all directions, seeking refuge among sympathizers or in jungle hideouts. Apart from the loss of two senior cadres, the worst deficit from this second meeting was the apparent inability of the resistance groups to meet and elaborate an agenda against the Japanese. It was clear the Kempeitai and their spy had a major objective: To thwart all efforts by the CPM to meet and coordinate their anti-Japanese activities. One after another, plans for a plenum were betrayed. No one had doubts now that a traitor existed and he must be a high-ranking party official, someone not just within the provincial leadership but someone inside the Central Committee, the inner sanctum of the party.

But who?

With morale eroded by the constant acts of treason, suspicion fell on everyone. Eventually the rumor passing through senior ranks was that the traitor was none other than the party's Number Two, Jhang Huang Shi. That rumor quickly evaporated when the Kempeitai captured and executed Jhang, apparently after a tip-off. Obviously the traitor feared that if Jhang were accused by the party and tortured, he might come up with the name of the real culprit in his efforts to exonerate himself. But worse was to follow. Jhang's capture was only the beginning. He had apparently talked. Within days the Japanese systematically dismantled the CPM's Singapore-based Central Committee, the party's backbone and brains trust. The arrests and the growing suspicion of a major leak in the CPM alienated those guerrillas who were not communists but had pledged to support the insurgency against the Japanese.

In the end the anti-Japanese resistance was never really coordinated and the "traitor" remained at large. The CPM leaders would boast about their anti-Japanese sacrifices in the years to come but in reality little was achieved despite the weapons drops by the British and the presence of British advisers who trained the guerrillas in a type of warfare that would become far more successful once the Japanese surrendered and the British returned to Malaya.

∎

The returning colonial masters had neither changed their attitude nor taken into account that the war had galvanized strong emotions for self-rule. One by one colonies had to be handed over to their natives, in Indonesia, the Philippines, Vietnam, India, Sri Lanka and across the African continent. But in Malaya, with its precious tin and rubber, military officers and planters acted in the same arrogant manner of pre-war days. British bureaucracy simply continued with the practices and regulations imposed on the country prior to the Japanese invasion. For those who fought or resisted the Japanese, this was unacceptable. Popular discontent was fueled by the ridiculous order to ban the Japanese currency from one day to the other rather than to phase it out gradually or to swap it for a new currency at a decent exchange rate. Peasants and workers, those who had no nest eggs tucked away in pre-war British banks, found themselves destitute, penniless, their savings and cash worth nothing. The majority returned to the ancient custom of barter trade.

The returned colonial masters wallowed in the aura of triumph from a war they had not won in Malaya, a colony they regained with a victory handed to them by the atom bombs on Hiroshima and Nagasaki. Still, behind the show of "life goes on as before", the British High Command had one nagging worry: The communist party and its guerrilla units could become a major obstacle to continued colonial rule by the Old Boys Club. The communists had to be neutralized. Again lack of creativity predominated. The officials pulled from their dusty drawers the durable recipe of awarding trinkets and imperial honors for native chieftains. The strategy had worked for centuries, why would it not work now?

One of those singled out for particular attention was Chin Peng, the dynamic young guerrilla leader who had often acted as the liaison officer between the Malayan resistance and the office of Lord Mountbatten, commander-in-chief of the virtually token British South-East Asian command based in the distant colonial safe haven known as Ceylon, today Sri Lanka.

In one of those ironies of war, Chin Peng was honored for his bravery in the service of the English Crown, with the Order of the British Empire (OBE). He also received two combat medals for courage under fire. In subsequent years the British did their best to erase these awards from public memory, especially after the authorities posted a quarter million sterling reward for the capture of Chin Peng alive and half that prize-money if someone brought in his corpse.

Other guerrilla fighters were awarded similar medals. To attract these young men to the side of the good guys, the British organized an elaborate victory ceremony in Singapore to which a number of key communist fighters were invited, including Chin Peng. The men were to be personally decorated by the commander-in-chief, now back in the colony. The jungle fighters, used to life in shelters, huts and on bare ground, were lodged at the swanky five-star Raffles Hotel, the best in town, and feted with food and official attention.

At the same time the guerrillas, as they had promised in the accord written on a page of a school notebook, publicly surrendered the weapons the British had airdropped for them during the war years. Following the order of their Chairman, Lai Te, 4,000 guerrillas handed in their weapons and then quietly melted back into civilian life, but with the tacit understanding they were to be activated again.

The order to disband puzzled the communist rank and file, which had always been told the battle would go on until Malaya became an independent communist nation. Yet no one questioned Lai Te's weird decisions and strategies. He was the boss. He was infallible. Even senior cadres including Chin Peng felt the party Number One, with his stunning knowledge of international affairs, was acting in coordination with Comintern decisions in the Soviet Union and China. Questioning his directives was like challenging the parents of the credo. And challenges could be fatal, as Siew Lau had found out when he proclaimed his own vision for land distribution.

In Singapore, the ceremony for handing over of some 4,000 weapons was duly performed. But British officers must have wondered at the small amount being turned in and were surely suspicious at the ever ready explanation that the rest of the weapons air-dropped and off-loaded from ships during the war had been destroyed in the anti-Japanese battles, which everyone knew, had been rather limited in scope.

In his memoirs, Chin Peng admits his men kept some 5,000 British weapons and buried them in jungle hideouts together with Japanese arms and ammunitions captured when Japan surrendered and no British troops were present to disarm them. These caches, located in secret stashes around

Malaya, were known only to one or two local commanders and, in view of the unidentified traitor's activity, their locations were not passed on to the Central Committee. As it turned out, these arms dumps would sustain the guerrilla war and become a major headache for the British military, which was constantly combing the countryside to find them. Hundreds of rural people were interrogated, not always with the methods permitted by the Geneva Convention, to glean information on the dumps' whereabouts.

Meanwhile in Singapore, the cheap charade to win over the hearts and minds of the guerrillas with trinkets went reasonably well until the British decided a group of senior guerrilla fighters including Chin Peng must participate in a military parade of British power in Singapore, not as trophies, of course, but as allies in the anti-Japanese resistance and now as the friends of Britain. The participation of the guerrilla leaders would show to the public that the communists were now peaceful and on the side of His Majesty's colonial rulers.

The jungle fighters balked at this. They could stomach the good food, the soft beds and even the medals but not a public display of their loyalty to colonial masters, whose return to the pomp and power of the old days, they had not expected would come about so swiftly. Worse, the returned masters had made no pledges of self-rule except some vague phrases of future home rule for Malaya. And they had not offered the locals a say in running their own country. Much to everyone's dismay the Old Boys club had simply moved back in, lock, stock and barrel.

The guerrilla leaders led by Chin Peng refused to attend the parade. The British were furious. But their efforts at persuasion failed. Neither he nor his comrades were ready to betray their firm belief in an independent Malaya governed by a Maoist style dictatorship of the proletariat. Being paraded with the British or being filmed visiting their headquarters would send the wrong signal to those combatants disbanded and waiting for new orders. All entreaties by the British, soft or stern, met with a firm "no".

Then, the unexpected happened. No one could quite understand or believe that bowing to British will would guarantee a period of peace during which the party could reinvent itself as a pro-independence movement exerting diplomatic pressure on Britain and, if necessary, military pressure. But this is how Chairman Lai Te explained his order to cadres that they must attend the parade and visit the British HQ base. As always, the comrades obeyed, angry perhaps and certainly puzzled and unconvinced, but aware that failure to obey was like signing one's own death warrant. The rigid and blind code to follow orders from above was perhaps the most destructive flaw in the CPM since it did not allow criticism, the lifeblood of any nation or organization that wants to gain strength and achieve improvements.

But that is how the party was run.

■

One of the early problems in a country running low in victuals was what to do with the large number of Japanese soldiers who had been ordered to surrender by their emperor in a part of Asia they had conquered and never lost. The majority of the Japanese followed their emperor's orders. Some officers committed seppuku. Raffles Hotel was soaked in the blood of Japanese officers who sliced open their bellies and spilled their entrails on the parquet floors. But hundreds of soldiers wanted to fight on, refusing to believe the emperor had issued such an order. Entire battalions offered to fight the British, rather than surrender. These troops preferred to change allegiance and if need be, embrace an honorable death as soldiers. This type of desertion became a major worry to the British command, still unsure how much they could trust their reluctant war-time allies, the communists. In the absence of any other military force, the Japanese troops had handed over their arms and ammunition to the guerrillas, reinforcing the military capability of the CPM. The colonial authorities also knew that hundreds of Japanese soldiers had thrown in their lot with the resistance instead of surrendering to the British. Though disarmed, these Japanese were being treated like guests by the communists in their jungle camps and village strongholds.

The truth is the Japanese and their hosts lived in harmony for months before one of the most disgusting episodes of the post-war period occurred, an episode that would haunt the CPM forever and highlight the main flaw in its existence. Even Chin Peng, years later, would express his "shame" at what was done to those Japanese soldiers who thought they had found shelter and an opportunity to fight the British with the guerrillas.

The order came from Chairman Lai Te personally to all regional commanders. It was couched in a pragmatic explanation: Due to the scarcity of food and shelter, it was impossible to host the Japanese deserters any longer. Therefore, it was imperative for every guerrilla unit hosting such deserters to take them out into the jungle in small groups and "eliminate" them. These orders had to be followed with utmost secrecy, could not be discussed and the participants in these eliminations were to be sworn to utter secrecy.

And that is what happened with chilling Chinese efficiency—and slavish obedience.

■

While the CPM had made a public show of disbanding and handing over its weapons, the cadres returning to civilian life worked relentlessly among an increasingly restless population suffering hardships and deprivations during the changeover from one colonial rule to another. Party activists were behind many of the public protests demanding higher wages and jobs. The British responded with brute force, shooting unarmed protesters in a systematic crackdown of the kind the police or troops would never dare carry out in their own country. For dissidents and activists, this was evidence, easily exploited and publicized, that Asian lives were not as valuable as the lives of white people.

In this volatile atmosphere the case of merchant Chan Sau Meng led to a showdown between the populist communists and the British Military Administration (BMA) over who runs Malaya. Chan was arrested by communist cadres and charged with profiteering during the Japanese occupation. The local CPM commander, Soong Kwong, ordered the merchant to pay a small fine and then released him. But Chan complained to the British. The colonial administration arrested Soong and put him on trial to show the public that post-war rule by the CPM (before the British returned) was over. Communist chiefs such as Soong no longer had the right to administer justice. But the public mood was not in accord. At the trial, two of the three native judges found party chief Soong not guilty—a verdict received with loud applause and cheers—highly embarrassing the British administration. The British ordered a retrial. Once again, two of the three civilian judges found Soong not guilty, reflecting public indignation with those who had collaborated and profiteered under Japanese occupation.

Determined to make their point, the BMA set up another court, this time headed by three British military judges. Needless to say, they unanimously found Soong guilty of misconduct and sentenced him to four years in jail. In a fit of anger and egged on by popular fury at the verdict, Soong took off his shoes and hurled them at the chief justice, a sign of utmost disrespect. (In a more notorious instance of such show of disrespect, an Iraqi journalist threw his shoes at President George W. Bush during a press conference in 2008.)

■

The case, combined with protests, strikes and anti-British pamphlets, made the colonial administration aware of the potential for an insurgency and the urgent need to retrieve the weapons supplied generously to the guerrillas during the war. These arms—and by all estimates there must have been thousands of them—could now be used against the British.

(Decades later the Americans in Afghanistan faced the same dilemma: The shoulder-held Stinger missiles the CIA had supplied to the Afghan Mujahideen during their fight against the Soviet invaders, might now be turned on the Americans. A few years before the allied occupation of Afghanistan, the CIA desperately tried to buy back these Stingers, offering double and triple the production costs—with scant success.)

The specter of a well-armed insurgency prompted the British to activate their main asset: Our Man in Singapore. He had been re-recruited as soon as the Union Jack flew over Singapore once again. Apparently he had switched back as easily from the Japanese to the British as a man changes his shirts. But this time his masters demanded more than he considered safe for his personal security. For once, however much he argued, his controllers were adamant: The need to locate the arms caches was more important than his safety. With heavy heart and foreboding, the master spy must have issued the order to list all arms dumps, an order that could unmask him or, at least, seriously jeopardize his position inside the CPM. That he did issue the order was evidence the British military was desperate to lay their hands on the hidden arsenals of the communists. In the endeavor to neutralize the CPM's military sting, the spymasters pushed their star informant too far.

Once Chin Peng and other senior cadres received the order, they could only guffaw: Whose idiotic idea was it to compile a list of all dumps and make it available, not to the Central Committee, but to the Chairman in person? And why was the list to be accompanied by the names of those cadres who knew the location of these dumps?

Yet the cadres, separated by bad communications across various provinces, had not much chance to discuss the unusual order with one another. Besides, such a delicate matter could not be discussed by telephone. Those who did manage to communicate with Chin Peng were so startled they began to express thoughts and suspicions that had been lurking in their minds for years: Was it possible he was the traitor? Had he betrayed comrades and the party for the last 15 years, the very man they trusted and loved like a father, their iconic Chairman Lai Te?

The evidence was overwhelming: The raids on party meetings, the arrest and execution of so many comrades close to the Chairman who could have raised suspicion; the order under Japanese occupation for workers to return to tin mines and rubber plantations—which is what the Japanese most desired; the disbanding of the guerrilla army—which is what the British wanted most; the arrest of 600 Chinese volunteers recruited by the communists and about to embark for Vietnam to help the Viet Minh fight the French, the execution of the Japanese POWs ready to fight against the British. And finally this ultimate betrayal: Surrendering the arms that gave the party its main bargaining power with the British. Without those weapons the party had no teeth.

If Lai Te was the traitor the scope of his betrayal was heinous, equivalent to a Mao working for the Japanese or offering the location of his Red Army to Chang Kai-shek, or the Emperor of Japan turning over inside information to Washington. In his memoirs, Chin Peng claims suspicion had existed for some time but the Chairman's position was so exalted no one had the courage to voice their reservations or question openly why Lai Te had been blessed with such good fortune that each time a raid occurred during a meeting of senior party members, he was late because his car had broken down, a bridge had collapsed or he had missed a rendezvous with a guide. Before the war he had also been absent when British colonial police pounced on high-level communist party meetings. He was not present each time the Japanese attacked jungle camps. At one stage he was even held up at a Japanese checkpoint for two hours—until the raid on a party meeting he had obviously betrayed was over. The dots, suddenly connected, provided a chilling picture of a man ruthlessly eliminating his companions without any feeling of guilt or remorse.

In his memoirs, Chin Peng narrates that once during a Central Committee meeting he mustered the courage to mildly criticize the Chairman for condemning an innocent cadre for treason. Suddenly Lai Te broke into tears. With sobs he confessed he had been ill for some time but had no money to seek a cure. Immediately the mood changed. Every regional cadre contributed to a "Save Lai Te" fund and Lai Te vanished for several months, absent on a health cure. Then there were the two Committee members promoted to the inner sanctum of the party by Lai Te despite tacit protests among the comrades that they did not merit such exalted positions yet. These two became his eyes and ears and angrily admonished Chin Peng for upsetting the beloved Chairman.

Lai Te was no fool. He knew that his demand for a list of the dumps and the men who guarded them had overplayed his hand. He had issued the directive under extreme pressure. He must have surely argued with his British handlers that such an order was akin to telling the party "I am the traitor". After all, the Central Committee, more cautious then ever, had previously issued an iron-clad directive that there was to be no list of dumps, nor were more then one or two people to know the location of any dump. In this way, even if someone was arrested, he or she could only betray the location of one dump, no matter whether they were tortured or induced to become informants.

The British refused to listen to Lai Te's reasoning. Neutralizing the weapon dumps was absolutely essential for the tranquil continuation of British rule in Malaya. The dice was cast and Lai Te obviously figured it was time to perform a vanishing act. He was not a poor man. A party investigation later found that he had siphoned off funds worth two million dollars, a fortune in those days. At least half of his pilfered money came from the sale of rubber stockpiles, which the guerrillas had confiscated when the Japanese surrendered. (The Japanese had "inherited" these stockpiles when the British fled. But they could not move the rubber to Japan for lack of transport.) With the Japanese surrender, every regional guerrilla commander expropriated as much of the rubber as he could lay his hands on, an easy task since there was no other law enforcement or military presence to prevent their confiscation. The rubber was kept in party warehouses until the price on world markets rocketed. Then it was sold. Regional commanders sent half the proceeds to the Chairman as party funds, keeping the rest to launch their own regional industrial enterprises and projects. All of these enterprises apparently failed, causing the wry comment from Malayan Chinese that the guerrillas were good fighters but lousy businessmen. In addition, much of the money was squandered. But not the money Lai Te administered. He had acquired property in Thailand and Hong Kong.

Once suspicion about his role had become a virtual certainty the party still remained paralyzed. No one had the courage to stick their neck out and raise the alarm for fear that denouncing him could trigger their own death warrant. No one knew how many party members were still loyal to Lai Te and would arrest the accuser by order of the accused.

The stalemate remained several weeks and Lai Te might have also survived this ultimate betrayal. But, for once, he lost his nerve or, perhaps, thought it wise to retire before he could be exposed. His disappearance made it legitimate to search for him. The longer he remained without trace, the more voices, first privately then publicly, were raised asking for an explanation. Led by Chin Peng, with the excuse of investigating the case of the missing Chairman, the party began to rummage through his private affairs.

The scope of what they found left everyone aghast.

He was not only married to a party comrade in Malaya but had three other women. He had a Chinese mistress in Hong Kong, set up in an apartment he owned. He had a Vietnamese wife in Bangkok in another apartment he owned and a beautiful Vietnamese mistress who had lost one hand in an accident. She ran a bar and restaurant he owned in Singapore and lived in an apartment he paid for.

Lai Te felt so secure and untouchable that during the Japanese occupation he drove a Morris 8 H.P. Saloon car with the number plate S4678. The car was the property of the Japanese military intelligence in Singapore, the Kempeitai. The Chairman stayed at the swanky Coliseum Hotel on Batu Road in Singapore, often accompanied by his stunningly attractive mistress.

While the war raged and people starved, Lai Te lived like a rich playboy, a kind of James Bond, but one who did not indulge in killing, delegating the dirty work to others. While his men survived on a bare minimum in often miserable conditions in the jungle, he stayed in the best hotels when he traveled. He had a car and chauffeur, ate in first class restaurants, pretended to be a well-to-do businessman, a cover he carried off as successfully as the use of his four fake names. Officially Lai Te had no face. Even some of the senior party members had never seen him in the flesh. This only added to the myth.

When Chin Peng, an important leader of the fledgling guerrilla army, had met Lai Te for the first time, the arrangements were so elaborate Chin was not even allowed to see the car in which the Chairman arrived or know the address of the house where they met. After all, he might have recognized the car as the one owned by the Kempeitai.

■

Once the enormity of the treason became known, the party hierarchy gathered on March 6, 1947, and quickly elected Chin Peng as their new General Secretary and Chairman. Chin was 24 years old, perhaps the youngest national communist party chairman anywhere in the world. He had survived eight years of purges and betrayals by his predecessor and inherited a party torn by dissent, suspicion, ethnic differences and constant treason, without visible weapons, though with an arsenal buried all over the country.

In times of internal crisis unscrupulous leaders often resort to armed conflict to unite their fractured forces, rekindle a sense of patriotism and deflect attention from economic or social woes. Chin Peng, anxious to unify his forces, decided to return to the original goal of the party: Malaya was to become a communist country run by the ethnic Chinese majority but with full rights and participation of the native Malay population. He had always encouraged the recruitment of more Malays but was being stalled by the growing rift and envy between the two main ethnic communities, a rift that would explode in racial riots and end with the secession of Singapore as a city state made up almost entirely of ethnic Chinese. As in other Asian countries where indigenous natives have taken a backseat in the theater of wealth, the Malays—laid back, less diligent in the pursuit of riches and not as clever in ethnic networking as the Chinese—watched with growing resentment as the Chinese took over commercial life, cornering, as their cousins did with the Dutch in Indonesia, concessions from the British.

This disparity in the ethnic distribution of wealth would result, a decade later, in the Bumiputra laws, which gave preference to indigenous Malays. But these restrictive regulations did not close the wealth gap between the two communities although they tipped the demographic balance in favor of native Malays or so-called "sons of the soil". Obviously the Bumiputra laws upset the Chinese community, which tried in vain to rescind the discriminatory regulations. Ironically, the Bumiputra laws did not to stop the Chinese (those not settled in Singapore) from dominating the economic life in Malaya and later the Malaysian Federation.

During those volatile post-war months, Chin Peng had married a comrade in the party, Khoon Wah. With party help, he concealed himself as an up and coming young businessman in Kuala Lumpur living in a fine home with all the trappings of bourgeois existence, including a piano.

He continued to be haunted by the betrayals of many good comrades, among them some of his best friends, who had been handed over or killed by the Japanese and later the British thanks to one man's cynical and callous self-interest. One of Chin Peng's first orders as chairman was to form a killer-squad to hunt down the former party chairman. But before the traitor was executed, Chin ordered, he personally wished to conduct an interrogation of his predecessor, a veiled indication the former chairman was not likely to have an easy death.

But Lai Te and his bags of money appeared to have vanished into the Asian maelstrom—but not before he struck one last blow against the man who succeeded him. Almost certainly he sold Chin Peng's whereabouts to the British. Chin escaped the police raid through a back window but he left behind his passports and a birth certificate, which proved he was born in Malaya—and not in China.

■

In the years to come, the British would rue the rash decision that exposed Lai Te as an informer. Under his chairmanship of the CPM, the British colonial forces were one step ahead of communist activities and plans. With the chairman providing intelligence, the rebels posed no real threat to colonial rule. In retrospect, ordering their master-spy to obtain a list of all weapon dumps and people guarding them proved to be one of the most stupid and costly decisions the colonial administration had made, far worse than the decision to ban the Japanese colonial currency overnight, which had left Malayans without money and lost them whatever savings they had made.

Had the British proceeded more patiently with the job of locating the dumps, they would have been able to dismantle all of them eventually. Chin Peng says in his memoirs that Lai Te's standing in the party was so sacrosanct no one would have objected or voiced suspicions if he had inquired from this or that regional commander about the location of a particular dump or had ordered the relocation of some of the dumps. Instead, the British wanted the entire arsenal in one consolidated list plus the personnel attached to it. This order broke the party's basic rule of secrecy and could not be explained away as easily as a broken down car.

Even with the astonishing demand for the list, it would have been difficult to connect all the dots of those years of betrayals had not Lai Te himself panicked, convinced his role as informer had been compromised. Not known for courage in the field, he simply vanished without a trace. This left the party's affairs to be run by Chin Peng and other members of the Central Committee, who began to make discreet inquiries with other regional communist parties without telling them the truth. In the search for their once beloved leader, the party cadres came across puzzling evidence: Lai Te had no connection to the Comintern, nor did he enjoy the confidence of either the Vietnamese or the Thai comrades.

Still, Lai Te remained nominally in charge of the CPM until the party members had realized not only was their chairman missing but so were the party funds.

Only then, almost reluctantly, did the party hierarchy make the logical deductions about betrayal and elected Chin Peng to take over as top leader. With his election, the party had a dedicated, fanatical and dynamic new chairman, a man who had sworn to fight the British and turn Malaya into a communist nation.

The Chin Peng-led insurgency would last until 1989, three decades after the British handed over Malaya to a new coalition of shrewd politicians and astute leaders who had no intention of giving the communists a legitimate role in an independent Malaya but continued to try and pacify them with pledges of amnesty and by keeping in Malaya British and Commonwealth forces to fight them. The pacification attempts failed, not due to any reluctance on the party's part to give up its clandestine existence but mostly due to directives from Beijing to fight on.

■

Chin Peng was one of those people who believe so profoundly in their credo, whether religious or political, that they dismiss anyone who disagrees as either an enemy or as lacking mental acuity. Be they Nazis, communists, neo-liberals, Zionists, sect members or missionaries, the majority of these people go to their graves convinced of the undisputable righteousness of their cause. For them it is almost impossible to admit they were wrong because such an admission would render their life meaningless. One meets these diehards often in life and usually brushes them aside with a compassionate smile. But when one of these fanatics attains power over life and death, then, almost inevitably, tragedy follows.

Chin Peng never attained the status of a Mao or a Ho Chi Minh, although he fought longer then any of them. The fault was mainly his lack of education, his isolation from the rest of the world and the absence of any ideological debate to modify or modernize his beliefs. He lived in the jungle, fought in the jungle and acted like a man in the jungle. His aim to defeat the British and later the independent State of Malaysia in order to establish a dictatorship of the proletariat never changed in light of global events. With characteristic Chinese stubbornness, he pursued his goal, exhibiting single-minded determination. His personal credo allowed no deviation from the chosen course. Like many of his kind, he became in the process a puppet of wilier and more ruthless string pullers—in Beijing.

The Chin Pengs of this world rarely make concessions unless one of their icons shows them the way. Once Deng Xioaping, as Mao's successor, had qualified the Great Helmsman as 70 per cent good and 30 per cent bad, Chin Peng too felt free to admit that his CPM had made errors, although he was anxious to qualify these errors as strategic rather than accept his guerrillas had carried out barbaric and brutal actions, difficult to justify even in a civil war.

But then he could claim the British too had never shied away from equally despicable actions. The worst was at a place called Batang Kali when Scots Guards mowed down 28 unarmed civilian workers in 1951. For 19 years the massacre was officially covered up as a gunfight to stop captured guerrillas escaping from custody. No one queried how not one of the unarmed escapees had survived. All had been efficiently shot dead. In fact not one of the dead was a fighter. All were workers, shot down in a My Lai-like incident as troops ran amok against civilians. Naturally, as happened at My Lai, Western media gives credibility to their government and military versions in times of war when patriotism and loyalty are invoked to silence criticism and cover up the excesses of those who use war to give free rein to their perversions. Sudden power over life and death is corrupting. Besides, psychopathic individuals are to be found in every nation, irrespective of the degree of development of civic consciousness. In times of war, dormant, psychotic urges are suddenly liberated and are easily justified. Men can turn into killers and justify their urges as being in the service of "the cause".

The guerrillas often executed innocent people as collaborators or as traitors. The British committed their own foul deeds, among them dragging the bodies of shot guerrillas through villages as a deterrent. In an identical event that horrified the world 50 years later, Somali guerrillas dragged the bodies of American pilots through the streets. A gruesome photo from the 1950s shows a uniformed and grinning British soldier holding in each hand the decapitated head of a guerrilla, one a man, the other a woman.

Under Chin Peng's chairmanship and with his determination, the fight against the colonial masters gained new momentum. Without their master spy to keep them abreast of events, the British began to suffer losses. Sporadic attacks against British troops and installations resulted in the declaration of what became known as the Malayan Emergency, a series of special laws and regulations to cope with the communist threat. The Emergency, a kind of civil war, became so extensive that Britain, short on personnel and funds after the drainage of World War II, asked for military assistance from its Commonwealth allies, particularly Australia and New Zealand. The inclusion of Australian troops was not popular in some London circles. Australians, who had bled for the British in disproportionate numbers during all major conflicts, were viewed with trepidation by many British commanders.

A 1948 memorandum by a high-ranking British officer to British Secretary of State for Commonwealth Relations, Philip Noel-Baker virtually urged him to forget deploying Australian troops in Malaya for both political and military reasons. Australian participation in Malaya would undermine British prestige and enhance Australia's growing influence in Southeast Asia. And one could not trust Australian troops to obey British orders. The memorandum, quoted in Chin Peng's memoirs, bluntly stated:

> *"... there is no doubt that Australians have splendid fighting qualities. But unless they are kept under the strictest discipline (which they do not like) they are too high-spirited to be really suitable for the kind of work for which they are likely to be required in Malaya and are liable to be at their worst off parade... ."*

The last quip was an obvious reference to the Australian habit when off duty to imbibe large quantities of alcohol.

The reservation was ignored and Australian forces did participate in the hunt for the communist insurgents. The Australians missed an opportunity to wipe out the main part of the insurgents including most of its leaders when their RAAF carpet-bombed the wrong side of a mountain ridge. In his memoirs, Chin says, had they bombed the other side of the ridge he and the bulk of his forces would have perished.

■

Even as he injected new vigor into the war, Chin never forgot those comrades killed, incarcerated or tortured as a result of Lai Te's betrayals. One of his main prerogatives was to make the traitor pay the same way others had paid for treason—with his life. Lai Te's betrayals irked him because he had trusted the man so long and thus, in a way, felt he shared in the blame for the death of so many comrades. In fact, the full scope of the Chairman's treason was never shared with the party rank-and-file. Full knowledge of the treason would not only dishearten the men and women but stoke the paranoia still lingering from the days of the Japanese invasion when scores of guerrillas or collaborators were executed for cooperating with the invaders or snitching on their comrades. Many of those shot dead were innocent, including David Chen, headmaster of Chung Ling High School in Penang and accused as collaborator by one of his students who obviously had a grudge against the much loved teacher.

Among the first actions Chin Peng took as Chairman was to create a killer squad. He appointed a senior party member, Ma Ting, to head the squad. Ma was the head of the Singapore Town Committee, one of CPM's most senior functionaries. Everyone in the squad was furnished with photos of the wanted man and the five false names he had used in the past, among them what many chroniclers later believed was his original name: Francis Lighter. The squad's sole task was to track down the traitor. Chin Peng specified, however, that before doing away with Lai Te, he wished to ask him a few pertinent questions, the most urgent being the identity of the British spymaster who controlled the Chairman before, during and after the war.

Chin never had the chance to ask those questions. He would have been shocked to find out that the man who controlled Lai Te all those years was the only British officer, a man called John Davis, for whom Chin Peng had developed a soft spot over the years of their association during the anti-Japanese struggle. Major Davis had been the officer Chin had personally delivered from a British submarine offshore to the guerrilla jungle camp during the war. And it was the Major who had coordinated the anti-Japanese cooperation between British Special Forces, known as Force136, and the communist guerrillas headed by Chin Peng. It was Davis who urged London to furnish the jungle fighters with British arms and training and who recommended Chin for the OBE and two medals of valor. Chin and Davis had developed a collegial relationship of mutual admiration during the war. Even in his memoirs, decades later, Chin had nothing but praise for the British Major who would become his enemy again after the war. Following the peace treaty of 1989 that officially ended the civil war, Chin even flew to London for the Major's funeral service.

Chin would only know the truth years after Major Davis died.

Admittedly it stunned him. Davis had not only controlled Our Man in Singapore, the very Chairman of the CPM, but in doing so had inflicted mortal wounds on a guerrilla movement and a communist party that might have, without the traitor, changed the history of Malaya and the entire peninsula. Deng Xiaoping had predicted Malaya would become another communist stronghold in the region, part of a Red Belt right across Southeast Asia from Burma to Thailand, Malaya, Vietnam, Cambodia, Laos, the Philippines and Indonesia. All of these countries would be part of a communist fraternity under the tutelage of Big Brother in Beijing. The prediction fell well short of its aim: Only Vietnam, Laos and Cambodia became communist nations and soon

Vietnam and Cambodia would be embroiled in their own fratricidal war.

For his own peace of mind and for the welfare of the party, Chin had been anxious to capture Lai Te alive and extract from him what secrets the master spy still possessed. Chin had no doubt Lai Te would fully cooperate as he had cooperated with the Vietnamese, the French, the Japanese and the British. Lai Te was a soft man who did not blink an eyelid sending others to their death but abhorred any violence on his own person. Chin remembered how the Chairman had broken down in tears on the one occasion he had criticized him. He gave strict instructions that Lai Te had to be apprehended alive and in "good condition".

However, the hit squad's search for the fugitive chairman and the party funds proved futile. Even his four wives, questioned under pressure, had no idea what had happened to him.

■

In the meantime and without the services of their master spy, the British struck back at Chin Peng's offensive with venom and some dubious methods in a kind of civil war against the communists. Strapped for funds and military personnel after a sapping World War and bogged down in India by the clamor for independence, London requested the help of its Commonwealth allies to fight the threat of a communist takeover in Malaya. By then it was obvious even to old colonial hardheads that self-rule was only a matter of time, just as in India and Ceylon. However neither Britain nor its allies intended to hand over the lucrative peninsula to the communists. By working hand in hand with the future ruling clique in Malaya, the colonial masters assured for themselves a role in the country, as advisors and military allies, well after granting self-rule in 1957.

Although Chin's energetic leadership had converted his guerrillas into a cohesive force and Malaya into a battlefield, the communists were running short of weapons and ammunition by the end of 1951. To replenish, they staged ambushes on British military personnel and supplies not as much for the kill but to scavenge their arsenals. Unfortunately the enemy had become savvy and the pickings grew thin. Anxiety over dwindling material and battleground successes can produce abject frustration among fighting men, especially guerrillas entrenched in jungle bases and dependent on food supplies from friendly villages and "liberated" areas. Only a major victory or a headline making triumph can alleviate this creeping depression.

Sometimes such a triumph comes when least expected and utterly unplanned.

■

Siew Ma was short and stringy, a veteran of the anti-Japanese war and one of the most celebrated guerrilla leaders. But even he had no idea the fortune that was about to drop in his lap would stimulate the insurrection and take the official reaction to a new level of violence. It would also send tremors through what was left of the rapidly vanishing British Empire and fuel a civil war that was to last another 40 years.

Ma had positioned his 36-men unit in heavy brush along the Gap Road leading to the popular expatriate resort of Fraser's Hill about 90 kilometers from Kuala Lumpur. A veteran of many skirmishes, he had picked his spot well. The road was climbing steeply for some 300 yards and any convoy or car had to change down gears and reduce speed to a virtual crawl. His target, he hoped, would be a convoy taking supplies to a military garrison. Like the rest of the rebel units, he and his men were woefully short of weapons and ammunition. The main armor he had mustered for the ambush consisted of two Bren guns and a Sten gun. Most of his men were unarmed or under-armed, carrying knives or a pistol. Some had a rifle. Their main task was to pounce on the captured supplies and carry off as many weapons and ammunition as they could to the base deep in the jungle. Siew Ma had organized his men into three charging squads to rush the convoy and pilfer its supplies. He expected little if any resistance, aware his unit was ill equipped to do battle in an encounter.

Now it was Saturday and his men had been lying in wait since Thursday. No convoy, not even a small one, had passed. Food rations had run out and patience, like an over-extended elastic, was about to snap. Traffic had been unusually light. Scouts had assured Ma the road was frequently used by supply convoys carrying guns and ammunition for the Royal West Kent regiment's operational area nearby.

By early Saturday the men were tired of watching British residents motor by on their way to a weekend at Fraser's Hill, their automobiles piled high with picnic baskets, children's toys and cartons of food on roof racks. Someone suggested holding up one of the cars to sequester its food supplies. Comrade Siew Ma was not amused.

The date was October 6, 1951, the day Joseph Stalin, in an interview with Pravda, ridiculed U.S. criticism of the Soviet Union's nuclear policy. But the day would be far more significant for Malaya when Siew Ma heard the crunching of gears.

■

As Mao and his successors discovered, directives and policy statements, just like texts in the Bible and the Koran, can easily be misinterpreted and utilized by zealots or miscreants to satisfy their desire for vengeance, their psychosis or their political or religious opportunism. Just as the law allows police powers and misuses never intended but appropriated, so the political campaigns of communist parties around the world led to excesses that were mostly unintended but appropriated and defended with the explanation that they were included as innuendos in the statement of the campaign. It is unlikely Mao expected the Red Guards to smash the artistic and architectural heritage of China when he proclaimed: "Destroy the old to build the new".

Often what is intended as a scare campaign or a correction of injustices can degenerate into unwarranted violence. This was the case in the CPM's directive to its regional cadres to crack down on "strike-breakers", those who cooperated with white plantation and mine managers to break the party's call to strike for fairer wages and better treatment. A crackdown meant, in party jargon: Kill the collaborators, make sure the people know what they can expect if they betray strike leaders or collaborate with the management.

The directive did not mean: "Kill the plantation managers who bully workers and undermine their justified demands."

But that's what happened.

■

The coordinated attacks on the Sungai Siput and Elphil plantations north of Sungai Siput town are blamed for the declaration of the Emergency, the de facto announcement of the administration's war against the communist-led insurrection against colonial rule. Chin Peng and the CPM Central Committee were stunned by the news that overzealous comrades had unilaterally extended the campaign against strikebreakers to include European managers.

The first to die was Arthur Walker, aged 50, already a kind of local hero because he had survived the cruel Japanese internment at Changi Prison. Walker and his wife were days from departing to England on home leave. Walker was known as a harsh manager at Sungai Siput plantation. He sat at his office desk when three local men entered and wished him "good morning". The trio had cycled up to the gates and without being challenged had casually ambled into Walker's office.

"Morning," the manager replied: "What do you want?"

The answer was a volley of shots. One hit Walker in the head, one in the chest. He lay dying on the floor, the keys to his safe beside him. The assailants fled, without taking anything.

The 12 "comrades" who simultaneously raided the Elphil plantation just two miles down the road were far more dramatic. The manager, John Allison, 55, and his assistant Ian Christian, 21, who had arrived only a few weeks earlier, were quickly immobilized and their hands bound behind their backs. The "comrades" then ransacked the office safe and took $1,000 in cash. For the next sequence the raiders frog-marched the planters to a bungalow verandah and tied them to two chairs. In full view of the plantation workers who had gathered, the two were executed with bursts of gunfire. Not content with their callous killing, the raiding party then located canisters of kerosene and poured their content around the smokehouse, which was packed with rubber—and lit it. The fire burned and smoldered all day and much of the night. It was reported later that the raiders had called out to the workers as they left: "We are only after European strikebreakers."

In his memoirs, Chin Peng laments the death of the 21-year-old Ian Christian who had arrived only recently and could not possibly have participated in the suppression of any strikes. But he had no regrets over the two managers who, he said, used mercenary thugs to keep their workers from demanding higher wages and better treatment.

The reaction to the killing of the two planters was startling: European managers all over Malaya left their plantations to seek refuge in towns until the authorities promised them protection and declared war on the culprits and the communist party.

■

The Land Rover, its engine whining around the bend, had on board six armed local police. Better six than nothing, Siew Ma thought, signaling to his men to wait until the Land Rover had moved into what was called in sniper jargon "the killing box", the area in full view of his Bren and Sten guns. Ma almost missed the next vehicle as it came around the bend. He was startled to see a shiny black Rolls Royce limousine. What was this limousine doing here?

He had no time to consider the question because his men had opened fire on the police, wounding all but one. The Land Rover skidded to a halt on the left hand lip of the road and the wounded policemen spilled out seeking cover in the undergrowth. Immediately they began to fire back at the raiders.

The driver of the limousine reacted slowly to the mayhem in front of his eyes. He swerved and stuttered to a halt nearly 40 yards behind the stranded Land Rover. Shots instantly peppered his vehicle. The driver, wounded, opened the door and rolled out. He sprawled on the road without moving. The shooting died down steadily until only intermittent shots rang out. At that point, to everyone's astonishment, the rear door of the Rolls suddenly opened and a skeletal elderly European wearing a light tropical suit stepped out. He was walking in the direction of the guerrillas hiding in the bushes. He had hardly taken three or four steps when he was felled by rifle fire. Pitching forward, he slid into a roadside gutter, face down, dead.

Ma was still in two minds whether it was worthwhile to flush out the policemen for their weapons when he heard more crunching gears. Next, coming around the bend, he saw a British scout car its Bren gun blazing.

Guerrilla warfare does not call for head-on battles, which are sure to lead to heavy losses in manpower and weaponry. So Ma ordered his bugler to sound the retreat. Two days lying in ambush had netted nothing and had expended precious ammunition. In his view, the operation had been an abject failure.

Only a day later would he be informed that the European sprawled in the roadside gutter was Sir Henry Gurney, the British High Commissioner and as such the colony's most senior dignitary.

Sir Henry's death, virtually by accident, would enrage the British. He became a heroic example of British chivalry after the media reported that he had stepped out of the Rolls Royce to save the life of his wife, a passenger. He had argued that since he was the obvious target of the assault, the raiders would stop shooting if he gave himself up. He did not realize he was neither the target nor did Ma and his men have any idea who that foolish white man was stepping out of the Rolls as if he expected to be saluted.

While the British bombed villages near the ambush site and harshly interrogated men, women and youths in the hunt for the perpetuators of the killing, the guerrillas in their jungle bases celebrated a major victory in their war against British occupation.

■

The killings of Sir Henry and the plantation managers offered the colonial authorities a convenient excuse to upgrade the severity of the Emergency laws. From now on any armed communist captured or any citizen found supplying food to the rebels would face the death penalty. At the same time the authorities issued wanted posters for Chin Peng with a massive 250,000 sterling reward for his capture alive, half that amount for the body. The British expected that the thumping "dead or alive" rewards for Chin and other senior members of the party would persuade their associates or sympathizers to betray them. Surprisingly, over the 40 years he lived clandestinely, no attempts were ever made by his comrades to assassinate or capture the Chairman.

Yet the most crippling blow to the insurgency was not the death penalty and the "Wanted: Dead or Alive" posters but the arrival of Lt. General Sir Harold Briggs. A distinguished veteran of World War II, Briggs unleashed a "scorched earth" policy. It called for burning down villages considered traditional suppliers of food for the guerrillas. The villagers were then transferred by force to areas completely controlled by British and Malayan forces. The new villages were surrounded by barbed wire fencing, flood lights and guards. Briggs might have learned his tactic from the Soviets who torched villages and crops to prevent them feeding the advancing Nazi army during World War II. Not content with caging suspected communist sympathizers in "New Villages", the authorities introduced central cooking, thus ensuring that all rations were controlled and accounted for.

The effect was disastrous for the rebels. Starvation became so common the guerillas even tried to eat rubber seeds until they received a message from Chinese scientists to immediately stop it as the seeds were highly toxic.

Unable to feed their men, commanders gave some of them permission to re-enter civilian life in villages and towns. Others deserted or turned informers to escape the hunger and deprivations in the jungle.

■

With their movement increasingly marginalized and separated from its civilian sympathizers, the party's executive committee turned more and more to China for aid. But help usually comes at a cost. There is no doubt Chin Peng and his politburo gradually slithered under Beijing's umbrella of influence. Shortage of food and finance were not the only reasons. The party members were nearly all Chinese. Their credo was a replica of Maoism. China, even before Mao took power, had included the CPM among its allies, a member of the group of communist parties in Southeast Asia, which, so the Chinese then believed, would wrest power from the capitalists and turn the Asian continent into a communist empire under Beijing tutelage.

Already in the late 1940s and early 1950s, Mao's China had generously accepted sick or wounded Malayan comrades for medical care on Chinese territory. The bulk of these evacuees suffered from tuberculosis, a byproduct, just like malaria, of jungle life. This Good Samaritan scheme took on a puzzling aspect when the Chinese kept these sick fighters for years beyond their recovery, no doubt subjecting them to Maoist indoctrination before allowing them eventually to return home.

By the mid 1950s Chin Peng realized—as he wrote in his candid memoirs—that neither Beijing nor Moscow saw any advantage in the continued armed struggle in Malaya. Once Britain had decided to grant home-rule to Malaya in 1957, the principal justification for the insurrection—the withdrawal of the occupiers—was no longer valid.

On the other side of the conflict London was not yet ready to abandon its lucrative foothold in a part of Asia that was crucial for continued and necessary British interests in commodities such as rubber and tin. As long as the communist insurrection was alive—or kept alive—the new Malaysian Federation would require British military aid. The new Federation's armed forces and police were not yet sufficiently trained and coordinated to confront the CPM rebels.

Britain had much to gain in maintaining a communist threat in Malaya, a threat that could be easily contained. Yet containment not only required a British presence in the former colony, but also help from its Commonwealth brothers. Australian, New Zealand and Nepalese troops were soon drafted in to fight a waning communist rebellion against the newest member of the British Commonwealth.

At the same time the CPM had a hard time explaining to people at large why it was still fighting against what was now a democracy with a vote for all. The excuse of fighting for a dictatorship of the proletariat was wearing woefully thin. More reasonable, at least among ethnic Chinese, was the unspoken understanding that if the CPM came to power or shared power, it would usher in a golden era for Chinese dominance in Malaysia.

In the war of propaganda, Chin Peng had no valid arguments except his stubborn belief in communism. Privately he admitted that neither he nor his senior cadres had any illusion they could win a military victory. Their main hope was to wear down the country with protracted rebellion to the point where the CPM would be given an opportunity to participate in the electoral process in return for surrendering their arms and pledging peace.

That dream was rapidly being ridiculed by London's public relations campaign, which labeled the communist insurgency "a foreign conspiracy". The argument cited the rebels' close links to China and the Soviet Union. This valid argument was further reinforced when Chin Peng visited not only China but also Russia. By classifying the insurgency as an ethnic Chinese grab for power and subservient to China, Britain sought to eliminate the guerrillas' main claim to legitimacy as a nationalist movement.

In fact the public relations campaign removed the mantle of a legitimate nationalist movement from the communists and hung it on the shoulders of Tunku Abdul Rahman, Malaysia's first president. This suave manipulator and negotiator had enticed Chin Peng to much publicized peace talks at Baling in 1955, less then two years before the British had set the date for Malaysia's self-rule. At the talks, Abdul Rahman gently rejected

Chin's proposal of an absolute amnesty for his guerrillas and a legitimate role for the communists in national elections. The Tunku wanted peace but he and his coalition partners were afraid a legitimized communist party would attract the ethnic Chinese vote. No matter whether the voters were communist sympathizers or not their first loyalty was to their ethnicity. Even if the CPM did not win a majority it could garner sufficient votes for the party to become a power broker and potential coalition partner.

The Tunku knew Chin Peng could not accept that after years of fighting, his men would be subjected to interrogation and possible persecution if they laid down their arms. Officially that was his argument in rejecting the Tunku's proposal. Behind the scenes there was another reason: The Communist Bloc was encouraged by the outcome of the Korean War, the Vietnamese resistance and the "conversion" of countries to communism in Eastern Europe and Africa. All over Southeast Asia communist parties were emerging, promising a better deal for the workers and the poor and an end to exploitation by the rich. Their message fell on fertile soil.

Once the Baling peace talks failed to give the CPM a role in the self-rule of Malaysia or complete amnesty for its fighters, Chin Peng pulled out. In secret he then traveled to Beijing, disguised as a peasant, wearing a false moustache and riding for hundreds of kilometers pillion on a motorbike. He needed to discuss with the Chinese leaders what to do next. Should he disband the guerrilla movement and seek a long-term political solution, or should he fight on?

The man who was running party affairs in those days was Deng Xiaoping (to be sidelined by Mao later, only to return eventually and become China's paramount leader). Deng, drawing attention to the growing fortunes of communism in the region, advised Chin to "keep fighting, victory is nigh".

And that is what Chin Peng did for another 30 years.

But beginning in 1969, he conducted the insurgency from safe havens in southern Thailand or stationed in China. In reality the rebellion against the newly founded Malaysian Federation was now guided by advice and financial support from Beijing. Like aid recipients all around the world, the Malayan communists submitted their annual wish list to Beijing. Although the Chinese were often generous with medical, financial and material assistance, they adamantly refused to supply the guerrillas with arms, afraid of the international reaction at a time when Mao's propaganda machine was giving daily grief to U.S. imperialist interference in Vietnam. In one of those ironies of war, however, both China and the United States indirectly nurtured the ethnic Chinese revolt in Malaysia, which continued without any legitimate grievance and on a gradually collapsing ideological platform. It was China that made available funds allowing the guerrillas to buy U.S. manufactured weapons and ammunition. American weaponry was freely available in southern Thailand on a booming arms market. All of the gleaming hardware on display to shoppers was either pilfered from the war in Vietnam or more likely came from supplies destined for the Vietnam War but de-routed to arms dealers by corrupt U.S. military officials or, more intriguingly, by plots within plots of secret services and power-brokers on all sides anxious to keep the region fighting on with all kinds of little wars. The communist guerrillas were particularly fond of U.S. M-16 assault rifles and—as Chin Peng admits in his memoirs—these were freely available at reasonable prices.

China also allowed the CPM to run a Free Malaysia radio station on its territory. The moment this became an embarrassment—when China moved closer to capitalism and to Southeast Asia in pursuit of trade—Beijing simply ordered the Malayan comrades to close down and remove their station from Chinese territory.

The Malayan comrades obeyed.

Just as the civil war was petering out into minor incidents, it did receive a last shot in the arm in 1975. Following student riots in Bangkok, more then 2,000 students flocked to the jungle camps of the Malayan communist party ready to boost the insurgency against capitalist regimes.

Unfortunately for the comrades in the jungle, the new recruits quickly proved to be useless city slickers horrified by the harsh environment and rigid training and indoctrination at these camps. Worse, a number of the recruits turned out to be informers for the authorities, rekindling the constant paranoia of betrayal inherited and perpetuated since the days of Lai Te. Amid shrill claims that as many as 90 per cent of the recruits were informers, the party launched another of its brutal purges. When the victims of these witch-hunts were tallied up, 91 recruits and guerrillas, some of them loyal old fighters, had been executed after impromptu courts found them guilty of treason. The bloodletting of the innocent was so widespread that angry relatives invaded the camps of the communist guerrillas after the war ended in 1989 and demanded the lives of the executioners. In the end the communists apologized publicly and compensated relatives of those innocently executed with a one time payment of $800 and a document admitting their loved ones had been unjustly put to death.

The reason for this large-scale massacre of traitors was the idiotic party policy of converting death sentences to imprisonment for those who repented and implicated other traitors. Few of those convicted had the courage to face the firing squad. Most of them sentenced to death simply pointed the finger at someone innocent to save their own lives. The irony of this harebrained scheme was that many honest communist fighters, wrongly accused, faced the firing squad rather than point the finger at an innocent comrade. In his memoirs, Chin Peng regrets that many of his bravest comrades lost their lives not by fighting the enemy but as the victims of paranoia. Why, as Number One in the party, he never outlawed this ridiculous hunt for traitors or why this witch-hunt for traitors often coincided with the fanatical purges in Maoist China, Chairman Chin Peng never explained in his elaborate memoirs.

But wars usually do have an end.

The visionary architect of the deal to end the four decades of civil war was Dr. Mahathir Mohamad who would become notorious in later years for his bold stand against the World Bank and the IMF, which he labeled U.S. tools and held co-responsible for the economic melt-down in Southeast Asia in the 1990s. Mahathir's economic policies and his healthy disrespect for Western market methods helped Malaysia escape the meltdown. For many his name became synonymous with anti-Americanism as well as the decline of the World Bank and the IMF as economic advisers and policy-makers in the developing world.

The leadership in Beijing, which has always shown a soft spot for Mahathir and his strong stand against U.S. hegemony, gave its blessing to the 1989 peace deal. It was signed six months after the killing of hundreds of students around Tiananmen Square, a shooting spree that left China looking like an ogre in Western eyes and slowed down, at least for a few months, the country's phenomenal economic growth.

The deal was generous. It offered not only amnesty but financial assistance for several years to the guerrillas, helping them adjust to civilian life. Those born in Malaya or Thailand were allowed to return home unpunished and without having to account for their activities.

All would go home except Chin Peng.

He was banned from returning to his hometown in Malaysia since he could not prove he was born in Malaya and not in China. His birth certificate and passport were left behind when he barely escaped a police raid on a bungalow where he stayed near Kampar in the early 1950s. Obviously, the documents were in the possession of the Malaysian authorities who had no intention of handing them over to its owner and by doing so removing the only excuse for keeping their most controversial citizen out of his homeland.

Unable to return home, Chin Peng now lives in one of those specially built villages for exiles along the Thai side of the border with Malaysia. The Thai government offered the villages as a contribution to the peace deal. After all, the insurgency in Malaya had also affected Thailand since the guerrillas had operated for years from its territory and at times clashed with the Thai military. From his home across the border he can follow the escalating problems of ethnic differences in a Malaysia today dogged by bribery and kickback scandals and the clamor of the ethnic Chinese that they are being unjustly excluded from mainstream business at the expense of the native "sons of the earth".

In recent years Chin Peng has requested the government in Kuala Lumpur a number of times to allow him to die in Malaysia, but to no avail. While his requests were strongly supported by ethnic Chinese organizations and leaders the Malay majority turned them down obviously convinced his return could serve no useful purpose and was certain to pour fuel on the simmering differences between the communities. The mere presence of Chin Peng, although 87 years old now, would surely galvanize Chinese aspirations and might serve as a launching pad for reigniting old grievances. His request went to the High Court, which also rejected it. The memories associated with the old man's stubborn war are still too fresh and sore for older Malaysians while the myth of his ideological struggle may turn him into a folk hero for the young.

■

Many mysteries remain unsolved in the often nebulous annals of the communist insurrection but none more so than the fate of the great traitor

Lai Te, the puppet-master who played great and small global powers against each other on a stage he dominated, a man who had no loyalty to anyone except himself. In his own way Lai Te may be considered a pioneer of the modern entrepreneur who deals with any nation or any ideological system offering lucrative profits, a type of entrepreneurship embodied in the existence of the ruthless pan-global conglomerates today controlling the existence of entire populations and ever ready to betray, to lie and to have people killed for profits.

Once exposed as a traitor, Lai Te maintained the same cold-blooded control over his fate, the same bravado in moments of extreme danger he had shown as CPM leader when he exploited the weakness of his party system and the ambitions and greed of the great powers in order to further his own career—and pad his pockets.

The mystery of Lai Te may never be solved completely but Chin Peng insists in his memoirs that the traitor received what was coming to him.

But did he?

For weeks the three-man killer squad led by Ma Ting, head of the Singapore Town Committee, staked out Lai Te's hang-outs and the apartments of his wives and mistresses—all in vain. The fugitive party chairman and his loot did not show up. In the end, grudgingly, Ma Ting had to report to the party that the traitor must have left Singapore and Malaya. He might be anywhere in the world now.

Weeks went by.

Finally, following the customary cumbersome arrangements shrouded in secrecy, the reshuffled party politburo authorized Chin Peng to travel abroad and explain to fraternal communist parties, especially the Thais and Vietnamese, how Lai Te had betrayed his own party and possibly also them. The delay in informing the regional "comrades" of the high treason was baffling since Lai Te was obviously also in possession of inside information compromising all regional parties. He was sure to be extensively debriefed by the British or whosoever he sold out to about what he knew. For this reason, informing the other regional parties immediately should have been a mandatory priority.

Instead Lai Te fooled everyone. He became untraceable to all sides, including his four wives. An urgent message sent out to embassy spooks from London indicates that his British controller was anxious to warn

Our Man in Singapore not only that he had been exposed but that the party had pronounced a death sentence on him and had dispatched killers to hunt him down. The message apparently did not find its target but it did indicate that the CPM's secrets continued to be as leaky as a strainer. Obviously the British were still being supplied with inside information on the deliberations of the party hierarchy.

But even the British could not locate their master spy.

That was left to an accident.

On his swing across the region to inform comrades of the debacle, Chin Peng also passed through Bangkok. Furnished with false documents, he checked into a cheap downtown hotel before making arrangements to meet both the Thai and the Vietnamese communist representatives in the city. He wanted to explain to them the situation and to request their help in tracking down the traitor.

The comrades promised they would issue a wanted notice in case Lai Te surfaced in their areas. At the same time, they helped Chin Peng obtain tickets and documents to travel to Hong Kong, his next port of call on his journey to alert allies.

At the end of a two-week stopover in Bangkok, a Thai party official escorted the Malayan visitor in a trishaw from the Thai party headquarters to the Cathay Pacific Airways office on Si Phaya road to buy a ticket for a flight to Hong Kong. Returning from the airline office in a rickshaw, Chin Peng recalls in his memoirs, he saw a familiar figure on the footpath bargaining with a vendor. After the trishaw had passed him, the man turned and Chin Peng, looking back down the road, realized it was Lai Te. He was standing there alone, enjoying the first puffs from a cigarette he had just bought. Worse, he was looking directly at the man in the trishaw.

Lai Te's luck in escaping dangerous situations still held. While the excited Chin Peng yelled at the trishaw driver to stop and barked at his Thai escort, "I've seen the renegade," Lai Te calmly boarded a Tuk-Tuk, one of those motorized tricycles, and vanished in a haze of blue smoke belching from the two stroke engine. Pedal power was no match for a motor, hard as the trishaw coolie tried.

Both excited and frustrated, Chin Peng headed for the office of the Vietnamese party on Sukhumvit to report that the traitor was in town.

The Vietnamese activated their paramilitary network in Bangkok with an order to check every hotel. But their efforts proved futile. Lai Te had vanished once again.

So Chin Peng continued his journey, flying to Hong Kong to inform the communist leaders there and on the mainland of the situation. It was while in Hong Kong that he realized how crippling the principle of secrecy could be, how antiquated inter-party communications were and how cumbersome the old system of face-to-face information had become. He was told Lai Te, obviously aware of the snail's pace of communications, had, in fact, visited the Shanghai communist party branch. He had spun the comrades a pitiful story of how he barely escaped a British trap that had left him with nothing but what he now wore. The Shanghai comrades dipped deep into their coffers and lent the traitor money. Then they helped him obtain a ticket back to Bangkok.

Chin Peng flew back to Bangkok to alert the Vietnamese.

From here on the Lai Te saga becomes foggy, smothered in that cloak and dagger atmosphere so popular in the early 1950s in an Indochina where men and women bartered their fortunes and their bodies for survival, pursued by the specter of nationalism and communism and flagellated by the greed and opportunism of their fellow men.

Two days later, the Vietnamese reported they had located Le Tai. The traitor must have been either suicidal or convinced that the Malayans were so embarrassed by his betrayals they had kept silent to regional comrades. This can be the only explanation for his audacity in contacting the Thai communist party asking for money and help to escape the apparently omnipresent British trap. That was the story he now seemed to peddle to everyone.

The Thais agreed to meet Lai Te in a shop house.

A few days later, Thai party chairman Li Chee Shin told Chin Peng curtly: "Lai Te is no more." He would not elaborate, not for another three years.

The story he told three years later concurs with the mystery surrounding the fate of a spy whose activities were just as murky and mysterious as his alleged death.

It appears the Thai comrades sent a three-man hit squad to apprehend Lai Te at the shop house and bring him back for questioning. The squad was young and inexperienced. As soon as their quarry entered, one of the men grabbed him from behind around the throat. A second man put the traitor in a headlock. Lai Te was small and feeble, even in his younger days. The youth who had him around the throat apparently became over-zealous and squeezed too hard. Lai Te choked to death.

The three men found a hessian sack, stuffed the body inside and dumped Lai Te into the fast-flowing waters of the Chao Phraya River.

Of course, no one could verify whether the body dumped was that of the traitor or whether a body was dumped at all. Perhaps Lai Te bought his freedom with some of the cash he had expropriated. Or British intelligence might have invented an elaborate plan to make their precious asset vanish forever with the help of paid comrades.

Whatever the reality, the news of his death terminated the hunt for the super-spy.

Still there are those who whisper Our Man in Singapore lived to a ripe old age, cultivating roses in the front garden of a quaint country cottage somewhere in rural England.

Who knows?

GLOSSARY

....

Kempeitai: Japanese Military Secret Service

CHAPTER 5

THAILAND: INTEGRATION OR DOMINATION?

Among the steady stream of ethnic Chinese who have trickled into the Kingdom of Siam since the 13th century, Seng Sae Khu was a latecomer. He arrived only in 1860. Yet by the turn of the century he had amassed a small fortune as a tax farmer. Like many of his compatriots, he had sought and obtained a concession to collect taxes at a price below the values of the tax revenues. The Thai monarchy, like neighboring sultans and colonial powers, had realized early that its Chinese subjects were highly efficient in the collection of duties and levies on royal or colonial monopolies.

Tax farming did not win the Chinese popularity. But rulers in those days were hardly interested in how the taxes were collected or how much was collected as long as the specified sum poured into their coffers on time. This left the tax farmers with the freedom to charge more than the required tax. The surplus could then be siphoned into their own pockets. Tax farmers were the most loathed class of people in Thailand, a loathing transmitted from one generation to the next.

Ironically, the collection methods did not differ much from rural China in those days or even today. Local tax and levy collectors have used the same stand-over and rough-up tactics their ancestors employed centuries ago. Furniture, livestock and land are, as it was then, still summarily confiscated and sold to pay taxes or local levies imposed by officials. And if nothing valuable is available, the tax farmer may still take away a member of the household, usually a daughter or son, in lieu of payment. These unfortunates can be held as hostages until the tax is paid or hired out as bonded labor, sold as concubines or prostitutes.

In the Kingdom of Siam, the tax collector became so despised that mobs often vented their desperation on all ethnic Chinese, a minority easily identified. Most ethnic Chinese had kept their original names although the majority had married Thai women and had gradually become integrated into Thai society. It became increasingly difficult to identify them by their physical features though not by their name. In a stroke of genius and to avoid periodic race riots against his Chinese subjects, King Rama VI (1910-25) passed legislation that required the Chinese to adopt Thai surnames in order to facilitate assimilation and make them less readily identifiable. The vast majority opted to become Thai.

By then Seng Sae Khu had lived and died in virtual anonymity. His wealth, profession and tax collecting methods were not unusual among an ethnic minority half of which could trace its ancestry back to Chaozhou prefecture in northern Guangdong. Nearly all of these ancestors had arrived without women and married Thais, one of the reasons their racial integration into Thai society went relatively smoothly and without the kind of bloody pogroms organized by the Dutch in Indonesia and the Spanish in the Philippines.

Seng became a posthumous hero as the patriarch whose fortune laid the foundation for the financial and political rise of his great grandson, Thaksin Shinawatra, considered in recent years Thailand's richest man. Backed by his financial empire and a populist campaign to bridge the gap between the rich and poor, Thaksin became prime minister in 2001 and was re-elected with a thumping majority four years later. His votes came mainly from rural followers whose income doubled because of his economic policies, among them micro-loans to villages and a policy of more self-sufficiency in agriculture. This helped reduce costly imports while raising local production and incomes. He won popularity from the poor with his 30-baht (US$1) health care reform. This offered medical care virtually free for the first time.

But the shrewd billionaire-prime minister suffered from the fatal flaw of many of his ethnic Chinese compatriots who, locust like, want everything for themselves and leave nothing for others. Buoyed by his success at the polls, his immense wealth and his popularity, he channeled lucrative contracts and monopolies to his own companies or those of his wife, son and two daughters. This was not uncommon among Thai leaders although in the past greed had always been tempered by allowing others to also make some profits.

Born into the rich and influential Shinawatra family in Chiang Mai (the name Shinawatra means "does good routinely"), the young Thaksin worked in the family's silk enterprises, then in its bus line transportation system and finally in running the chain of cinemas owned by his father. His first leap to national prominence was not due to his commercial acumen but a popular movie "Baan Sai Thong" he made after he had left the Royal Thai Police Force, in which he rose to be lieutenant colonel. In 1980 he married Potjaman Damapong, the daughter of a police general. By then several of his personal enterprises had failed. But he struck gold when he started a telecommunications firm, the Shinawatra Company, which initially supplied computer software to the police department and then rapidly expanded into pager services, cable television, satellite communications, data communications networks and finally a virtual monopoly on mobile phone services. His company went public on the Bangkok Stock Exchange in 1990. That year he also signed a 20-year deal with the Telephone Organization of Thailand and changed his company's name to Shin Corporation.

Now a wealthy tycoon, Thaksin entered politics in 1994 as minister of foreign affairs and four years later founded his own Thai Rak Thai (Thai Love Thai) Party whose populist agenda found ready followers. The party dominated the next elections.

He quickly honored his campaign promise to help Thailand's rural poor although his critics argue he actually allowed them to slip deeper into debt by offering easy loans they found difficult to pay back. Once he became Prime Minister in 2001 Thaksin made some startling moves: He paid off the International Money Fund's 72 billion dollar loan to Thailand (granted after the 1997-98 Asian economic crisis) and then kicked the IMF out of the country. He started a universal health care system that allowed people to be treated for the equivalent of a dollar, imposed a moratorium on the payment of farmers' debts and created a $25,000 fund that could be used for any project chosen by the village.

His decisive style won over the electorate despite criticism that he was autocratic and endowed with a streak of cruelty. In fact his campaign to stamp out narcotics trafficking in the capital cost the lives of an estimated 2,500 drug-related victims, many of them rounded up and summarily executed by, apparently, official death squads. At the same time Thaksin's tough offensive against Islamic separatists in southern Thailand turned brutal when 80 unarmed militants captured by the army inexplicably choked to death in the back of army trucks. This massacre gained Thaksin and his methods international condemnation.

But he quickly redeemed himself in the eyes of his compatriots with strong leadership in handling the effects of the devastating tsunami, which lashed Southeast Asia at the end of 2004. He tirelessly toured the flattened coastal towns and delivered swift relief to the survivors. Partly on the accolade for that relief operation he won a second term in office.

He seemed to have found a formula for political success. His politics were nationalistic and populist. His northern Thai accent and criticism of what he dubbed "the Bangkok elite" won the hearts of rural folk and the urban poor. His initiatives came at a time when the inequality between countryside and the city became increasingly clear. Rural workers in the 1960s had earned one sixth of the wages of urban workers but by 2001 they were earning only a 12th of the income of urban workers. Poverty had become mainly a rural phenomenon.

Of course his escalating popularity upset the country's entrenched elite which felt threatened. This elite, supported by the urban middle class, habitually used the law and the military to cut any power usurper down to size. Early in his first term, Thaksin faced an investigation by Thailand's Corruption Commission. He was accused of failure to reveal all his wealth while he was deputy prime minister in 1997. The inquiry also wanted more details on why he gave shares of his Shin Corporation to his drivers and maids once he was forced to give up the stock after entering politics. But Thailand's Constitutional Court acquitted him of the charges by an 8-7 decision. It was not a good idea to convict a prime minister who had engineered a 22 per cent jump in Thailand's gross domestic product. The economy continued to grow but his critics warned the country was debt-riddled, the result of his largesse with loans, a charge that now appears to have been leveled for political reasons rather than facts. By 2010, analysts, including The Economist weekly, found Thailand's fiscal situation was healthy by the time Thaksin was removed and his much criticized health reform was fiscally viable, contrary to claims by his opponents.

Despite the campaign to damage his credibility, Thaksin's party won 375 of the 500 seats in parliament in the February 2005 elections, the first Thai election won outright by one party without the need to seek coalition partners. With this solid mandate, Thaksin was expected to make good on phase two of his election promises—education for the poor and expanded credit programs by creating new banks.

But his business interests quickly caused new problems with the 2006 sale of the Shinawatra family's share of Shin Corporation to Temasek Holdings, an investment company owned by the Finance Ministry of Singapore with a portfolio estimated at US$127 billion. The sale virtually gave the government of Singapore control of telecommunications in Thailand and caused bitter protests, although Thaksin argued the sale was in response to criticism his family holdings caused a conflict of interest with his job as prime minister. This excuse looked ludicrous when the sale took place hours before a new Thai law would have prevented the transaction and Thaksin had made sure before the sale that the Taxation Department changed the rules to exempt him from paying taxes on the deal. This type of manipulation brought accusations of insider trading although these charges were dismissed by a court later.

Unable to be rid of him in a democratic way, in 2006 the Armed Forces cut short Thaksin's term in office. The generals removed him in another of their bloodless coups, alleging he had accumulated what was described officially as "abnormal wealth". In a melodramatic turn of events, he was convicted, sentenced to two years in prison and released on appeal. Finally, he fled abroad, a positive solution for both sides. Thaksin apparently had no stomach to spend time in a Bangkok jail while his enemies had no intention to convert him into a jailed martyr for his loyal followers.

This is when trouble began.

The people Thaksin labeled in his campaign speeches as "the Bangkok elite" had made sure for generations that no single strongman could emerge to take total control for too long. This elite, among them a predominant percentage of other ethnic Chinese, soon realized Thaksin was shoveling the country's wealth into his own pockets while launching populist credit campaigns at the expense of their profits. A similar modus operandi was not unusual in Thai politics. However a tacit understanding existed that the spoils, if not divided evenly, were at least to be shared to some extent.

In other Southeast Asian nations, the disproportionate domination of politics and the economy by one ethnic Chinese usually resulted in race riots by the indigenous population of that country. Not so in Thailand where the integration of the ethnic Chinese in the modern era has allowed them to move without racial backlash into the highest political, academic and military positions, even to the inner circle of an iconic monarchy. (Thais still see their monarch as the exalted father figure of the nation whose counsel must be followed, who can never be criticized or blamed for any hardships or disasters. The law of lese majeste is still valid and woe to those who should dare insult the king in public.)

Thaksin's populist run was terminated in 2006 during his second term as prime minister. The Thai elite and middle class saw his courting of the rural and urban poor as a growing threat to their dominance and a certain recipe to class conflict, an assumption that proved to be correct. As usual when a government displeases the ruling forces, the law is activated to indict the prime minister and if that fails the military acts as a savior of the nation, removing the prime minister and his government in what generally turns out to be a bloodless coup. This is followed by an interim reign of the generals who eventually and often under international pressure agree to democratic elections and then return to barracks. This civilian-military swap administration is so ingrained in Thailand that Thaksin's 2001-2005 term as prime minister was the only democratically elected government to complete its term in office. And despite criticism of his autocratic ways, he was re-elected.

Given the economic and political predominance of the Thai-Chinese minority, the process of racial integration in Thailand is nothing short of amazing if one considers that between 1930 and 1950 the country suffered frequent race riots over charges that the ethnic Chinese dominated the retail and food industries and set prices at will. Even more amazing is the number of ethnic Chinese prime ministers and politicians over recent decades. Among the most prominent was Chatichai Choonhavan (prime minister 1988-91) the son of Marshal Phin Choonhavan. Chatichai fostered international trade and improved relations with Cambodia and Laos before a military coup deposed him. His successor was Chuan Leekpai, twice prime minister (1992-95 and 1997-2001) whose rags-to riches life caught popular imagination. Born into a Chinese family of 11 siblings, he was brought up in a house with a grass roof and walls made of betel-nut wood. The soil was the floor. He came to power on popular acclaim and without the traditional nod from the aristocracy and the military.

Between Chuan's two premierships fell the one year long government (1996-97) of General Chavalit Yongchaiyudh, another Thai-Chinese whose election was considerably facilitated by his control of 126-military run radio stations and two out of the country's five television networks. He resigned under pressure during the 1997 financial crisis but regained prominence recently when in February 2010 the ousted Thaksin named him chief commander of the People's Army.

Even Abhisit Vejjajiva, the young prime minister who replaced Thaksin after the military kicked him out of office, comes from a prominent Thai-Chinese family. He is notorious for his controversial political juggling, including a call on King Bhumibol Abdulyadej to replace Thaksin with a royal appointed prime minister. In a rare public speech the aged monarch replied: "Asking for a royally-appointed prime minister is undemocratic. It is, pardon me, a mess. It is irrational."

With the ethnic Chinese population figure in Thailand still estimated at only 14 per cent of the total, the dominance of Thai-Chinese in running the country and owning its resources is a tribute to the determination of a people who have never slowed down in their endeavors, no matter where they are, to acquire power and wealth, often under circumstances not favorable to their ambitions.

Prime ministers in Thailand falling and being replaced by others from the same racial mix might be reminiscent of the ancient warring states in China when provincial warlords fought each other in bitter struggles over the acquisition of more territory and wealth once the riches of their own territory had been exhausted and no further profits could be squeezed from their enterprises.

Is it not the same in Thailand today where Thai-Chinese strongmen accuse Thai-Chinese prime ministers perennially of corruption, mismanagement, siphoning public funds into their own pockets or precipitating economic disasters so they can replace these ethnic rivals with their own choice for prime minister and so feather their own nests as well as the fortunes of their families and clans—only to be replaced in time by the next Thai-Chinese pretender?

Throughout history, Chinese clans or provincial warlords had a habit of turning on other clans or warlords in their quest to accumulate more power and more wealth.

But first conditions had to be right.

It was another Thai-Chinese prime minister, Plaek Pibulsonggram, who revoked the acquired stranglehold of the ethnic Chinese community on the country's vital commodities. He acted in the 1950s to prevent further anti-Chinese demonstrations by removing the cause of these disturbances, which had dated back to the 1905 recession, a setback that lasted ten years. That recession, like subsequent economic downturns, was blamed on the prices charged by, and hoarding by, Chinese millers and rice traders. Even before the 1905 recession, anti-Chinese resentment had exploded periodically. The ethnic Chinese—although only about 10 per cent of the total population at the turn of the 19th century—employed secret Chinese societies to collect taxes. The Chinese were also the preferred agents for royal trade monopolies and dominated domestic commerce.

Faced with popular anger and the peril of an anti-Chinese pogrom of the kind taking place in neighboring Indonesia, prime minister Plaek removed the main cause of the discontent. He created state corporations to take over the rice, tobacco and petroleum monopolies from all private business. His legislation ushered in a period of relative racial peace allowing the economic and political fortunes of the integrated ethnic Chinese to flourish as never before.

But by 2010, Thailand was torn asunder by rivalry between these Thai-Chinese factions. Over the previous year the majority of the establishment had rallied behind the token figure of Prime Minister Abhisit, who took over his post by sleight of hand and party loyalties in parliament. This phalanx of mainly Thai-Chinese clans confronted the followers of the self-exiled Thaksin, who managed the confrontation from abroad. He broke with the custom of previously deposed prime ministers who quietly melted away to temporary obscurity—perhaps to make a come-back years later—or devoted themselves to business interests. Using his charisma, his money and his record as a champion of the poor, Thaksin garnered such fierce popular support, mainly from the rural and urban poor, that Bangkok remained under a virtual state of siege in 2010 between his red-shirted supporters and the yellow-shirted mobs loyal to the administration. How many of these support demonstrations were orchestrated rent-a-mob crowds or legitimate followers remained a mystery. What is no longer a mystery is the fact that Thailand's poor and rural people, marginalized for centuries by a royal oligarchy and pacified by Buddhism and a paternalistic monarch, are no longer willing to return to their designated role in society. Thaksin may have lit the flame of protest but the fire he kindled is already burning further than his own ambitions envisaged and has turned Thailand into a virtual state of civil war. He may even be discarded in the foreseeable future by radical socialist leaders who will relegate him to the ranks of the have-alls and the traditional exploiters of the proletariat.

Another victim of this clash of classes is sure to be the ailing monarch who has wisely kept silent during the turmoil in 2010. He may have realized silence was his best option to ensure he remained king if either side won. However the almost divine role of the monarch as the infallible and unquestionable head of the nation is likely to be considerably reduced in the near future if not abandoned after the death of the current king. There is something utterly anachronistic about a country in 2010 where criticizing His Majesty or any of his family is automatically punished by heavy prison sentences for Thais and expulsion for foreigners.

The 2010 crisis has plunged a flourishing economy in one of Asia's most harmonious and culturally independent nations into an uncertain future as Thai-Chinese interests battle for the leadership of a nation in which the elite and the middle class suddenly find themselves pitted in the streets against the nation's poor. In Thailand, where class differences were always glossed over by an accommodating Buddhist religion and a patriarchal monarchy, militant class consciousness is a novelty and has now been awakened, just as has the vast gap between rich and poor.

At the root of these current troubles and those yet to come was, no doubt, the insatiability of one man who believed, like many of his fellow ethnic Chinese, that enough is never enough.

EPILOGUE

ARE THE CHINESE COMING?

When Chinese academics and politicians in Southeast Asia began to trumpet the concept of "Asian values", the majority of the uninitiated believed their proclamation was the Asian equivalent to Black Power, the assertion of an Asian identity and the arrival of Asia as a key global player. Or was it an Aryan-like claim to racial superiority?

Instead, Asian values turned out to be a doctrine, not unlike communism or capitalism, a belief that individualism must come second to collective welfare. Taken to its logical conclusion, this doctrine means an individual can be sacrificed for the benefit of the rest of society and individual human rights are automatically suspended if they impinge on the wellbeing of the majority.

Not surprisingly China embraced the doctrine with gusto. After all it contained the basic ingredient of its Communist Party, namely power by an omnipotent oligarchy, a group so small academics believe no more then 300 to 400 inner sanctum officials are running China today. This oligarchy exerts its authoritarianism not only on domestic political and economic decisions but also on a Diaspora that may have foreign citizenship but in its heart of hearts remains attached to the Motherland—and its economic potential. In many ways the relationship between China and its Diaspora is reminiscent of the Jewish Diaspora which also flourished in many countries, especially the USA, but retains a strong emotional alliance to the Jewish State, an attachment so powerful many Jews, both in leading corporate and political U.S. circles, maintain American and Israeli passports. This poses the question then: Who enjoys their real loyalty, particularly when the issue is the Middle East where for decades U.S. policy has uncannily coincided with Israeli policy? The same question can be asked about the Chinese Diaspora whose members are equally attached to their ethnic roots and whose Motherland, though not publicly, considers them pioneers of its overseas ambitions.

To impose a doctrine it is necessary to create a code of laws. The draconian regulations and decrees most Asian nations impose on their citizens were thought to be justified by the second equally important principle of Asian values—the prevention of chaos at all costs since chaos is considered the biggest threat to an Asian society. It becomes logical then that individuals or groups considered a threat to public order must be arrested, jailed or even executed. Therefore any citizen or group of people opposed to or critical of the government must be fomenting chaos—and thus has to be neutralized.

The idea of Asian values did not originate in post-Mao China as one would expect, although China embraced the doctrine whole-heartedly to justify the dictatorship of its omnipotent Communist Party (which today, more then ever, controls all aspects of private and commercial life) but in former prime minister Mahathir Mohamad's Malaysia and more vigorously in the pristine city-state of Singapore. Back in the 1990s, the idea of Asian values was vigorously nurtured by Singapore's supreme ruler since 1959, Lee Kuan Yew. Today Lee is a backseat emperor, officially retired but operating from behind the scenes, just like Deng Xiaoping did in China until his death.

Not surprisingly, Asian values became a buzz-word following the bloody student uprising at Tiananmen Square in 1989 which, so the logic went, had to be smothered in order to forestall chaos. Proponents of Asian values today still promote social harmony over dissent and hail socio-economic progress as far more important than human rights and civil liberties. They argue that single party rule is preferable to political pluralism with its disturbing populist turbulences, such as we are witnessing in Thailand and in, to some degree, Malaysia today. No doubt the concept of Asian values borrowed heavily from the teachings of Confucius. He preached loyalty towards all forms of authority, including government, parents and teachers—in short patriotism and filial obedience.

The Asian economic meltdown and the populist concept of more democracy and less autocracy in Thailand and Indonesia all but silenced the clamor for Asian values, except in China where the post-Mao helmsman, Deng Xiaoping, virtually adopted Singapore as a role model. He sent senior cadres to study administration in the tropical Chinese city-state notorious for its draconian laws, its fake façade of democracy and its boast of being the world's most pacific and egalitarian society, a true peoples' paradise on earth.

What Beijing's cadres still find today in Singapore is an Orwellian mini-state where Big Brother watches through surveillance cameras if a citizen fails to flush a public toilet, spits on a public sidewalk or carelessly tosses away a cigarette butt; a state where dissidents are jailed, free speech is limited to one's private home, the gathering of more than four people is banned and the death penalty has been imposed on nearly 500 people over the last decade. This is a mini-nation where bureaucrats are matched to marriage partners according to IQ tests and the national birthrate is regulated. (The two-per-couple rule was so successful the government had to urge educated people to try and make it three because the population had declined below the mark set by the demographic planners.)

The leaders in the Chinese motherland admired these Singaporean straitjackets. These included control over the media which is now owned by two state companies and the practice of elections, held every five years, although opposition candidates are arrested and charged with defamation if they express criticism of the government. Candidates unable to pay the exorbitant fines for defamation are declared bankrupt and sent to jail. And should any constituency stubbornly vote for the tolerated opposition, it may find the underground train no longer stops at their local station.

In this Hobbesian paradise, caning for robbery, vandalism and rioting continues and is mandatory for rapists and visiting foreigners overstaying their visas. As a concession to human rights, the cane is first treated with antiseptic to prevent infection and dunked in water to prevent it splitting.

In Singapore, superannuated air conditioners must be traded in for new models after a certain date. Still, reforms are not unheard of. In 2004

Singapore relaxed the ban on chewing gum, allowing the use of "therapeutic gum". Three years later, private and consented sex between same gender individuals was no longer considered a criminal offense.

For those who can live with these intrusions into their privacy, there are rewards: Education and health care are virtually free, no one pays more than 20 per cent in taxes; a once illiterate population of workers is now literate; annual economic growth rate is an average nine per cent in this micro-managed society and priority housing is available within a mile from the home of elderly parents so they can be looked after by their children instead of being dumped at the expense of the state.

Visitors to Singapore may discover shopping is the city's main pastime; Indian shopkeepers are everywhere; public transport is super-efficient, buildings and streets are pristine, beggars are invisible, bars are orderly and inebriation in public is quickly stifled—and fined—by ever present guardians of law and order.

Life in Singapore is so regulated and orderly the city has been hailed as a model not only by China but by many of its neighbors. Chaotic East European states have held it up as a society to be emulated.

They ignore warnings by sociologists that the Singaporean model is in danger of fostering regimented societies totally subservient to orders from above.

Asian values lost some shine after the Asian economic melt-down of the late 1990s but the credo has been gaining credibility again with the recent economic surge by China and India. The numerical superiority of these two giants has always scared a Western world which took the concept of autocratic Asian values far more seriously than the Asians who, after all, have lived with it as far back as their history books remember.

Chinese people traditionally follow opportunities rather than political philosophies unless these philosophies can be used to improve one's fortunes. Pragmatic and earthy Chinese see opportunities where others have already given up.

In Australia and the United States in the 19th century, Chinese gold miners dug up fortunes on claims white miners had already evacuated because the gold veins had become too poor and too difficult to work. Today the developed world has virtually given up Africa as a basket case, but not the Chinese, who are heavily investing in the continent in return for trade and mining concessions. Similar investments—usually followed by a wave of Chinese migrants arriving on business visas—are now gushing into forgotten Pacific island nations, among them Fiji and the Solomon Islands. Chinese corporations and investment groups are heavily buying into U.S., European and Australian companies and are accumulating government bonds.

After near-bankrupt Greece was bailed out in 2010 by the European Union, the Chinese government offered to refinance Greek debts, buy bonds and invest heavily in Greek industry. This will give Beijing a significant foothold in Europe and access, via Greece, to European markets. Already Chinese-made vehicles are replacing European cars in Turkey after Ankara forged a special relationship with Beijing. Turkey also has extraordinary market access to, though not membership in, the European Union (EU).

Other weak links in the EU, such as Ireland, Portugal and Spain, are already targets for Chinese investment capital and industries, a blessing to the faltering economies of those countries. This role of savior of financially troubled states was previously a prerogative of the United States, which today has its own economic problems at home and no longer the funds to finance rescues abroad. Besides, bloated with cash reserves, China is offering far softer terms than did the far more avaricious U.S. investors via the World Bank and the International Monetary Fund (IMF). After all, for the Chinese the expanding foothold in Europe will pry open the door for their merchandise into the European Union—without quota and tariff restrictions.

After the Chinese push into Africa, where they bought up land to extract oil and minerals, Chinese manufacturing interests have gained the most solid footholds in Greece and Ireland. In Athlone, central Ireland, a consortium of Chinese investors is buying a £40 million sterling (US$60 million) plot of land to import 2,000 Chinese workers and turn the area into an industrial zone, already dubbed a "Beijing-on-Shannon", for Chinese manufacturers. This industrial zone will also employ 8,000 Irish workers, an irresistible carrot for a region where a fifth of the workforce is unemployed or underemployed following the credit crunch. The new Chinese manufacturing hub in Ireland, like those elsewhere, would gain access to Europe for its products, bypassing tariffs and quotas.

Meanwhile in Greece, a cash-strapped and virtually broke

government has already signed deals to allow Chinese shipbuilding and hotel constructions, all under Chinese management and with Chinese workers. Chinese investors are also bidding for the Greek railway system, which is up for sale to raise funds for the national treasury. Athens has become a main target for the billions of dollars of trade surplus languishing in Beijing's treasury. During a visit to Athens in October 2010, China's vice-premier Zhang Dejiang signed a series of industrial cooperation deals which strangely coincided with the announcement that Greek bonds had been downgraded to junk status by credit rating agencies. Zhang's pledge that Beijing would 'encourage' Chinese businesses to seek investment opportunities in Greece fell like a soothing lotion on the bruised Greek economy, desperate to attract any kind of foreign investment for its debt-ridden economy. At the same time China is anxious to acquire a solid European base for the export of its consumer goods. Cosco, the giant Chinese shipping group, has pledged to go ahead with a US$3.5bn plan to build a massive container-handling facility at the Greek port of Piraeus and turn it into a regional hub as well as a huge logistics centre from where trucks would move containers around the rest of the continent. The Chinese construction firm BCEGI signed a €100m agreement to develop a hotel and shopping mall complex in Piraeus. China wants to bail out the Greek railway operator OSE, the airports and even the postal service. Joint ventures, a favorite Chinese recipe from the days when European and American companies flocked to China, are now seeking Greek partners on Greek territory in a variety of commercial interests ranging from telecommunications to tourism and olive growing.

In the give and take of commerce, the Chinese have already gained. The powerful Greek ship-owner fraternity has placed a signed order for 15 bulk carriers to be built in China. In 2009 Greek shipping companies placed orders for 80 bulk carriers in China, which is vying with Japan and South Korea today for the title of the world's biggest shipbuilder.

Although U.S. officials denounce the Greek deals, saying they are part of Beijing's strategy to increase its global power, American industries have been deaf to political warnings, jumping on the Chinese bandwagon. In March, Ford agreed to sell its Volvo subsidiary to Chinese company, Geely, for US$1.8bn, kindling a trend to shift the world's car industry from west to east. German carmakers are also franchising many of their models on the boom-market in China where the majority of a 1.3 billion population dreams of owning a car.

Even Britain, also short of funds, is advertising assets for sale. The Chinese are particularly keen to buy Britain's air traffic control system. In fact Britain has become a favored target for Chinese companies. Statistics from the Think London investment agency indicate the British capital has attracted 34 Chinese direct investments since 1997 because the Chinese view London as a major door into Europe.

The fortunes of the Chinese have improved dramatically over the last two decades, ever since Deng opened the Middle Kingdom to trade with the outside world and told his one billion citizens: "To get rich is glorious" and the communist party, run by a small executive cupola, decided to ruthlessly micro-manage every aspect of industrial and public life.

The days of Chinese boat people are long gone. When the Australian Navy locates asylum seekers in boats offshore today, they rarely find a Chinese citizen among them. The Chinese do not arrive stored in cargo decks or on rickety fishing boats any more, but fly into Australia and Europe on business and student visas or on family reunion permits. One of Australia's great ironies today is the tug-of-war between political parties over how to prevent a few thousand ragged asylum seekers slipping through the backdoor on rickety boats every year. The hunt for these illegal backdoor arrivals is heralded loudly on the news almost daily while tens of thousands of Chinese and other Asians are flying into the country quietly through the front door—on legitimate visas. The Australian government spends millions of dollars to keep the "boat people" housed and fed in refugee camps telling its public it is successfully eliminating illegal immigration while in reality the number of Chinese and other Asians immigrants is snowballing annually. In other words, the government trumpets an anti-boat people campaign to placate public fear and outrage over an Asian invasion while the invasion is already in full swing.

The reality is this: Over the past few years, the Chinese have become Australia's most numerous annual immigrants. Diligent, industrious and highly motivated, they already occupy senior positions in business and academia. Chinese investments have boosted Australia's mining industry and sent the real estate market sky high. It is an irony of history that Australia was the only nation in the South Pacific which successfully fought

Chinese proliferation on its territory by a cruel law banning Chinese women from entering the country and banning the Chinese from owning land. Yet these restrictive measures did not prevent the Chinese in Australia from multiplying in so-called Chinatowns in Sydney and Melbourne. Many of the women were smuggled in as boys or came in as boat people dropped off along the country's vast shoreline and picked up by triad-type people smugglers. Like elsewhere, the Chinese went into retail and there is hardly a nook in Australia without its Chow-House—a Chinese restaurant.

Arguably the biggest success story of the Diaspora is Thailand where ethnic Chinese for centuries have integrated by marrying Thai women and adopting Thai names. Ethnic Chinese have attained leading positions not only in the economy but in politics and the military. Many prime ministers were Thai-Chinese. And Thailand's current crisis is caused mainly by a power struggle between Thai-Chinese interests.

China's growing power has straightened the backbones of all Chinese, whether at home or in the Diaspora. The rise of China as a mercurial force has converted the Diaspora into a valuable asset abroad, an asset that has become a broad bridge to the outside world and a vanguard for ambitious Chinese schemes to gain access to industries and raw materials overseas. The Diaspora has become a pilot force for China's state and private enterprises with international ambitions. These joint ventures are making new fortunes for both sides. Diaspora managers, experts in local conditions and dealings, place the investments and supervise the projects. The financial powers behind these Diaspora managers are the state and private corporations, which accumulated vast foreign currency reserves thanks to Chinese goods flooding the world market.

China seeks and needs access to raw materials. These are vital if Beijing is to maintain its phenomenal economic growth rate. Keeping the economy on a roll is a prerequisite for the Communist Party to retain absolute power. As long as the system offers opportunities for a better life and access to modern gadgetry and diversions, the population is unlikely to challenge the Party's omnipotence or its draconian security and judicial apparatus that arbitrarily decides the fate of citizens.

Only a revolt by China's marginalized rural population, a two-thirds majority, could halt or retard the country's triumphant march on the road to becoming the world's leading economic power. Should the peasants Mao empowered but Deng's open door policy disenfranchised run amok, China may return to the civil wars between provinces and between warlords, conflicts that always were the country's worst nemesis and were responsible for retarding its role as a leading contender on the world stage.

No doubt China's rapid transition from a backward, largely primitive society to a nation endowed with the technology and comforts of developed nations was accompanied by some negative aspects. Chinese people, almost overnight, found themselves catapulted into a modern material world without the mental preparations enjoyed by Europeans and Americans whose values, technology and outlooks on life were gradually changed and shaped over two centuries of disastrous wars and revolts, always followed, however, by surges of idealism and more freedom to express them.

In the annals of slavery and persecution, the slaves, once unshackled, have often become the masters of their masters, treating the newly subservient with similar cruelty and the same lack of compassion they or their ancestors suffered. For generations, the Chinese were subjected to racist discrimination, abuses and often death at home or in their adopted countries in Southeast Asia. But today Chinese minorities dominate these countries economically to a point where the proletarian labor force of these nations have often become the servants of the Chinese.

On any Sunday morning in Hong Kong and Singapore, tens of thousands of Indonesian, Filipino, Thai, Sri Lankan and Bangladeshi maids and nannies gather in central areas for picnics or social chats on their day off. Their number is so vast that locals usually shun these meeting zones. These women, most of them married with children back home, are the so-called Overseas Workers. Their monthly remittances are the lifeline for entire families and clans back home. (Remittances from nine million Filipino Overseas Workers are the country's main revenue earner.)

Their harsh, often brutal, taskmasters are the newly rich Chinese, notorious for paying low wages, expecting long working hours and exacting more than they paid for. The work of these domestic helpers, often physically and sexually abused in the bargain, allows Chinese wives to be employed or work in the family business. Back home, it allows the children and cousins of these domestic helpers to go to school and ensures timely food and care for elderly parents.

In the often small and crammed apartments of Hong Kong and

Singapore, many domestic workers sleep under stairwells or in alcoves. Their stories, rarely told in public because most are ashamed their families might hear about the way they are treated, are the dark side to the Chinese people who have not shown much compassion for the less fortunate or those considered lower classes. The Chinese tend to treat underlings with the same indifference that has always been part of the behavior of the landlord, mandarin and communist cadre in China. Scant consideration is shown towards anyone below one's social level or for that matter for the welfare of animals—unless they can be eaten, once fattened up.

If one takes a Chinese guest to a restaurant, the most enjoyable part of the outing seems to be the selection of the live creature about to be consumed, whether it is a duck, a chicken, a snake or a fish. Any decent Chinese restaurant gives customers a wide choice to select from. I have waited for half an hour as my guests watched fish swimming in an aquarium, making up their mind as to which one the waiter should extract for dinner. The pragmatic idea, so I am told, is to see which fish is liveliest: that one will be the freshest and therefore the tastiest. The same applies to the live animals kept in cages at restaurants. No Chinese would pick for their meal a chicken dozing half dead in a corner of its cage—or a dog with mangy fur or a duck unwilling to ruffle its feathers in anger if provoked by a stick poked through the mesh wire to see how lively it is. One may well ask what is enjoyable about tying strings around a bird's legs and then allowing it to fly high into the air, making it believe it is being set free. Instead its tormentor will pull it back to earth by the string. Flying a bird is a favorite pastime of youngsters.

One of the basic concepts of Asian values is the belief among many Asians that the rest of the world has never understood their culture or been willing to make concessions to Asia's contributions to humanity's evolution. It is true the Chinese invented many useful things, among them paper and gun powder, but like the achievements of the Egyptian, Greek and Roman civilizations, these innovations are buried in history. No one today kowtows to the Greeks or Italians for what their ancestors achieved or left as heritage for all humanity. One must then ask whether the veneration of Asian values is not really intended to serve as a call to nationalism, patriotism and even racial superiority—a dangerous dish in our volatile nuclear era when hundreds of millions of people seek a livelihood and new habitats while others are being convinced their hour of destiny has arrived—thanks to past achievements and the power of numbers.

The world is witnessing today the greatest transmigration since the Dark Ages when Central Asian and East European tribes invaded a crumbling Roman Empire. In our era, hundreds of millions of people seek new frontiers, a livelihood, a refuge from civil wars, an opportunity to sink roots, a chance to make fortunes or simply the need to feed themselves and their families. This push into the wealthy portion of the world has kindled xenophobia among the inhabitants of those countries which see the newcomers as a threat to their jobs, wealth and security.

This fear of "the intruders" has its paradoxes.

In northern Italy hardly a family exists in which the father or grandfather did not migrate to other European countries or America in search of work or a better life after World War II. Yet nowhere in Europe is the rhetoric about the evil immigrants more bitter than in northern Italy where a political party, La Lega (the Northern League), has become the country's leading political force in just a few years by stoking xenophobia. The party blames outsiders for crimes and shortages of jobs. It bombards its electorate with racial prejudices, among them the ridiculous claim that the taxes of the north of Italy feed the south and therefore the country should be divided into federated provinces.

Not surprisingly, unscrupulous politicians collect votes by paying lip service to this xenophobia. Behind the scene however demographers and industrialists welcome this immigration as cheap labor and a necessity to maintain, at least for the time being, high living standards for societies with more elderly non-working people than ever before. Progress in medicine and abundance of food has helped people live longer. And if "white" societies like Australia's have recently opened more doors to the Chinese, it is not because they have discovered a sudden love for the people of the Middle Kingdom but have realized, just like the Dutch in Indonesia did 200 years ago, that Chinese hard work, drive and dedication will be beneficial to the country's economy while serving as a counter-balance to the laid-back lifestyle of its "white" citizens.

Unlike in the days of the Huns and Visigoths, these migrations will not come en masse and with deadly armory but gradually, steadily, accelerating as numbers double and triple over short periods. The invasions are world-wide and will defy the shrill xenophobia of groups such as La Lega, which would like to see migrants if not hung from lamp posts, at least chased out of the country with sticks and curses—naked, if possible.

Whenever I think of the unstoppable presence of the Chinese, I am reminded of Venice, Italy where I now live part of the year. In Venice, the Via Garibaldi was always a backwater of drowsy open air cafés and small shops run for generations by the same family. With its head to the lagoon and its tail on a canal, the Via was a local hangout, distant enough from St Mark's Square and historic sites to avoid the elbow-to-elbow and shoulder-to-shoulder rub of mass tourism. The locals, fishermen, shopkeepers, glass bead stringers and artisans were notorious for their "red" political views. The Italian Communist Party's Venetian headquarters was located in an alley just off Via Garibaldi.

Then, overnight, the Chinese moved in.

They did not arrive en masse or with fanfare but stealthily, almost imperceptibly. By the time people noticed them, their numbers had already multiplied.

One morning a single bar on the posh lagoon end of Garibaldi was manned by Chinese staff and run by a portly Chinese manager with a fixed smile and a gold incisor tooth. Initially the regulars joked with the Chinese waitresses about their missing 'r's and halting Italian. But the locals came back and brought along friends. The drinks, the coffee and the food were cheaper than in neighboring cafés and the Chinese staff were friendlier than the grumpy and lackadaisical Venetians, who seem to be at pains to let customers know that serving on tables and cooking meals is beneath their dignity and intellectual capacity. Soon a second bar opened next door run by the Chinese and then a third and a fourth —all of them underselling the traditional Venetian bars whose prices have been grossly inflated by greed and by mass tourism that brings an average half a million visitors a week into the relatively small City on Water.

Such quiet takeovers are not unusual on a larger scale world-wide. Already the haute couture industry in Naples, once a mainstay of the local economy, is practically controlled by Chinese migrants who possess residency permits. They spare no expense: The Chinese have bought out Neapolitan tailors to teach their high fashion know-how to imported

Chinese workers, some legal, some illegal. In European ports such as Naples, a large portion of imports from China are now being handled and controlled by Chinese middlemen or, as some would have it, by Chinese muscle. In such ports, shirts and garments made in China, Vietnam or Cambodia arrive with the buttons missing. The buttons are sewn on locally so the garments can be labeled "Made in Italy". This escapes import tariffs and triples or quadruples sale price.

The buy-out of shops and businesses is not confined to Italy but is happening in the rest of Europe as well. At the core of the rapid expansion of Chinese interests and investments is a ubiquitous nucleus of the Chinese Diaspora—with residency or citizenship papers—serving as the foundation on which compatriots in China build fortunes abroad.

Europe is not the only target for Chinese economic expansion. The Chinese are seriously into Australian mining but their real target these days is Australian real estate for speculation and as holiday homes for China's burgeoning multi-millionaires. Hardly a real estate auction is held these days in which the winning bid is not made by Chinese interests. The bottomless funds of the Chinese Diaspora have driven the cost of homes in Australia sky high, making it almost impossible for young couples to acquire homes at a reasonable cost and forcing the government in 2010 to halt the purchase of real estate by foreign investors.

No one is sure who funds these Chinese ventures, although academic surveys indicate that southern regions in China such as Fujian, a traditional exodus point for migrants, have created their own enclaves in Eastern and Western Europe as well as in Africa. Flush with money from booming Chinese exports flooding world markets, Chinese corporations and provincial entities are investing their profits abroad using as go-betweens and door-openers the ready-made front of local Chinese who are usually from the same provincial areas, towns or neighborhoods.

More convenient still, these enterprises can dispense with local labor: They have a reservoir of workers at their disposal from among Chinese students abroad or illegal migrants seeping into Europe through the eastern member states of the European Union, such as Hungary, which made a killing in the past by furnishing the Chinese with visas that gave them access to the rest of Europe.

Unlike the migrants from Africa, highly visible because of their color, dress and boisterousness, the Chinese have merged into Europe quietly. Their presence in Europe (half a million in Italy alone) becomes an issue only when headline making incidents occur—such as the one at Dover in 2000 when 58 illegal Chinese choked to death in a container lacking ventilation. Or when 23 Chinese cockle pickers drowned in incoming tides in Lancashire. British Immigration had no record of the existence of five of the drowned while nine others were asylum seekers but had permits to pick cockles. Some had fake IDs.

Unlike immigrants from Africa, the Chinese have sophisticated support networks active all across Europe. Most western countries including the United States and Canada have Chinatowns or Chinese quarters.

In a rapidly changing world, the threat of invasion by migration has kindled xenophobic reactions in most developed countries, especially in Europe where the Chinese are part of tens of thousands of migrants from impoverished nations trying to sneak in by road or by sea each week. In a bygone era Chinese migration was a private enterprise, facilitated by snakeheads or triad gangs ferrying migrants to their destination in return for years of bonded labor. The system is still alive but now the facilitators are often state or corporate enterprises. While yesterday's migrants eked out a miserable initial existence for years before their grandsons and great grandsons had access to laboriously accumulated wealth, the injection today of funds from China into overseas enterprises has tremendously accelerated Chinese expansion abroad. The Chinese of yesterday were prone to periodic anti-Chinese pogroms in their adopted countries. Today no government would dare stoke or tolerate the massacre of local Chinese or the confiscation of their property. The reason is not Beijing's modernized military muscle but more significantly the large trade deficits western nations have accumulated with the People's Republic. Not surprisingly the media frenzy about illegal migration has precipitated a fear of newcomers, of losing jobs and of having to work harder because the immigrants work more and for less. This xenophobia mixed with an economic downturn and declining job opportunities has re-inflamed the West's simmering sinophobia—the fear of the 1.3 billion Chinese who may dominate our world by sheer force of numbers and overwhelming economic clout. Sinophobia is no novelty. For hundreds of years Western literature and later cinema depicted the Chinese as a cruel, greedy and crooked people.

Epilogue: Are the Chinese Coming?

Sometimes, in a nightmare, I see masses of Chinese coming down an empty road, steamroller-like, slowly but steadily and inexorably, bringing along the realization that nothing will stop their progress. This is not an unusual nightmare for someone who has lived in Asia for 16 years, eight of them in China, and watched tidal waves of banner-waving humanity demonstrating for weeks along the Avenue of Eternal Peace during the Tiananmen student protests in 1989 or listened to awed Vietnamese and Korean former army officers tell tales of endless waves of Chinese soldiers overrunning their defense lines during the Korean War and the 1979 invasion of Vietnam. Who would not be impressed by watching a seemingly endless avalanche of bicycle riders in the old days roll down Beijing avenues before the bicycle was replaced by the motor car? Wherever you go in China, cities, towns, villages are bursting with humanity, 1.3 billion members of humanity, an awesome number for any Westerner or someone like me brought up in Australia, a country which in my youth had barely reached a population of ten million for the entire vast continent, a country where the peril of a Chinese tsunami-like military invasion hung over everyone's head like a Damocles sword.

There is an air of purpose about the Chinese, a quick wittedness, a curled-up feline readiness to pounce, exploit openings, squeeze through loopholes, legal or material, in order to advance their fortunes or academic ambitions. In all my travels and residencies during 40 years as a foreign correspondent, no people have impressed me as much as the Chinese by their ability not only to survive and progress in adverse conditions and amid racial prejudices but to retain a pride and often arrogance that comes with the knowledge of being bigger than the rest and the nurtured belief of being smarter than the rest, more diligent, more willing to face danger and death for a chance to improve one's position in life. The Chinese are gamblers, not only at the casino table and the race courses, but in the game of daily life, where they are willing to gamble their possessions, their future and even their life for more money, greater prestige, more acquisitions, more space and greater power.

The people on Tiananmen Square in 1989 were not democrats but opportunists. Many members of the Communist Party threw their lot in with the protesters because if the protest succeeded, it would have catapulted them up the party ladder. These party turncoats were fully conscious the gamble could cost them their neck—which it did in some cases.

Similar to America, whose main ambition is access to resources and guarantees for investments, the Chinese will become partners and often dominators in our economies, whether we like it or not. And, of course, like it or not, the Chinese will become part of our populations, leaders in academia, the economy and politics, if only because their commercial acumen and their ruthless determination to succeed has made them the new settlers of the world.

One might sum up the Chinese mentality with one of their own pithy sayings: "Sheng zhe wei wang, bai zhe wei kou." Loosely translated it means: "Winner take all, loser is a mug."

As to the question "Are the Chinese coming?" the answer is: "They are already here."

ULI SCHMETZER

Born in Germany and educated in Australia, Uli Schmetzer was a well-known foreign correspondent for almost 40 years until he retired to write books. For ten years he reported for Reuters news agency from Latin America and for 25 years for the *Chicago Tribune* from Europe, the Middle East and Asia. He is the author of *Times of Terror*, a hard-hitting memoir; and *Gaza*, a novel set in the Israel-Palestine conflict. During his colorful career Schmetzer covered the world's major news stories—among them periodic spells reporting the Israel-Palestinian conflict between 1988 and 2004. He lives part of the year in Italy, Australia and the Philippines. He comments on world events on his website: **www.uli-schmetzer.com**

ALSO BY THE AUTHOR

TIMES OF TERROR: NOTEBOOKS OF A FOREIGN CORRESPONDENT
A startling memoir, spiced with revealing anecdotes and disturbing insights. Schmetzer pulls no punches about how news is manipulated and massaged and how executives bow to profits, politics and lobby groups.

GAZA
A novel that follows the journey of three friends through Israel and Gaza. Through them we see the suffering and the manipulation of public opinion during the 60-year-old Israel-Palestine conflict.

"Schmetzer's scope and detail deliver deep and practical truths... *Times of Terror* is a wide-awake memoir, that marks world changes in a lifetime's observations and clarifies ours."

DR JACK DEMPSEY
Historian, Bentley University, USA

www.ingramcontent.com/pod-product-compliance
Lightning Source LLC
Chambersburg PA
CBHW060116170426
43198CB00010B/910